Heart of the Storm

Heart of the Storm

My Adventures as a Helicopter Rescue Pilot and Commander

Colonel Edward L. Fleming

WILEY

John Wiley & Sons, Inc.

Published by John Wiley & Sons, Inc., Hoboken, New Jersey
Published simultaneously in Canada

The Author gratefully acknowledges the following for permission to use photos in this book: Fleming family: pages 115, 116 bottom, 119 top and middle; 106 Rescue Wing, Nyang: pages 116 top, 117 middle, 118 bottom, 119 bottom, 120 top, 121 top, 122 bottom; US Air Force: page 116 middle; Walt Wheeler, Department of Military and Naval Affairs: page 117 top; Don Spering: pages 117 bottom, 118 top; Frank Klay: page 118 middle; Lt. Col. Jim Finkle, 106 Rescue Wing, Nyang: pages 120 middle and bottom; Dave Dunster from Flightline Photo: page 121 middle; 109 Airlift Wing, Nyang: pages 121 bottom left, 122 top and middle; Dr. Jerri Nielsen family: page 121 bottom right.

For general information about our other products and services, please contact our Customer Care Department within the United States at (800) 762-2974, outside the United States at (317) 572-3993 or fax (317) 572-4002.

Wiley also publishes its books in a variety of electronic formats. Some content that appears in print may not be available in electronic books. For more information about Wiley products, visit our web site at www.wiley.com.

Library of Congress Cataloging-in-Publication Data:

Fleming, Edward, date.
    Heart of the storm : my adventures as a helicopter rescue pilot and
commander / Edward Fleming.
        p. cm.
    ISBN 0-471-26436-9 (cloth : alk. paper)
    ISBN 978-1-68442-584-6 (paperback)
    1. Fleming, Edward. 2. United States. Air Force—Officers—Biography.
3. Helicopter pilots—United States—Biography. 4. United States. Air Force—
Search and rescue operations. I. Title.

    UG626.2.F573A3   2004
    358.4′0092—dc22

                                                            2004002609

Printed in the United States of America

For Lucy and Ella

Contents

CONTENTS

Photo gallery: pages 115–122

Acknowledgments

I owe so much to so many people. First, my grateful love and thanks for the support and inspiration from my immediate family, Jean, Cavan, Keith, Alex, Lucy, and Ella. I also acknowledge all of my supporting family far and wide.

Thanks for the immeasurable literary inputs from Keith Fleming and Walt Wheeler as I wrote the initial manuscript.

I appreciate the patience of all my manuscript readers, particularly Jean. In addition, the input from Peggy Mancarella was tremendous.

I greatly appreciate Jim McGettigan, my mentor, for his friendship and advice during this long process.

Thanks to Marilyn Allen and Bob Diforio for guiding me.

Also I want to thank Nick Taylor for his ceaseless efforts and considerable literary skills necessary to make this book a reality.

I owe a particular note of appreciation to John Wiley & Sons, namely Tom Miller for keeping the project on track—and for his patience. And also thanks to Kellam Ayres for her assistance.

And, importantly, I give my unwavering love and respect to all the men and women who risk their lives in performing public service. The military, first responders, police, and fire just to name a few—I offer my acknowledgment that this is their story as well as mine.

Author's Note

I have taken pains to ensure that the facts of my career as recounted in this book are accurate as I remember them. Some of the names are changed, however, in an effort to protect the dignity of former colleagues in the rescue service and to preserve the memories of those they left behind.

I

Headwinds

We value the individual supremely, and nature values him not
a whit.

—Annie Dillard

We'd left the storm behind on the way out into the
North Atlantic. Now, as we returned in the December cold and darkness, with one nearly dead Ukrainian sailor in the passenger bay, we flew back into it. Suddenly, ferocious headwinds hit the helicopter and yanked the controls nearly out of my hands. The helicopter turned into a berserk rocking horse, its nose pitching violently up, then slamming down. Rain drove against the cockpit glass. It found the openings in the windscreen seals and invaded the cabin, where avionics control boxes, radios, and circuit breakers were all getting wet.

I was wrung out. I'd been flying since before dawn that morning, with almost no sleep the night before, on a mission to rescue the crew of a sunken freighter, *Salvador Allende*, 820 miles at sea south of Newfoundland's Grand Banks.

The aircraft's vibration had worked its way into my hands and feet. Now it was drilling its way into my brain. I didn't know whether I was shivering from my cold, wet flight suit or from the helicopter's shuddering. But we were headed home. We'd taken our last fuel from one of the tanker planes flying overhead and we were bearing down on the coast of Nova Scotia in formation with a second helicopter.

Back in the bay, the pararescue jumper who'd fished the sailor from the ocean was trying to keep the sailor, huddled in a sleeping bag, and loose rescue gear from crashing around the cabin in the turbulence. The flight engineer sat behind us on the jump seat straining to hear sounds of trouble from the jet engines and the transmission that channeled the engines' power to the slashing twenty-six-foot rotorblades. *Jolly 14*, like every MH-60 helicopter, was supposed to get major maintenance after ten hours in the air. We'd been flying for thirteen.

Jolly was the universal call sign for all air force rescue helicopters, followed by the last two of the numbers on its tail. Jolly originated as a nickname; the MH-60's predecessor, the HH-3E, was a big, blunt bird with an engaging roundness, and the air force models all were painted a dull green. Somebody called it a Jolly Green Giant, and the name stuck.

We'd expected as many as seventeen survivors, according to the briefing we'd received before we left that morning. We found just one that day. He'd been in the water almost forty-eight hours when we picked him up seventy miles from where his ship went down. He spoke enough English to tell us the water had been warm. The Gulf Stream had kept him alive, but it had killed his crewmates. The sharks just hadn't gotten to him yet.

It made me sick to see them, the predators tearing at the bodies in the water, and I knew those men were dead because we hadn't gotten there in time. Rescue was like that. I'd been elated at saving one victim and crushed at the same time because we hadn't saved more. There wasn't a man in our crew who wouldn't remember the sight of the sharks attacking the bodies in the water.

Another gust hit. The helicopter shimmied, then dropped two hundred or three hundred feet before I could level it. "Hold your altitude, sir." The copilot's voice came through my helmet headset over the cacophony of rotor and transmission noise and engine whine. I looked at the altitude gauge among the dozens of instruments I had to scan constantly on the control panel and reflected how I'd never gotten used to the feeling when the weather takes the bottom out and you're falling through space in eleven tons of metal with no idea of where or when you're going to stop.

It wasn't just the drop. I was becoming frightened. We had been awake for nearly forty hours, and I was fatigued, almost to the breaking point. Can't show your fear, though. Fear's contagious and it can be fatal. It was important to keep focused for the crew and for our families.

I forced my hands to stay light on the controls and slowly climbed back to an altitude of about 500 feet.

Jolly 14 labored and lurched into the headwind, jerking us against our harnesses. The rain kept finding a way in, joining and forming lines of moisture that trailed away from the edges of the windscreen. The severe turbulence we'd hit forced us to fly low. Above 500 feet, the rain changed to sleet and blowing snow, creating the possibility of rotor icing.

We flew for half an hour without speaking, each of us lost in his own thoughts. Mine were of the thrill I always got from taking human beings out of harm's way—more than 250 so far by a rough count—and of the end of my career. It was 1994, I was forty-seven years old, and I'd flown rescue missions for nearly twenty-five years. I sensed that I was nearing the point where I would have to leave the cockpit. I hated deskwork, pushing papers. But I owed it to my wife, Jean, and our two sons to get out before my skills deteriorated—to walk away and not be carried. Too many of my friends and colleagues had lost their lives in helicopter rescue. It is one of the most dangerous jobs there is.

2

An Unexpected Turn

Go . . . where there is no path and leave a trail.
—*George Bernard Shaw*

The idea of the helicopter has been around for more than fifteen hundred years. The Chinese had a version of a top that was a stick fixed with a propeller on one end. They'd spin the stick between their hands or with a string, and it would soar into the air.

The evolution from toy to immensely valuable and highly dangerous tool of modern life took most of those fifteen hundred years. It was not until World War II that Igor Sikorsky's experiments produced a helicopter that consistently got off the ground. From then on its promise vied with the impulse to take the machine beyond its limits, an impulse that, combined with the fine balance of elements in its design, has made the helicopter three or four times more dangerous to fly than military fixed-wing aircraft and about ten times more dangerous to fly than commercial fixed-wing aircraft, based on crash statistics.

The irony of the helicopter is that its greatest blessing—its versatility—is also its greatest curse. Because they can do so much, flying in and out of the tightest spots under the worst conditions, helicopters often are flown into situations where the safety options diminish exponentially, leading to peril and, frequently, death.

* * *

It was a possibility I lived with every day of my career. But at the beginning, when I knew the helicopter's gentle origins only because I was a Chinese history major at the University of Buffalo, helicopters were the furthest thing from my young mind. Then the Erie County draft board ordered me to report for a preinduction physical.

Up to then, February 1970, I'd led a predictable life. I grew up Irish American. My first memory was of my great-aunt, my mother's mother's sister, gauzed in an oxygen tent as she lay dying in a bedroom of our small house. Someone held my hand and led me in to her, the old woman wanting to see the young ones a last time. My father, Edward Joseph Fleming, was a telephone lineman who worked his way up to foreman. He walked to work at the company offices 2 miles away, and we didn't own a car until I was in the fifth grade—a '49 Ford, purchased in 1958. Mother, when she wasn't taking care of her aunt, and later her mother, taught at St. John the Baptist, the Catholic elementary school where I learned the rigid discipline of priests and nuns. I ate dinner each night at a table peppered with the strongly voiced opinions of my parents and three sisters. In football, tennis, and track and field at Cardinal O'Hara High School, I lettered but never starred. By the time I entered the University of Buffalo as a day student in the fall of 1966, I had learned the art of detachment from the world's confusions.

I disappeared, mostly into sports. Classes with a few hundred students in them didn't need me there to answer roll call. I did my reading, showed up for tests, and received gentleman's C's for my lackadaisical efforts. The rest of the time, my friends and I ran, lifted weights, drank beer, and killed time. We sought out amateur track meets and tennis tournaments around Buffalo, and drove to them in the salt-rusted Ford Falcon I'd bought used with 118,000 miles on the clock. I kept its radio permanently tuned to the station that played Neil Young, the Moody Blues, Dylan, and the Stones.

As much as I tried to turn away, the world kept intruding. The civil rights movement and the war in Vietnam were steady themes of conversation at our dinner table. My father was a veteran of World War II. He'd grown up in the Little Dublin section of Saratoga Springs, New York, where working-class Irish lived. The Irish were the people who forked hay and groomed, walked, and otherwise supported the race horse industry and the health resorts that brought the town such glamor in the summers. After moving to Buffalo and marrying my mother, he joined the army. He fought in New Guinea and the Philippines. By the time I knew him, his main pastime was gardening, but he was still a natural athlete who could pick up a sport—he bowled, played golf, and now and then shot pool for money—after months without practice, and he could hold his own with the best. His intelligence far outweighed his education, which ended with high school. He taught me the importance of serving when the country called, but he believed that the endless morass of Vietnam was not a way to fight a war.

Against the backdrop of the struggle in the South for equal rights and the increasing clashes over Vietnam that peaked at the national political conventions in 1968, when more than half a million Americans were fighting in the war, we contended at home with a more immediate concern.

My sister Lynne, the youngest of the four siblings, had been diagnosed with Hodgkin's disease when she was a sophomore in high school. Lynne was the brightest of us. She read eagerly and displayed what she learned with the sheer joy of knowledge. More than that, she faced the cancer with a fighter's courage. I was a year older than she was. It was because of her example— fighting through high school and winning a scholarship to Canisius College despite the cancer—that after my first two slacker years at Buffalo I began to pay attention.

Jean Brady was the other factor in my renaissance. Jean and her family lived less than a mile from us, but I had never met her before I walked into an economics class one day in the winter of my junior year. She was wearing a pea coat, scarf, and boots, standard Buffalo winter gear, and had some books I'd been looking for. Three months later, I wasn't dating anybody else, and in December of my senior year, I gave her a ring.

Neil Armstrong's one small step onto the moon the previous summer had been spectacular, but for draft-age men in 1969 the big news was the draft lottery. The first drawing was held December 1 and the number for my birthday, April 16, came up low. My student deferment would run out as soon as I graduated the following June. So when the notice for my physical arrived six weeks into 1970, I expected that soon after graduation, I'd be in Vietnam.

Before long I was driving my rusted-out Falcon through Buffalo's gray streets to City Hall, where the physicals were conducted on an upper floor. There were throngs of us there on a Saturday morning, and every one of us checked our dignity at the front door.

It was the mother of all medical exams, and at the end of it I decided there had to be something better in the way of military service. I had taken my father's point of view that serving my country was a privilege whether one believed in the war or not. I just didn't want to do it in an army uniform. I talked to my parents and Jean and decided to check out the other services.

Two days later, I visited the air force recruiting station in the Buffalo suburb of Tonawanda.

The recruiter sized up my situation right away. He said he could get me in the air force, but there was one small catch. I had to sign up for a career field where he was having trouble filling his quota of recruits.

"You interested?" he asked.

I said I thought so.

"Good," he said heartily. "Because I'm not recruiting fliers, son. I'm recruiting heroes. The air force is starting a new training program for the Air Rescue Service. We need men to fly helicopters. When a plane goes down, when an American military man is trapped behind the lines, when people are in trouble anywhere, a lot of times a helicopter is the only way to get them out. You'd spend three months in OTS doing your officer training. Then you'd get nine months of army helicopter training. And then you'd come back over to the air force for three more months so we could teach you how to really fly. Still interested?"

Flying was never one of my ambitions growing up, let alone in helicopters. I had more of an academic career in mind. I had never been in a helicopter. I knew little about them, other than about their Chinese origins. They struck me as mechanical monstrosities that were as likely to shake apart as they were to lift off and fly. Watching news reports from Vietnam, I was always struck with how *vulnerable* they seemed, chugging along above the treetops. I had not then seen the horrifying statistics of helicopter casualties.

"Have you ever flown in a helicopter, sir?" I asked, looking for something personal beyond the quota-filling sales pitch he was giving me.

"Never have, son," the recruiter answered. "Not that I wouldn't. Just never had the opportunity."

I didn't hear in his words a ringing endorsement of helicopter flight. Still, the idea of helicopter rescue sounded interesting. I envisioned rescuing stranded people, and the thought produced a surge of satisfaction. The wheels of my career turned and gyred. "Let's do it then," I said, and signed the papers on the spot.

I graduated from college that June. Protests against the military over Vietnam surged to new levels of fury and disillusionment, with the escalated bombing of North Vietnam and the deaths of four students at Kent State University the month before.

In July, Jean and I were married. We honeymooned briefly on Lake Champlain in Vermont. Then I entered three months of officer training at Lackland Air Force Base in Texas, and emerged as a newly minted second lieutenant in the air force. And in December, less than a year after I had confronted the idea of flying helicopters for the first time, Jean and I began the long drive from Buffalo to Fort Wolters, Texas, for the first stage of my pilot training.

It's easy for a child to leave his parents, especially when he's married and has a new life ahead of him. Jean had written me in OTS to let me know that she was pregnant, so we had that to look forward to as well. What's harder is leaving a sibling you've doted on and cared for. Lynne remained for me an example of courage. Unlike my father's Signal Corps service in the Pacific, which I knew more from history books than from the few sketchy stories he reluctantly shared, I had seen Lynne's courage first-hand. I'd seen her fight debilitating chemotherapy and radiation treatments for the inoperable cancer. I'd watched and helped her study while she was weak and wasted, and I saw her pain transcended by her pleasure in learning. Leaving removed a layer of her support.

Even when we said good-bye, she was courage personified. She told me she'd be fine, she was going to keep fighting. She told me she loved me and Jean. And she told me to always follow my curiosity, because knowledge was a strength that nothing and no one can take away from you. I left her reluctantly, hating that I'd be far away, but I knew that our parents, and our two older sisters, wouldn't let her fight alone.

Fort Wolters sat in a hot patch of Texas about an hour west of the cloverleafs and burgeoning skylines of Dallas and Fort Worth. We were a few miles out when I glanced up and noticed with a start that the sky was full of dragonflies. They seemed to be everywhere, darting and swooping in movements with no pattern evident to me. I pulled over to watch and point them out to Jean. As I watched, I suddenly realized that they weren't dragonflies flitting close to the car, but small helicopters in the distance. There must have been hundreds of them, flying in all directions like bits of metal in suspension. They hovered, moved in circles and straight lines, and darted up without warning from the fields close to the highway.

Jean and I sat there and just stared. Reality seeped in for the first time, and suddenly I felt anxiety. For the next several months my life would be up there in the dust-blown Texas sky. I felt like the boy who had broken a window in a scary neighbor's house, and now was knocking on the door to offer retribution, not knowing what would happen. Finally I took a deep breath, Jean and I squeezed hands, and I pulled back onto the road and drove the last few miles to my waiting future.

3

I Fly

Aeronautics was neither an industry nor a science. It was a miracle.

—*Igor Sikorsky*

Dempsey Army Airfield was the main training field at Fort Wolters. That's where many of the helicopters were maintained, and where, early each morning and afternoon, the little bug-eyed trainers lifted off in a mass ascension like a cloud of locusts. They'd fly out to several staging fields where the actual training occurred.

The countryside around was runneled with dry streambeds. They could rage with water in a thunderstorm, but it only rained three months a year. The rest of the year it was dry, and the helicopters raised enormous dust clouds.

There must have been five hundred of them launched and flown in any training period. Even at that, a lot of groups were training at Fort Wolters, and there weren't enough helicopters for us all to fly at once.

Helicopters had emerged as significant combat aircraft in Vietnam. They got shot down a lot, but for every one that was shot down, five crashed for reasons not related to enemy fire. I was at the beginning of my learning curve. I didn't know then just how complicated and uncompromising helicopters were. And I hadn't yet grasped that they were routinely thrust into hazardous missions under conditions that would keep airplanes on the ground. This combination caused relatively high losses whether in combat or not. Nobody talked about the losses much, in any case. But we knew that was the reason why helicopter pilots were in such demand, and why, even with American troop strength in Vietnam declining, the army was pushing so many of them through Fort Wolters.

Captain Carlsson, my flight instructor, was the strong, silent type, quiet to the point that it was eerie, but at the same time utterly professional. His quiet reflected a calm that came through in his instruction. He used analogies to explain the mysteries of helicopter flight and hovering.

"Have you ever seen a person riding on a unicycle and then seen that person stop?" he asked. "His arms and legs are working pretty hard. Well, if you can balance on a unicycle, using your arms and legs for different purposes all at once, you might be able to hover. It's a lot of work to stay in one place." The analogy made a weird kind of sense, and he went on, bringing the helicopter's controls into the picture.

It hadn't been that long since I was a teenager learning to clutch and shift my old Ford Falcon. Controlling a helicopter was going to be a whole lot harder.

A helicopter pilot sits on the right side of the cockpit, straddling a lever that rises up from the floor. This is the cyclic, and it's controlled by the right hand. (It typically requires an exaggerated forward lean that eventually leaves instructor pilots hobbling around with bad backs.) The cyclic is the directional control. It tilts the main rotor. If you move it to the right, for example, the main rotor tilts right, and the helicopter moves in that direction.

The left hand controls the collective, a tubular lever with a throttle on the end located to the left and forward of the pilot's seat. Raising it increases the power in the engines and the torque and lift of the main rotor. With an increase in collective, you increase the flow down through the rotor, which results in power to climb, fly faster, or maneuver the aircraft more aggressively. Lowering the collective does the opposite—it decreases power to slow the aircraft, descend, or land. Every movement of the collective requires a throttle adjustment.

Helicopter pilots will sometimes tell you the controls are placed on the aircraft's right side and arranged the way they are because Igor Sikorsky was left-handed, but I don't know whether that's true.

Two pedals lie at the pilot's feet. These control the tail rotor, which is the small rotor on the back of the tail that prevents the body of the helicopter from spinning under the main rotor. The tail rotor helps stabilize the aircraft.

The secret of flying a helicopter, like the secret of the stationary unicyclist, is to use all these together, to balance the competing forces to keep it in the air. The other secret is to do it all without thinking. That takes a while.

Carlsson explained all this in terms both eloquent and terse, as was his style. They flew by me in a jumble of words I wasn't yet familiar with and actions I had yet to put into practice. It seemed to me that piloting a helicopter required all the actions of the unicyclist he described, and then some. It was as if the unicyclist not only was balancing on his one wheel, but also juggling buzzing chainsaws at the same time, plus sword-swallowing and breathing fire. The combination of activities was impossible to follow. I couldn't have repeated what he told me, and I felt dizzy trying to imagine doing it. He ended with a warning. "Remember, this isn't a dance," he said. "You don't go one-two-three, one-two-three. You do it all at the same time. The helicopter is impatient to smack the ground. It won't wait for you to think about it. What do you think?"

Silence, as I tried to grasp it all.

"Let's go try it. It's a real lot of fun," he said.

The captain didn't give me the controls that afternoon. That's probably why I'm still alive.

That night I sat down with Jean and described my session. "Let's try it," she said. She sat me at a kitchen chair and told me to go through the motions. So I sat leaning forward in the awkward position of helicopter pilots with my left arm cocked at my side and my right arm resting on my right thigh, both poised to work imaginary controls. My heels were on the floor, my toes pointed to the ceiling. With my left hand I raised and lowered an invisible collective while I twisted an imaginary throttle. I moved my feet on imaginary pedals and shifted an imaginary cyclic, while Jean coached me by reading the sequence from my instruction book. It was quite a hover.

I practiced like that for several evenings. I got to the point where I was handling the kitchen hover pretty well. I was still having some difficulty in the aircraft.

I was one of nine air force second lieutenants in my training class. The rest of the class was army; Fort Wolters was an army post, and the army was conducting our training. There were about thirty-five in my class, veterans from the infantry, artillery, and other army specialties who had volunteered to learn helicopter flying. They were older than we were, and they had been around. Most had done tours in Vietnam. They called us "zoomies" and some treated us with polite condescension.

We trained in Hughes-built TH-55s, the small two-seat helicopters I'd seen filling the sky when we drove into Fort Wolters and nearby Mineral Wells. Even up close, they looked like mechanical insects, with the two front windscreens bugging out on either side like eyes. Nothing altered that impression when they were in the air; their engines buzzed like a fly on the wrong side of the screen, and they darted like the dragonflies I'd thought they were.

Each class was assigned to fly mornings or afternoons. You'd fly in the morning for a while, then you'd switch to afternoons, a plan that to my thinking was cleverly designed to assure that you got little relief from the grind. When we weren't trying to master the challenges of rotary wing flight, we listened to classroom lectures or busted our humps in physical training.

Fort Wolters made no distinction between army trainees and those from the air force. We all trained as if we were getting ready to fight a ground war. The army tests demanded that we crawl under barbed wire, climb hand over hand, walk on balance beams, run three miles at a minimum, and throw dummy hand grenades for accuracy, all in full combat gear. This was a lot of fun for the army trainers, who took sadistic pleasure in bringing the zoomies up to infantry standards.

One day early in our training we were in the briefing room preparing for flight. Some of us had started to solo, but I hadn't yet. The room contained a blackboard, a wooden podium, and about forty square tables with three straight-backed metal chairs at each. Overhead, fluorescent lights in the ceiling lights flickered and hummed. The setting was U.S. Army utilitarian.

An instructor and two students sat at each table. I had been paired with an army lieutenant, Joe Dunn, for training, and we sat with Captain Carlsson. We were discussing the various maneuvers and emergency procedures we were going to tackle on the day's flights when suddenly the safety officer burst into the room. He stood at the podium and waited. Slowly a silence fell across the room. Carlsson seemed to sense that something had happened. Such an interruption was unusual.

When he spoke, the officer's words were abrupt. "I'm sorry to have to tell you, but Lieutenant Pike was killed this morning. His helicopter came apart in flight."

I was stunned. Airmen and soldiers alike sat in silence. Steve Pike was one of the zoomies, but his death didn't know air force blue from army green. He was a pleasant guy and an eager flier. We weren't close, but his death brought home the dangers of helicopter flying. Unlike fixed-wing training aircraft, our aircraft came with no ejection seats or parachutes. As we progressed in training we realized that every emergency, no matter how severe, had to be ridden to the ground.

"What happened?" someone asked.

"The rotor system disintegrated and flew off the aircraft. When that happened it just came apart like a starburst. His body was recovered, but it was badly dismembered and partially shredded,

as it was forced through the metal of the instrument console."
The officer was using a more macho tone than I had ever heard
from him before, as if he were using the accident to remind us of
the constant dangers posed by helicopter flight. "In fact, we
couldn't identify the pilot until we found his wallet at the scene.
The tower operator said he got off one cry for help over the radio
but he had no chance. It happens. Okay," he said. "Get back to
work and get ready to fly." The officer turned and left the room.

The instructors must have been hardened to such accidents,
but the students all looked at one another. It was a frightful
moment of reality for all of us. For the first time, fear truly trick-
led into the equation. We all knew, intellectually, that military
helicopters were the most dangerous form of flying. It hadn't
taken long to learn that the combination of forces needed to get
them into the air and keep them aloft was a tricky balance of aero-
dynamics and mechanical legerdemain. One loose link could lead
to its unraveling. But we hadn't seen the danger manifest itself.
Surely, with the catastrophic disintegration of an aircraft, the training would stand down to investigate and check the other helicopters. We were wrong. Captain Carlsson returned to the day's
flight plans. Thirty minutes later, I was walking out to the aircraft.

I wondered if the news of a fatal crash would reach the
trainees' families before we got home that night. Would Jean
know for sure I was alive before I showed up at the door of our
rented trailer to provide the proof? With the thought of the aircraft disintegrating around me, a jolt of anxiety struck me. I took
a deep breath to drive away a bout of dizziness. As I opened the
tiny helicopter's door, my hand trembled. I hoped it was the winter cold.

After eight hours of training, I was still responding to danger cues
with overly aggressive control inputs. The helicopter would spin
or plummet or take off to one side. Captain Carlsson would take
the controls, level it out, and I'd try again. The tension that built

up with my successive failures produced adrenaline and my touch on the controls got worse. I needed a surgeon's hands and a dancer's feet, but what I had were the hands of a bricklayer and the feet of a grape-crusher.

Wives' Day came. This was a day cooked up by army public affairs to show the officers' wives just how safe helicopter flying was. One of my classmates put an end to that. He made some miscues while he was trying to hover and crashed. Luckily, it was a low hover and he walked away. I don't think the wives were reassured.

Captain Carlsson and I ran through our practice routine the next morning. As usual, I put too much force into the controls, and he had to recover the aircraft. We landed, and the captain stepped out of the doorless trainer. I figured he was going to relieve himself of the morning coffee until he leaned back in to gather his helmet bag and his personal gear.

"Well, Lieutenant Fleming, it's time," he said. "You've got it by yourself now."

"But sir, I've never hovered this," I answered.

"You will, I'm sure of it."

He stuck his helmet under his arm and walked away.

I felt suddenly exposed like the kid in the class play waiting in the wings for my big entrance but not sure I knew my lines. The spotlight was waiting. I rifled my brain for everything I'd learned, trying to review it before I stepped onto the stage. I didn't want to let the captain down and his attitude of calm and confidence encouraged me. On the other hand, I noticed that he got a safe distance away before he sat down and lit a cigarette. I took a breath and tried to concentrate on what I had to do.

I slowly rolled on the throttle to get the rotor rpm up to flying speed and slowly began pulling on the collective. As the aircraft got light, trying to lift, I sensed it wanting to turn over like a top spinning on its side. Instructions crowded into my head and fought for attention. *Move the cyclic right. Left pedal. Let's go try it, it's a lot of fun.*

Suddenly, I felt the helicopter as I never had before. I felt more keenly aware of all its tricks, the way it signaled its response to the forces of Newtonian physics—the actions and the opposing reactions—that were employed in lifting it and keeping it aloft and steady. The copter cleared the ground and started to spin right, but I stopped it with the left pedal. It started to drift left, but I caught it in time with the right cyclic control. And then— the miracle! It held and balanced, stationary in the air. It wasn't impossible after all. I could do it! I would have shouted out loud if I hadn't been so busy.

Anyone watching would have seen a helicopter hovering, basically still. But there was a lot of motion going on inside the cockpit. I was the unicyclist, balancing with my arms, legs, wrists, and head, to say nothing of my racing mind, all moving feverishly to keep it still. I wasn't working from instinct—not yet, anyway. But the control movements were entering my working memory.

It's impossible to say how good it felt. What moments before had been cloaked in mystery had revealed itself to me. The secret was mine, and with it a new world had opened. I was in control of the machine for the first time. I felt exhilarated and calm at the same time, the calm that comes from moving from doubt to certainty. And Captain Carlsson had been right. It *was* a lot of fun.

I was feeling pretty proud of myself, almost smug. But to get credit for the solo, a pilot had to fly three takeoffs and landings. I landed and started to take off again. But when I added power, this time I forgot to add left pedal. The helicopter listed and took off sideways, while my helmet bag, extra gloves, and thermos with the dregs of the morning's coffee flew from the console and out of the cockpit. I added pedal, and that was the worst of the damage, except to my recently inflated pride.

The rest of the three patterns went okay, and I took the copter down for the third time with the sense of having cleared my most important hurdle.

Captain Carlsson emerged from the heliport's small training building as I hover-taxied to the apron in front. His chiseled face wore an expression that I'd call slightly pleased. He put on his helmet and climbed aboard, and I took off to fly from the stage field back "to the barn" at Dempsey.

I figured the captain was going to congratulate me on passing my first solo test and waited for him to say something. Instead, he quietly reached into his helmet bag and pulled out first my gloves, then my helmet bag, and finally the thermos, which was dented but intact. He put them all on a small console just to be sure I didn't miss them. Then he looked at me, smiled slightly, and gave me a thumbs-up.

"You got out of that corkscrew maneuver real nice, Lieutenant," he said.

I knew better than to be too full of myself, to get too swelled up about one day's worth of solo hovers. But the captain's praise made me glow inside. I appreciated for the first time the set of skills that went into successfully piloting a helicopter, and I knew—felt, really—that I had entered a small fraternity of pilots who could get the complicated and sometimes obstinate machines off the ground, into the air, and safely back to the ground. It was no small thing. I had a great deal more to learn; the small trainers were no match for the larger helicopters I'd be flying when my training was complete. But it was still a skill set I could be proud of, something to build on. I smiled in response to the compliment and said, "Thank you, sir."

You didn't rest on your laurels. The next morning I was at the controls of the TH-55 in the helicopter gridlock that took place every morning going out of Dempsey. I was now alone in the cockpit, in a line behind a hundred or more other greenhorn pilots, hover-taxiing to one of the four takeoff pads to go out to our training fields. And there were another hundred behind me. It was an airborne rush hour.

A helicopter naturally wants to turn its nose into the wind. In our tightly packed traffic pattern we had not only a 25 mph breeze across the Texas plains to deal with, but also the erratic winds generated by hundreds of helicopter rotors. The copters swung back and forth like a ragged chorus line as they advanced. No air traffic controllers were on hand to sort this out. "See and avoid" was the only rule. I guided the trainer through choking clouds of dust. Now and then a blown stone pinged off the windscreen just to let me know the world was out there.

Now I was in the air with a bunch of other rookies, all trying to keep from flying into one another. The day's exercise was to navigate to one of the satellite training fields while flying. We were supposed to take out a map, read it, and follow the correct route to get where we were going. We looked like little fish, wheeling and darting and diving to avoid a predator, but with a hundred or more helicopters in the air, the predator was us.

I forgot the map to concentrate on staying alive. When the swarm thinned out, I looked around to realize I'd flown far from my planned route. The map wasn't any help. It showed rivers in blue, as if they had water in them. The dry Texas spring had turned them into dusty ruts. I had no precise idea where I was.

Then I spotted a line of army buses. I knew the buses carried instructors and second-period students who would take the helicopters for the afternoon training session and then return to Dempsey in a P.M. version of the morning rush, this time with everyone trying to land at the same time. I thought one of the buses might be going to my training field.

I throttled back, maneuvered over the buses, and followed the line until one of them turned into the right training field.

I set up my practice patterns, finished my training, and landed. When I went into the building, I found Captain Carlsson waiting. He gave me a look. "How was the map reading?" he asked.

"Difficult with all the helicopter traffic, sir."

"Did you keep an aggressive lookout for the other traffic?"

"I sure did."

"Bus traffic also?" A smile flickered on his face. "You're learning to think on the fly, Lieutenant. You'll need that skill in the future."

I had no idea how true those words would turn out to be.

4

Deadly Webs

Take nothing for granted.
            —*Accident Investigation Manual, U.S. Air Force*

One crash haunts me relentlessly.

It happened in Korea, where I was stationed on my second assignment in air rescue. It occurred in conditions I'd been in too many times to count. It was a training flight, simulating survivor recovery in the treacherous Korean mountains. The pilots and crew were wearing night vision goggles. Rainstorms raked the night. The rescue mission could have been for real; it was the kind of night that planes go down and monsoon-flooded villages crumble into rushing torrents.

The hypothetical survivors were at the end of a steep, narrow valley, the kind of valley that is often crisscrossed with a web of wires overhead, carrying electricity for the conveniences of modern life into the hinterlands. As the crew flew into the valley, the pilots and scanners typically chose a route through the obstacles of rock outcroppings and ridges and noted an escape route out at the same time. As maneuverable as they are, helicopters can't always stop and hover; nor can they always fly backward—they can wind up trapped in dead ends. But the crew peered forward and to the sides as they advanced, not overhead, where the wires would have been.

Night vision goggles intensify photons of available light and create an image in the phosphorescent tubes the crews look through. But in stormy, overcast conditions, the definition fades. On this night, the valley, mountains, and sky would have blended together into a single shade of green.

Rain drummed at the aircraft with a noise deepened by its forward speed. Resonating with the engines and rotor noise, it mimicked a never-ending roll of thunder. The noise made crew communication difficult. It ate away at the crew's focus and produced the conditions for confusion.

The valley narrowed, closing off one option after another for escape. The rescuers were flying in a dark tunnel formed by the stifling closeness of the rock walls, the rising valley floor, and the thick knit of unseen cables over their heads. Soon there would be no way out.

The flight engineer was the first to sense trouble. His communication was recorded at the rescue air base operations center as he spoke to the pilot. "Sir, we've got to get out now, it's getting too tight to turn. We're too heavy to hover. Something is wrong. I feel it."

Feel counts for a lot when you've dodged death before. But he got no response, only silence, frequently a sign of workload and stress. Meanwhile, the storm and darkness were slowly causing the images in the goggles to blur and fade away. The almost imperceptible fading of subtleties in the "green on green" visual field of the goggles went unnoticed. Then one of the crew realized that he was seeing nothing through the NVGs, just a green wash instead of the faint silhouettes of mountains or valley floor that earlier showed their way.

"Sir, right scanner, my goggles have shut down!"

The copilot chimed in. "Copilot's goggles are gone, too. We need to get out of here."

The helicopter was traveling at 150 feet per second. It takes a well-trained pilot 2.8 seconds to notice something is wrong, and another 2 seconds to take corrective action. In that time the crew had flown another 720 feet filled with unseen obstacles.

With their options narrowing, adequate time to make decisions was a departed luxury. Instinctive response prevailed over reasoned actions. The vise tightened. Instinct told the crew to climb.

"Clear right and above! Climb! Shit, we've got to get out of here!"

The pilot moved the controls to climb out of the valley, and the Jolly Green Giant helicopter roared with the added power. Lightning flickered and lit the valley walls in sharp relief. They were too close. The only option was to climb. But among all the miles of threatening ridges and hilltops, the overhead cables were the easiest to miss in the blinding, deafening rain.

The pilot must have noticed the cable just before he hit it. The helicopter's path contorted in a violent evasive maneuver. It hit at 100 knots airspeed, 45 degrees left bank turn, and in an extreme nose high attitude that indicates a last-ditch attempt to escape the snare.

Huge parts of the main rotor blades, which are the helicopter's wings, sheared off on contact with the cable. The blades and main rotor hub failed and disintegrated. Two-hundred-pound shards of blade sliced down through the cockpit at nearly the speed of sound, cleaving metal and flesh. The blades sheared the cockpit and the two pilots away from the body of the aircraft. Then the tail failed from the violent forces of the decapitation.

From inside, to the doomed crew, the aircraft must have appeared to explode. The separated sections spun forward through the air. Centrifugal forces pinned crew members to the metal cabin walls. Pieces of the cockpit, the two pilots strapped inside, remained airborne only briefly. The cabin section hit the mountainside 1,000 feet beyond the cable strike. There were no survivors.

The potential for a quick and violent death was always there for all of us.

5

Turnings

The beginnings and endings of all human undertakings are untidy.

—*John Galsworthy*

In the spring of 1971, as I was acquiring the basic skills required of a helicopter pilot, the world outside kept turning. President Nixon's policy of "Vietnamization," adopted the year before to reduce the number of Americans in Vietnam and force the South Vietnamese to fight their own war, was producing steady declines in American troop strength. In the lurid realm of crime, much of the nation was transfixed by the burning eyes of convicted cult murderer Charles Manson.

Close to home, I was experiencing the joy of anticipating Jean's delivery of our first child, an event we both looked forward to, as did our family back in Buffalo. As April and her delivery date neared, I found it difficult to concentrate on flying. In a way, it was good practice, because piloting a helicopter demanded that you block out distractions and pay attention to the machine and the controls.

Keith Patrick Fleming was born before dawn on a morning early in April at the Fort Wolters Army Hospital. Jean realized he was coming about midnight. The complicating factor was that I was scheduled for my first checkride the next day. I wore my flight suit when I drove her to the hospital and spent the night pacing the floor and catnapping on a waiting-room couch.

At about six in the morning, a gruff army nurse appeared with a bundle and I looked down at our son. I was shocked at the little purple apparition. I guess I'd imagined a baby in the Gerber ads, a baby whose system had calmed down from the stress of birth and his new exposure to the world. This one was newly minted, with tiny purple fingers and a scrunched-up purple face, and as I watched him in absolute wonder, I suddenly realized what a miracle every new baby represents. *He's here*, I thought. He's really real.

Then, having no choice in the matter, I stumbled off for my first U.S. Army checkride. I got through it okay, then rushed back to the hospital, where I saw Jean for the first time after the birth. Keith was now a normal baby color. Jean and I just sat there and admired him, and I admired both of them.

The joy of our first son was tempered by remembering—as I did every day—that Lynne was locked in her fight with Hodgkin's disease.

What I didn't know was that my father was battling cancer, too. He probably didn't know it either, then. He didn't like to go to doctors. Edward Fleming's natural athleticism, his uncanny ability to play a sport well without practicing, had always seemed like vitality to me. Among the legends that surrounded him for me, his only son, was the fact that he and his brother Bill had, as youths, played semipro basketball to help put money in the family till. His skill at golf, again a sport he rarely practiced, was such that he had given lessons to Saratoga's well-heeled summer denizens, and he won driving contests from them on the side. He had always seemed so hale and vital to me.

The first inkling that something was wrong came in a routine phone call. We didn't have a phone in our trailer but instead made calls from a phone bank on the base. I spoke to my mother, and when Dad came on the phone he spoke to me warmly, but his mind seemed somehow absent. The words came out slowly, with a hollowness that frightened me. He showed caring and concern, but the optimistic energy that I was accustomed to was gone. He didn't speak or allude to any problems, but I sensed that things were very wrong.

When I hung up the receiver, I looked at Jean and said, "My father is dying."

Later, when my oldest sister, Joanne, called to say that Dad had cancer that had spread throughout his body, I said, "I know."

My father was a quiet patriot who never waved the flag outside the American Legion hall. But he set an eloquent example when it came to the sacrifices that freedom demands of its citizens. I always thought of him with pride when I put on my dress uniform.

It was with this mixture of joy and sadness that Jean, Keith, and I left Fort Wolters in June to move to Fort Rucker, Alabama, for my advanced training.

It was great to be back in the East, in a part of the country with trees thick with green leaves and streambeds that actually had water twelve months of the year. We liked the statue of the boll weevil that greeted us in the Enterprise, Alabama, town square, too. But I seemed to have run out of luck when it came to instructors.

In contrast with the quiet competence of Captain Carlsson, my teacher at Fort Rucker was an instructor from hell. His name was Stone, and he was mad at the world. He didn't like zoomies from the air force. Whatever lay behind his attitude, he was curt and sarcastic and a poor teacher on the ground. In the air, he was worse.

We were training now in TH-13s, helicopters like the ones television viewers are familiar with from the opening scenes of *M*A*S*H*. It was an unstable aircraft with finicky throttle control. Its instruments were rudimentary. But instruments were key to this phase of my training, because having learned to keep a helicopter in the air, I was now learning to fly it without visual cues, only instruments. This meant flying under a hood.

Hooded flight is hard enough. The vibration and flickering light through the rotor system and the hood can cause a strobe effect and, potentially, flicker vertigo. Flicker vertigo, at its worst, brings on convulsions in the same way that strobe lights can cause seizures in some people. I wasn't affected in that way, but Stone screamed abuse and obscenities from the beginning of a flight to the end.

"Zoomie," he yelled, "you assholes will never learn to fly these things! You in particular, Lieutenant, will be a smoking hole someday! I'm never wrong!"

I developed a visceral aversion to him. It was such that if he'd been sitting next to the only open seat in the officers' mess, I would have eaten standing up. He was the kind of person you'd cross the street just to avoid having to greet—and he was also the kind of person who'd notice that and cross the street just to confront you.

I quickly learned to tune him out if I was to keep the aircraft in the air. It was my second lesson, after anticipating Keith's birth, in tuning out the noise and distractions that can be fatal not only to a pilot and crew on a rescue mission, but that also can sabotage the best efforts of any enterprise.

Naturally, Stone noticed it when I was able to ignore him and treat him as white noise. Then he'd rap me on the helmet with a ruler. If I made the mistake of glancing in his direction, he'd scream louder.

"I'm talking to you, you worthless piece of shit! You better damn well listen!"

Two pilots in an army training helicopter sit hip-to-hip. You'd be lucky to sit that close on a first date. When you're sitting that close to a guy who's screaming in your headphones, calling you names you can't say on TV, and banging you on the helmet with a ruler, it's not just no fun; it's also dangerous.

Alabama's summer thunderstorms added to the fun. Every afternoon the hot and humid air—95 degrees Fahrenheit outside, and probably 10 degrees hotter in the cockpit—would generate huge thunderstorms. We stayed out of them, but the swirling air around them still bounced the helicopter like a toy. Stone fed like a parasite on their gusting, crashing energy and turned up his volume and abuse.

Finally, I had enough. I made an appointment with the air force colonel who served as one of the liaisons with the army helicopter training program. I planned to ask him for an instructor change. When I entered his office, I knew I had entered a place of deep weirdness.

The day was bright but the blinds were drawn. The colonel sat behind a very large desk in the dim light wearing dark aviator sunglasses. His face was expressionless. I couldn't tell if he was even looking at me.

"What's your problem, Lieutenant?" he began. "Why did you want to see me?"

"Sir, I'm having difficulty learning the instrument procedures with Mr. Stone," I said. "He's got no patience for me or any air force officer. Many of the army students, I've heard, also find him difficult to learn from."

The colonel swiveled in his chair, his dark glasses utterly opaque. "And what do you want from me, Lieutenant Fleming?"

"Sir, could you assist me in getting an instructor change?"

He picked up a pen and placed it on a blank notepad, then shifted them around. He said nothing for a moment, then looked up. "Lieutenant, you reschedule this meeting," he said. "Before you come back to see me, I want you to trim your mustache. I want you to trim it, and trim it, and trim it again until I can't see it anymore."

"But sir, I thought they were legal."

"Maybe they are. But not if you want help from me. I don't want any of my air force officers looking like army aviators, do you understand? Trim that mustache until it doesn't exist, and then I might help you. That is, if you convince me when you come back that you even want to be here."

"Yes, sir," I said, snapping off a crisp salute. I then wheeled in a smart about-face to head for the door. I was confused at first. Then I was discouraged. Here was a bureaucrat who didn't care about air force regulations, only his own interpretation of how the rules should read. Instead of caring about fliers under his command receiving the instruction they needed, he just cared about appearances.

That was the last time I ever saw the colonel. I kept my mustache and I never went back to ask his help.

Stone rode me without mercy for the rest of my instrument training. I wanted to kick him out the cockpit door, but his abuse helped me, too. It taught me to filter out the noise and listen to what the aircraft and the instruments were telling me. After three months, I graduated with the rest of my class in air force dress blues.

After the ceremony, I was standing with Jean and the air force lieutenants with whom I'd gone through the past nine months when Stone sauntered up for a last word. "Lieutenant," he said, drawing the word out with a sarcastic smirk, "I gare-ron-tee you will never amount to nothing in the helicopter world."

The hell I won't, I thought. I'll not only be something in the helicopter world, I'll also do everything I can every day I'm a part of it to erase the memory of people like you. I'll make sure when I start teaching I don't abuse my students, and I'll make them better fliers than you ever could.

My father's health was quickly declining, and as 1971 wound to a close the family gathered at his bedside. Jean and I came home and brought Keith in to see him. He struggled to sit up. I was shocked to see how frail he had become. I wore my dress blues with my pilot's wings, and we spent a few moments alone together. We talked quietly, and he studied me with eyes that were tired and full of pain, but I also saw a look of satisfaction. "I'm proud of you, son," he said. "I wish I could have seen you fly."

"I wish you could have, too," I said.

Later, when more of us were at the bedside and the painkillers were having their effect with Dad, I glanced up at him in one random moment and met Lynne's eyes across the bed. Her expression told me that she knew his fate would be hers, not tomorrow or the next day, but soon. She showed a profound understanding of the approach of death. I could hardly believe her courage.

Dad died on the last day of the year. His death released us from our vigil, and him from his suffering and pain. We had a good Irish wake full of the celebration of his life he would have wanted, with a measure of the sadness we all felt. And not long afterward, as he would have wanted, I returned to my duties in the helicopter world.

6

First Rescue

Leadership and learning are indispensable to each other.

—*John F. Kennedy*

I was an air force officer the army taught to fly. This made me either a hybrid or a bastard, depending on your point of view. I thought I could fly a helicopter blindfolded, but I was also in the dark about the way the air force did things and what it expected of its officers.

The air force meant to change that. I received orders to Hill Air Force Base in Ogden, Utah. There, my training group would get our introduction to the famous Jolly Green Giant. The Sikorsky HH-3E was the air force version of an amphibious model that the navy used for minesweeping and search and rescue. It was a big workhorse of a helicopter. It weighed 11 tons fully loaded, and its two 1,500-horsepower jet engines powered a five-blade main rotor that scythed a 62-foot circle, a sweep only 10 feet shorter than the Jolly was long.

The Jolly had been around since the sixties. It had earned a rough affection from the crews who flew it, many in rescues under fire in Vietnam, where they'd saved many lives. Its nickname was apparent to anyone who had seen it lumbering over the treetops in camouflage green. It was the machine I'd be piloting in actual operations, and I looked forward to taking its controls.

For all its strengths, the Jolly had one big shortcoming. It was designed as a troop carrier with space for twenty-five combat-ready soldiers, but the Air Rescue Service modifications had added armor plating to resist small-arms fire; external fuel tanks; and an aerial refueling system. All these added extra weight. The extra weight had reduced the power reserves to the point where the HH-3E couldn't carry more than six or eight in addition to the crew in high or hot conditions. The Jolly Green Giant was like an obese man without the power to carry a full load. As a result, the air force had phased it out in Vietnam and replaced it with the more powerful HH-53, dubbed the Super Jolly Green Giant. Yet the HH-3E was still struggling to operate safely in places like the Philippines.

While I was looking forward to testing my new skills against the Jolly's idiosyncrasies, I was destined to be disappointed. At Hill, nobody could keep them flying. Many of the Jollys and the other helicopters at the base were broken on any given day. They were waiting for repairs or replacement parts. And if they weren't, the Rocky Mountain winter howled in and grounded us.

Finally, the air force decided it was going to have to train us on the job. After three months of waiting in vain for helicopters that were fit to fly or breaks in the weather that would allow us some training time, new orders arrived assigning me to the 31st Aerospace Rescue and Recovery Squadron (ARRS) at Clark Air Base on the main Philippine island of Luzon.

The 31st ARRS was a long-range rescue unit positioned to support Clark and the Subic Bay Naval Station, the two largest U.S. military facilities in Southeast Asia, including Vietnam. Clark's hospital also was the largest in the region. The combination of facilities meant that I would encounter a lot of real-world situations as the air force brought my training up to speed.

Jean and Keith had accompanied me to Utah. Now I had to say good-bye to my family. They would return to Buffalo. The only comfort I took from leaving them was the knowledge that they would be at home, where my mother was coping with life in my father's absence, and where Lynne continued her struggle against Hodgkin's. Jean understood that we'd be apart for a long time, and the hug we shared went on a while. Keith, only ten months old, didn't yet know the meaning of departure. He was all smiles and happy sounds when I gave him a good-bye kiss.

I arrived at Clark in February 1972, after a twenty-seven-hour flight from Travis Air Force Base in California.

Clark was the main transit point into and out of Vietnam. Even in those days of declining American involvement, with U.S. troop strength below 140,000 and bombing raids on the North taking up the slack, the air base teemed with personnel. My first impression as I stumbled off the plane was that I was in a hot-house full of flowers. The air was heavy with a sweet aroma, and I was sweating before I reached the bottom of the stairs.

Dazed from the long trip and the suffocating heat, I joined a long line for inbound processing. Almost every flier knew Clark by reputation, and I was eager to get through the orientation and see what the place was like. I was also itching to get back into a helicopter's cockpit. I looked at the massed humanity around me and saw expressions that ranged from eagerness to resignation. We all had one thing in common: we were all eager to get to the front of the line. What happened then, I supposed, would take care of itself.

I was a dozen people from the front when I noticed a couple of officers peering at name tags. They looked at mine and one of them asked, "Are you the Lieutenant Fleming headed for the 31st ARRS?"

I hadn't expected a welcome party, but I was grateful for any-thing that would speed me through the processing and into my orientation with my new unit. I shook his hand and said, "Yes, sir, Lieutenant Fleming, arriving on station as ordered, sir."

The older of the pair was Lieutenant Colonel Bud Green, the rescue squadron commander. The colonel limped slightly, from what I later learned was a broken back suffered in a helicopter crash; he'd just been released from the hospital after several months. With him was Captain Rich O'Dell.

They had come to the terminal to make sure I got settled, so they drove me around the base on an impromptu tour. The colonel spoke softly. "Ed, we Americans have a complex history here, and for some there is only distrust and hatred for us. There are indigenous guerrilla movements here that we sometimes get involved with. Our helicopters and HC-130s have been known to take ground fire."

O'Dell said they all had their own reasons, that a lot of "little wars" were raging in the Philippines—and they had been going on, with Americans involved, for nearly a century. The Philippine-American War, much longer and more costly in terms of lives lost than the Spanish-American War, had left deep anti-American scars among Filipinos throughout the twentieth century.

There were the Huks, a deeply rooted antigovernment guerrilla movement that had been active on Luzon since resisting the Japanese during World War II. The remnants of an agrarian revolutionary movement whose name in Tagalog meant People's Revolutionary Army, they had fought side by side with U.S. forces during that war, only to be rewarded by becoming the target of U.S.-supported Philippine government counterinsurgency operations in the 1950s.

There also was the New People's Army, a group of Communist guerrillas active in central and northern Luzon. Their leanings also were anti-Marcos and anti-U.S. "imperialism."

In addition, there were Muslim separatists who were active mostly on distant islands to the south.

We worked with Negritos, a small pygmy population of hunter-gatherers who had been marginalized to poor lands. The Negritos we worked with lived on the side of the active volcano Mount Pinatubo and supported our jungle survival training as instructors.

There were headhunters in northern Luzon, often linked under the generic term Igorot. Although Christian missionaries claimed there was no active headhunting, anthropologists reported it as a central fabric of the culture up through the 1970s and later. Taking a head was an essential status symbol for a young male, and as reported by scholars, the head served as an urn in which the warrior could carry his sorrow and aggressions. The practice would not die easily.

All of these varied groups had one thing in common: they distrusted, with good reason, central government authority in general and the authority of Ferdinand Marcos' government in particular. And unfortunately, U.S. operations were often linked with those of the Marcos government.

The islands weren't safe, which is why Jean and Keith had stayed at home. I missed them already, but hearing of the various insurgencies, I was glad they were in a safe environment.

We rode in the heat past Clark's central parade ground and along its palm-lined golf course. CABOOM, the Clark Air Base Open Officers' Mess, looked like a country club with a striped awning at its entrance. The base was the ultimate gated community—a world of chaos and violence outside and a secure, unthreatened life within.

O'Dell had just pointed out the peak of Mount Pinatubo to the west when Colonel Green asked a surprising question: "How much experience have you had flying the HH-3E, Lieutenant?" he asked.

I told him I had never sat in an HH-3E, let alone flown one. I explained the problems at the rescue school at Hill.

"Well, Rich, you have your work cut out for you," the colonel said.

Under Rich O'Dell's guidance, I quickly learned maneuvers that in those days were exclusive to the Air Rescue Service. The first was aerial refueling, a maneuver that for helicopters was developed in the crucible of Vietnam, as pilots were shot down in the North, outside the Jolly's range. By the mid-1960s, the air force had adapted the HH-3E for aerial refueling with a probe that could be extended from the nose. Skilled pilots learned to mate the probe with a funnel-shaped assembly called a drogue at the end of a fuel hose trailing from the wing of a C-130 Hercules, a four-engine turboprop military airlift plane modified for use as a tanker. Since then, midair refueling had become vital to air rescue and special operations.

Aerial refueling made it possible to reach survivors who couldn't have been reached before but it didn't guarantee their rescue. That happened on the scene, usually under bad conditions. Rich introduced me to the pleasures of night water hoisting—hovering over water in darkness while a pararescueman dropped down to retrieve survivors to be raised on a hoist cable to the helicopter.

Once I'd absorbed these rescue maneuvers, one demonstration remained. Lieutenant Colonel Dick Smith wanted to show me "settling with power." It sounded innocent enough, but it was quickly clear it wasn't. He said, "I want you to get a feel for this, Ed, because it's a condition you want to avoid. Once you're in it, chances are good you won't get out of it, so it's better not to get into it in the first place."

The technical name for settling with power is the vortex ring state. It's what happens when tight conditions keep you from flying the helicopter forward and you're forced to hover, while at the same time heat has thinned the air, reducing rotor lift, or you're flying a machine that's short on power. You're unable to rise or maneuver, and you might have to take the aircraft straight down in a barely controllable descent. The heat in the Philippines was made to order for it. Combined with the HH-3E's marginal power, knowing the conditions of settling with power was a necessary part of my survival skill set.

Demonstration day arrived. It was hot as usual. We drew *Jolly 24*, a particularly sluggish helicopter that the squadron had nicknamed the "Plastic Pig." This helicopter was heavier than the others for some reason. Colonel Smith took the controls and flew the helicopter up to an unusually high 10,000 feet. Then, in a blue sky with intermittent clouds, he pulled the aircraft into a hover.

The helicopter slowed, then began to shake and groan. Then we started to sink. The colonel said, "The nose is up, so it's going to feel like you're falling backward. That's an illusion. We're going straight down. That's what it feels like. Got it? Good."

Immediately he tried to put on the brakes. The engines roared and the rotors throbbed as he called on all the power the helicopter had. I expected it to stop falling and start flying again, but we kept falling, faster and faster. Helicopter rotors, its wings, produce downward vortices of air. To fly up, the rotors must force this air down. But if you overtake your downward airflow, the air moves up through the rotor, not down. Every instinct shouts at the pilot to increase power to fly out of the downward spiral, but increasing power to gain lift with the reversed airflow has the opposite effect—you're driven downward faster. Adding power with the reversed airflow makes you power yourself toward the ground with ever-increasing speed.

I glanced at the instrument panel. The rate-of-descent gauge showed us falling 2,000 feet per minute. As I watched, it clicked to 4,000 feet per minute. I knew with a stab of fear that we'd reached the dangerous state where the helicopter had overtaken its downward airflow. Instead of the main rotor forcing air down through the blades, the air was moving up, accelerating our descent. This was more of a demonstration than I'd wanted.

The aircraft yawed violently, on the edge of control. The gauge showed us plummeting at 5,000 feet per minute, then 5,800, then 6,800. Then the gauge pegged. We were falling faster than it could register.

To say I was nervous wasn't the half of it. I was tight against my safety harness with the plummeting helicopter falling out from under me, and all I could think to do was watch Colonel Smith. I looked desperately for any sign that he could make the aircraft fly again. He appeared calm, but he'd stopped talking. His hands on the controls moved faster and more forcefully.

When we'd started, we were above the mountains. Now they rose into view, displacing sky and clouds. The nose-high helicopter kept snapping back and forth. I had no idea how close we were to crashing, but I braced myself, and a picture of the shock and sadness on Jean's face when she got the news flashed into my brain.

Colonel Smith pushed the cyclic forward. Nothing happened. He jammed it to the right. Nothing. We weren't going to get out of it. The earth was hurtling up at us and I was glad I couldn't see it. I thought how much I was going to miss seeing Keith grow up. Promises flooded my brain, the ones I'd keep if only I could live: to always tell Jean how much I loved her, to hug my little boy at every opportunity.

Now he jammed the controls full forward and out of sheer desperation held them there, motionless, willing the helicopter to respond. Finally, straining and groaning, the machine began to move, slowly, like a creature waking after a long sleep. It lost its backward tilt, leveled, and tipped forward in an attitude of flight. Shuddering as if it would break apart, the helicopter gained forward momentum. The rate of descent started to slow. It began to fly again.

I saw earth and trees through the windscreen. The dial on the altitude gauge pointed to 800 feet. We'd been less than ten seconds from crashing. I was shaking with relief and gratitude for having the remainder of my life back.

Colonel Smith's voice came through my headset. "There you have it, Ed," he said calmly. "Settling with power. You see what I mean about getting out of it. Not so easy. Better not to go there in the first place."

"No, sir," I said faintly.

He landed the helicopter and we went to the debriefing room. The colonel sat down and let out a long breath. "You know," he said, "for a minute there, I didn't think we were going to make it." I looked at the flight engineer who'd been up there with us.

He raised his eyebrows. "You looked awfully calm to me, sir," I said.

"Well, I didn't want to make you nervous," he responded, "but I was trying every trick I knew, and I used up most of them. Maybe all of them. But staying calm helps everybody focus on their jobs. Nervousness is contagious. Once it spreads, nobody can do their jobs and then we're all in trouble."

It was almost an afterthought, but I came to realize that that was as valuable a lesson as avoiding the conditions for settling with power. Nobody goes into life-threatening positions without feeling stress and strain. People fear for their lives; it's natural, and if you don't, maybe you shouldn't be in charge of leading people into battle or any dangerous mission. But showing fear is a distraction. Conveying the attitude that you can handle what a mission throws at you tells the people around you that they can handle it, too. The teamwork you train for works only if everybody's in a mental state to get the work done.

As for settling with power, or the vortex ring state, it's a significant contributor to helicopter crashes—so much so that years later, after I was an instructor pilot, the air force changed its training procedures to recognize the danger. The maneuver ceased to be taught in flight, and was relegated to flight simulators.

I moved into the regular rescue rotation. But since I was still officially in training, I had to fly with an instructor pilot.

Lieutenant Colonel John J. McGuire was in the copilot's seat the day I performed my first rescue as a Jolly pilot. We'd been summoned by the Philippine Constabulary, the national paramilitary force, to a site near Tarlac, north of Clark. The area was a hotbed of insurgency. Just a few days earlier, we'd had a helicopter take numerous hits from automatic weapons fire there by the Communist New People's Army. One of the pilots, Charlie Holman, was just back from a rescue rotation in Vietnam. He'd taken no fire in the war zone, but in Tarlac the helicopter had taken thirty rounds. The other pilot in the aircraft, Bo Adcox, had a round blow off the right side of his helmet. The wounded Jolly fell into a dangerous descent until Charlie grabbed the controls and wrestled the aircraft to the ground.

Our mission was to go back into the area for a mutilated constabulary member who was clinging to life. Mutilations by machete historically had been the tool of persuasion and coercion among some of the insurgents. That had happened to this constabulary member.

Colonel McGuire told me some history as we flew over the jungle. Tarlac was the site of Camp O'Donnell, the notorious prisoner-of-war camp at the end of the Bataan Death March. Thousands of American and Filipino soldiers taken prisoner died on the forced march in cattle cars that took them a portion of the journey or in the camp itself.

I thought of my dad, fighting in the Philippines, and the sacrifices of his generation. It was hard to imagine the entire world at war, battling over different concepts of civilization. The men who fought that war were all someone's sons, and many were husbands and fathers. Yet few of them questioned the purpose of their fight. The purpose was clear. That was why they had been hailed as heroes when they came home. Vietnam was such an enormous contrast, its mission debated and protested, and its soldiers reviled and spit upon, unfairly, when they returned home to their country.

Camp O'Donnell had been an outpost of the Philippine Constabulary before the war. The constabulary had taken it over again when the war was over.

Below us, the jungle broke to reveal Spanish-style tile roofs and I set the helicopter down. On the ground, the buildings showed age and hard use. Vines and creepers clawed at the edges of the compound like hungry animals trying to get in. The rotor wash stirred air thick with heat and the sickly sweet smell of jungle flowers. On the ground, the flower smell seemed to change to a pervasive, pungent combination of soil, sweat, and death. I couldn't decide if it was the history of the place or if it was real.

As soon as the helicopter settled, a crew of constabulary men in uniform burst from one of the buildings carrying their wounded comrade on a stretcher. They handed the stretcher into the passenger compartment. Colonel McGuire gave the order to lift off.

I handled the controls, and the helicopter rose to the level of the jungle canopy, where it stopped climbing. The rotors seemed to slip in the heat-thinned air. The Jolly shuddered and its belly scraped the trees.

Before I could overreact at the controls, McGuire started talking, coolly. "Keep your power on. Watch the rotor rpm, don't let it decay. The rotor is slowing down, bring the rpm back with collective. Milk it nice and easy, Ed. Don't worry. This is what we call a normal risk in this kind of weather. Out here you just have to learn to handle it." He kept talking, his calm voice telling me and the crew through the intercom that we were under control. But the helicopter acted differently.

The Jolly sank some more, staggering into the treetops. We sank into the jungle canopy, parting the crowns of trees as we carved through them as I tried desperately to get some flying speed. My body poured with flop sweat on top of the heat sweat I was already feeling.

I was scared of several things at once—of killing the crew, of wrecking the helicopter, of denying the mutilated constabulary man a chance at life, of failing. Of them all, failing was the worst to me. I clenched my teeth and managed through sheer will to keep my hands calm on the controls. Finally the helicopter gained critical forward speed and encountered additional airflow that helped it rise again. In another instant it recovered enough lift to rise slowly, putting precious feet between the helicopter and the treetops. Then we were clear. All of a sudden the wind through the helicopter's windows actually felt cool.

Half an hour later, I set the Jolly down in Manila on a hospital's helicopter pad. Medics ran out and grabbed the stretcher, and the wounded man's buddies scrambled after them into the hospital.

I watched them go, and suddenly realized that I'd helped save a life. I wished I'd known the man's name, but then I knew it wasn't that important. The satisfaction came not from keeping a roster of the rescued, but from completing a successful mission, fitting into a team of brave professionals all of whom counted on one another to do their jobs and keep them safe and alive. It was a heady feeling, worth all the months of training. For the first time since I'd visited the air force recruiter back in Tonawanda, I knew, really knew, that I'd made the right choice.

7

Monsoons and Mines

My forefathers were warriors. Their son is a warrior.

—Tecumseh

Family housing on the base and in secure areas outside was in short supply. But at last I cleared the waiting list for a house in a walled and guarded subdivision a few miles from the base next door to John and Jacquie Sfeir. John had been my friend since Officer Training School, and Jean and Jacquie were friends as well, having gotten acquainted starting at Fort Wolters. I excitedly called Jean to tell her that she could make plans to come out with Keith.

The weeks of waiting dragged by. I continued flying. In my off-hours I did my best to spruce up the three-bedroom house, but I could only do so much with rattan, the furniture of choice in the Philippines. And in a walled and barbwired compound, watched over by heavily armed Filipino guards, it would never seem like a home.

Their arrival date neared, and my excitement about seeing my family again grew with each passing day. I knew that even with the security problems in the Philippines, the islands were lush and beautiful, and there were a lot of things a family could do to enjoy the surroundings. The foliage alone deserved a lifetime of study. I imagined strolling with Jean among the beautiful surroundings. I needed her close, to sense her breath near mine, to feel her touch. I was aching to see how Keith had grown in the

43

months since I'd seen him. My strength was my family, and I dearly wanted to be reunited with them.

They arrived at Clark in late May 1972. Jean looked exhausted when she got off the plane. I could only imagine what the long flight must have been like with a fourteen-month-old to wrangle. Keith was oblivious. He blinked in the sunshine and wrinkled his nose at the heavy smell of flowers. He had more hair than I remembered.

On their heels came some of the most devastating monsoons in the history of Luzon. The rains went on for seven weeks. Ten inches fell on some days. From our compound's walled extremity, Jean and I looked out on moving water that every day gnawed its way closer to the houses. Valleys filled and became lakes. Animals and humans alike fled to what dry land there was above the waterline.

That was when I really learned to fly. The conditions would have been unflyable if we hadn't been trying to save lives. We flew in strong winds and zero visibility. It rained so hard that the wipers on the helicopter windscreens couldn't handle it. We learned through trial and error to fly cocked about fifteen degrees sideways, like a car with a bent frame. From that angle the slipstream cleared the side window better than the front. It was the only way to see.

The floods placed a huge load on the squadron, but our humanitarian operations went on nonstop. The 31st and a squadron of marines in CH-46s—a huge, Boeing-built helicopter that looked like a flying bus, with equally sized main rotors at the nose and raised tail of the aircraft—flew sortie after sortie. We delivered food and medical supplies to isolated villages and to refugees who huddled on islands of high ground. Much of the time we had to fly in an envelope of visibility that was only thirty feet below the low clouds and the rain-soaked surface. We hoisted flood victims out of pockets where they had no way to reach dry land, and evacuated them to hospitals or clinics.

The monsoons ended, and history crept along. Nixon was re-elected in a landslide, winning forty-nine states against George McGovern.

By the end of 1972 there were fewer than seventy thousand U.S. troops in Vietnam. The B-52s had resumed pummeling the north with bombs in a futile attempt to gain South Vietnamese forces an advantage in what was increasingly their war. January 1973 brought the signing of the Paris peace accords and the exit strategy designed to get the last of the troops home. The POWs started their journey home from the prison camp they had nick-named the "Hanoi Hilton," dark humor for the brutal treatment they endured. Clark and its hospital were the first stop in their journey, and their stories of mistreatment and torture further defined the ill-considered war.

The Paris agreement called on the navy to remove mines it had laid the year before in Haiphong Harbor. Ten wood-hulled minesweepers sailed for Haiphong in February 1973 to do the job.

Days after they arrived, an accident aboard the U.S.S. *Leader* injured several sailors. The 31st got the call that afternoon, task-ing us to evacuate the injured to Clark's hospital. As I led a crew scrambling across the tarmac to be in the air inside of thirty min-utes, my first operation as a qualified HH-3E pilot and aircraft commander had begun.

Planning for a long-range mission happens in the air. With lives at stake, there's no time to map out routes and plans around a conference table. The need for speed demands that you think and make decisions on the run, and as events change, you reeval-uate. It's an ambiguity you live with.

I steered the helicopter on a route that would take us across almost a thousand miles of open ocean. An HC-130 took off at the same time, to refuel us over the long route. I figured we'd have to pick up the injured sailors by way of a night hover over *Leader*. Given the Jolly's 164 miles-per-hour cruising speed, it would be dark long before we reached the minesweeper. Night vision goggles weren't in use yet. We'd perform the operation using a searchlight.

As we flew west toward the sun with the ocean slipping by beneath us, things suddenly unraveled. The helicopter's automatic flight control system (AFCS) failed. One second, my hands were relaxed on the controls; then the aircraft was jerking in a series of violent spasms. There's no such thing as an automatic pilot on a helicopter. You can't set it and forget it. The AFCS only damps the motions that would otherwise make the aircraft almost impossible to fly. Without it, the helicopter was yawing, rolling, and porpoising, all at the same time. I could barely keep it under control and in the air.

Once I realized what the problem was, my first thought was the mission. How were we going to get to *Leader* to lift off the injured sailors? I wanted a success in my first mission as aircraft commander. I wanted it badly. I could fly the helicopter, but air refueling or precision hovering over a ship for a night hoist would be all but impossible in the fishtailing, porpoising machine. The flight engineer tried everything he could to bring the system back to life, but it was gone. I felt a mixture of disappointment, anger, and frustration as I wondered what the hell to do. Part of me wanted to press on regardless. Legends were made from pilots who had brought battle-scarred Jollys home through desperate feats of flying. Then I remembered a story I had heard when I was still in training.

The thrust of the story was choice—making the hard decision not to attempt a rescue that could put your crew in danger. A rescue pilot at Niagara Falls was trying to rescue a couple floating toward the falls. His helicopter could take only one person at a time, but the couple were drifting too fast for him to take one person and return in time for the second. The couple chose to plunge over the falls together. It was a tragedy, but it would have been worse if he'd tried to save them both, and the helicopter and crew had gone down, too.

I ran over the circumstances together in my mind. Ahead of me, across hundreds of miles of ocean, navy crewmen were awaiting rescue. With me in the bucking, pitching helicopter were four men whose lives might depend on my decision. We were out of radio range, I was in the pilot's seat, and the decision was all mine. With luck we might make it, but no flier wants to depend on luck. I wasn't sure I could get my crew there and back safely, let alone the injured sailors. I didn't have enough experience. And to get that experience, I'd have to survive my early decisions.

I knew it was the right thing to do, but I still felt the gall of bitter frustration as I told the crew, "Let's call it off." They seemed relieved when I turned the helicopter around, but that didn't make it any easier. I thought of the injured sailors, not knowing if the extra hours to rescue would mean the difference between life and death.

After I steered the bucking helicopter to a landing back at Clark, doubt and failure still nagged at me. Colonel Smith, with whom I'd survived settling with power, was the operations officer. I was afraid he'd think I let him down. I walked into his office and waited for him to express his disappointment. But he surprised me, saying my decision was the right one.

"No crew would have survived an eight- or nine-hour mission like that," he said. "I wasn't quite sure about your experience level for an operation like this, but I am now. I can trust you to make those tough calls and not end up killing both the crew and survivors. Welcome to the club."

The colonel's words filled me with gratitude. I knew I'd done the right thing by not risking the lives of the crew in what turned out to be an unflyable aircraft. That boosted my confidence in my ability to command.

There were still survivors waiting for us, and we returned for them in a fresh Jolly.

*   *   *

Removing the mines from Haiphong Harbor was one of many events as the war in Vietnam wound down that allowed the nation to direct its attention homeward. Watergate had become a full-blown scandal undermining Nixon's foreign policy accomplishments. White House resignations and Senate hearings were carried live on television. Even at Clark, an ocean away from the United States, you couldn't pick up a newspaper or turn on a television set without being aware of the gathering storm.

Jean was pregnant again, due to deliver in the fall of 1973. As the date approached, I felt a renewal of the anticipation and concern for her welfare that I had experienced when she was pregnant with Keith. We knew more about what to expect this time, but that lessened none of my nervousness over what might go wrong.

She went into labor on an October night that was pitch black and drenched in monsoon rain. The monsoons had cut off the main roads to Clark and the hospital there. Only dangerous and insecure back roads were open, turning a 5-mile trip as the crow flies to an hour-long ordeal. Military curfew prohibited us from traveling off base at night—to move about in a civilian vehicle would subject you to dangers from the constabulary or the guerrillas or both.

To make the run to the base we needed protection. We didn't have a phone but the Sfeirs did. I went quickly to their house to call for security.

Soon two combat-ready jeeps showed up, manned by security police and mounted with M-60 machine guns. I piled Jean and Keith into the Mustang. I stayed between the jeeps in a high-speed run along the rain-swept roads to the base hospital, where our second son, Cavan, was born on October 4, 1973.

In retrospect, it was a dizzyingly historic month, in which war erupted in the Mideast as Egypt and Syria attacked Israel, Nixon fired the Watergate special prosecutor, and Vice President Spiro

Agnew resigned over tax evasion charges. But we had our own little bit of history to celebrate.

Attending Cavan's birth was more fun than Keith's. I was able to fully enjoy the arrival of our second son. I was wide awake, for one thing, with no checkride the next day. I knew the beauty of birth, and I knew that a new presence in our life would only make it better. I wasn't shocked when I saw Cavan, ruddy in the moments after birth, as I had been when I saw Keith. Jean, too, had the advantage of knowing what to expect, and we shared the calm and joy with Keith as we introduced him to his little brother.

8

Korea

I dream of journeys repeatedly: Of flying like a bat deep into
a narrowing tunnel.

—*T. Roethke*

In April 1974 I got a new assignment. It was in South Korea,
where I was to serve as the chief instructor pilot and flight
examiner of a rescue detachment at Osan Air Base, south of
Seoul. Detachment 13 was a unit of the 41st Air Wing out of
Hickam Air Force Base, Hawaii.

I greeted the assignment with mixed feelings. It would be a
challenge and a good step in my career. Flying in Korea's rugged
mountains was an acid test of any helicopter pilot's skills. But with
the Communist army of the North massed at the 38th parallel
that was the cease-fire line dividing the two sides in the Korean
War, Korea was an area of "potential hostilities." That meant off-
limits to families. Jean, Keith, and Cavan would have to return
home for the length of my assignment. I didn't relish the idea
of being apart from them, especially with Keith at one of the
most fascinating stages of his young life, and Cavan too young to
remember me at the end of the year-long absence I knew this
would be.

Jean knew the drawbacks of a military life. She would be
strong in my absence and would handle the children by herself.
But knowing that didn't replace her presence. She was my confi-

dante and my companion. I relied on her wisdom and her warmth, and I knew I'd have to fight bouts of loneliness when she wasn't there.

We discussed the country she'd rejoin after nearly two years in the Pacific. In many ways, Clark was just an extension of America. In others, it was rarefied and set apart, a function of its military presence and the civilians who supported it. At home, passions were freer and more random. The tide of Watergate kept rising around Nixon no matter how many sandbags he threw up. The furious Yom Kippur War the previous October, in which Israel had defeated the Egyptian and Syrian attacks, had led to an Arab oil boycott in retaliation for America's support for Israel. Gasoline prices had climbed but now, with the boycott over, they were falling back again. The last American troops were out of Vietnam, but the residue of bitterness remained. And from what I could tell from reading and watching television, young people in the United States were taking the advice of sixties guru Dr. Timothy Leary and tuning in, turning on, and dropping out. In many ways, I didn't envy Jean returning home. The overseas news made it seem as if the whole country was in a rather unpleasant state of searching for something elusive, out of reach.

We said good-bye on the edge of a runway at Clark. I kissed and hugged them all and boarded an air force bus that would take me and other travelers to the plane headed for Korea. When I had my seat, I waved at them through the window for a long time. The bus just sat there, with no one allowed to get on or off. I felt like I was trapped in a goldfish bowl. Then, after twenty minutes of longing to hug and be near Jean and the boys, the bus moved, and I had my last glimpse of my family for a year.

A few hours later I arrived at Osan and Detachment 13. The officer who greeted me at Osan had a heat-scarred pistol resting on his desk. It looked as if somebody had stuck it in a furnace and pounded it when it was red hot. The bullets had exploded in the chamber.

"You're wondering about the pistol," he suggested.

I told him I was.

"This is from Colonel Mudd's crash," he said.

"Yes, sir. We heard about it down at Clark, but I don't know all the details."

"We lost four men," he said. He went on to explain how the detachment commander, Lieutenant Colonel Mudd, and a crew of three had crashed on a night approach into the air base. They'd merely extended their traffic pattern to complete some checklists, then on the way in hit a mountain. They knew it was there, embedded in the blackness beneath them, but according to their aviation chart they expected to pass well clear of it. But the chart lied. It showed the mountain as 100 feet lower than it actually was. The aircraft struck its crest, pitchpoled, exploded, and burned.

"Four feet. Four lousy, stinking, miserable feet." The officer spoke suddenly with a sad resignation that revealed the emotional toll a crash takes out of a unit. He said investigators who climbed up to the crash site had found that the helicopter had missed clearing the ridge by only 4 feet. "They would have seen the airfield lights and felt confident they had a straight path toward home. They never knew what was in the black just underneath them," he said bitterly. "That pistol you see there belonged to the flight engineer."

The officer's recollection sobered me. I thought back to an escarpment in Lubang that John Sfeir and I had cleared by 4 or 5 feet. We made a living flying close to the ground, day and night, and just a few feet often meant the difference between life and death. Then I looked ahead and I wondered about longevity in my line of work.

I quickly learned that the crash had put some members of Detachment 13 in a blue funk. The faces I saw in the hooch I shared with other officers, in the operations room, and on the flight line were numb with grief and weariness. Four men lost out of sixty was a blow. Everyone in the detachment had lost friends and trusted crewmates. And in the aftermath, workloads had increased. The lost helicopter hadn't yet been replaced, so two were doing the work of three. Everybody from flight crews to mechanics were struggling to stay ready physically and mentally and to keep the Jollys functioning.

Larry Brooks helped ease the burden. He was a copilot I'd met in the Philippines when he was attending the Jungle Survival School at Clark, and he had preceded me to Osan. Larry knew how to grab life by the horns. Stocky and muscular, he was a demon basketball player and a great fan of a concocted game called combat golf, where you played with only two or three clubs and ran from shot to shot. I once saw him dismantle the hooch kitchen to catch an invading rat, and then serve supper with the live rat as a centerpiece under an upended glass bowl. Larry had a way of keeping even a tragedy such as the Det had suffered in perspective. He called me by the nickname he'd heard at Clark, "Easy."

Larry dismissed my interest in studying Korean history and the language, saying breezily, "Can't study, Easy. Libraries are too dangerous. Why, books have been known to fall off shelves and kill people!"

When Jean's letter arrived about a month after I reached Osan, telling me that Lynne had died, Larry was a source of sympathy and comfort. He invented distractions, insisting that we go running, lift weights, or play a round of combat golf so I wouldn't dwell on the loss of my little sister.

I had known that it was inevitable, that Lynne wouldn't be able to fight the Hodgkin's forever. Still, the reality was hard to take, and most of all I missed the fact that I hadn't been able to be there for her. Half a world away, I felt her absence deeply. I knew that a rare and beautiful spirit had been removed from the world.

Lieutenant Colonel Travis Wofford arrived at Osan and was the new commander of the detachment.

Colonel Wofford's reputation as a hero and a recipient of the Air Force Cross for courage in Vietnam preceded him. His warmth and self-assurance were a match for the fatalism that had infected some in the detachment after the crash. His confidence was soothing, and his enthusiasm for the job of flying was infectious.

"Ed'ard," he said to me soon after he arrived, speaking in a twang that I never could quite locate, "Ed'ard, you're the chief pilot. You've got to ensure that all these young troops know how to fly in all conditions safely. You've got to teach them to mountain-fly. We've got to assure them that they will have the flight skills to survive the year they're going to spend here."

I committed myself to the task.

The mountains that had killed the Det's earlier commander and his crew were the challenge we all faced at Osan. With night and bad weather, you couldn't always see them, but you could always feel their presence. You never forgot them if you wanted to survive. And you couldn't have forgotten them even if you wanted to—they were always there. Every morning when I emerged from the hooch I could see the flat bowl of land we occupied, the base runway and the valley beyond it where the hills started to rise. In the valley, in the right light, I could see the antiaircraft batteries, concealed in camouflage netting, manned by Republic of Korea soldiers keeping a watch north toward the demilitarized zone. I could see and smell farm fields that were fertilized with human waste. Terraced rice paddies segmented the low hills.

Then there were the mountains, dark and razor-sharp. They were a maze to navigate. Not only were they steep and creviced, they also were, in effect, booby-trapped. Cables and wires crossed over the deep-cut mountain valleys like a cat's cradle of yarn. Day or night, they were all but impossible to see, and each one had the potential to bring an aircraft down.

The weather was often implacable. Korea is known as "the land of the morning calm," but you could face bitter cold, howling wind, or torrential rains, and sometimes all three, on any given day.

Veteran Korea rescue pilots said that in the mountains, you flew less like a bird than some mechanical animal, steering the helicopters through steep, narrow tunnels in an act that seemed more like burrowing than flying. Soon their warnings were borne out.

Summer is typhoon season in the western Pacific. Typhoons are cyclonic storms associated with low-pressure systems. They generally travel at 25 to 30 miles per hour and are 500 to 1,000 miles in diameter. Their paths are often quite predictable. That summer we were in such a path. A huge storm in the Sea of Japan spread violent weather over much of South Korea. At its height, the storm shut down commercial air traffic at Seoul's Kimpo Airport, inundated the valleys with devastating mudslides, and isolated some villages. Military flights in and out of Osan Air Base also were halted. Rescue crews don't count on sleeping in such weather, and we were typically busy.

I was the aircraft commander on alert when the call came on a Wednesday night. Rainstorms had triggered flooding in a mountain valley south of Taegu, toward the southeastern tip of the Korean peninsula. The mountains were steep and the floodwaters forced into narrow channels carried a destructive force. My quick briefing told of a farming village that teetered on the brink of being swept away. Thirty or forty villagers were stranded and Korean ground rescuers couldn't get to them. We were the rescuers of last resort.

Travis arrived at the Det as he did for all operations. I told him that as many as forty people were in danger, that we needed another aircraft and a second crew. "Who do you think would come out and fly formation off of me in this?" I asked. Torrents of wind-lashed rain drummed against the darkened windows.

"Why, Ed'ard, I will," he said. "You'll be the mission commander and formation leader. I'll fly off you. Don't worry, Ed'ard,

I won't run into you." He gave a muffled chuckle and we charged out into the wind and rain.

"Scramble" meant we had thirty minutes to get into the air. Time already had elapsed, and we'd have to do our mission planning after we were airborne. I flew the helicopter while Larry Brooks studied maps in the copilot's seat. We flew on instruments to South Korea's Kwan Ju Air Base and then flew the last fifty miles into the dark valleys, staying under the clouds, with just a searchlight and a map to guide us.

Larry had picked a road to follow that would get us to the village. It wound along a mountainside near the bottom of a deep, steep valley. Below the road, the mountain dipped to the valley floor and then climbed again, just as steep on one side as the other. I led the formation into a tunnel-like slit of air, with rocky mountains on both sides, and the stormy cloud deck no more than 100 feet above the surface.

Gale-force winds slammed the helicopter toward the valley wall. I quickly swerved away before hitting it.

The winds kept knocking the aircraft and searchlight off course. Every gust that hit us sent the aircraft toward the mountain. One second we flew along the lit road ahead, the next the light would arc wildly into the clouds and we would drift toward the rock walls again. When the beam lit the mountains, they were always too close. You instinctively wanted to pull away from them, but there were more on the other side.

Slowly we worked our way up the valley, staying below the clouds, at times flying no higher than 30 feet above the road. Floodwaters cut away at the embankment that supported it. I was concentrating on following the road when we rounded a curve, and a blaze of headlights appeared to bear down at us head-on. A bolt of fear hammered my heart and sent a shot of adrenaline through my body as I powered the helicopter to climb above the approaching bus. Below me, the bus veered toward the mountain with its headlights flashing frantically as the two huge Jollys thundered overhead. With only our two searchlights to be seen, I suspect he thought we were a huge vehicle on a collision course with him.

Travis's voice came on the intercom from the trailing helicopter. "Ed'ard, if I didn't know better I'd swear I saw a bus fly by us. Nah!"

The village finally appeared, cut off from the road by a slashing torrent of floodwater. Trees pushed up above the rooflines of the houses, and between the shadows thrown by the trees thrashing in the wind, the searchlights picked out clusters of people— men, women, and children—huddled on the rooftops, waving at the lights. Water coursed among the buildings. In one narrow channel water sprayed like it was spewing from a fire hose, leaving nothing of a house in its path but a jumble of ribs sticking up.

I hovered on the sight of the standing houses. You need a stable reference for hovering; if I had tried to fix on a point in the water, I would inadvertently have let the Jolly drift with the water and hit something without even knowing we were moving. But one by one, the houses disappeared. Travis's searchlight backlit our position, creating moving shadows that interfered with my limited vision. I was worried because I couldn't see Travis behind us, but I knew if I drifted backward just a few feet, we'd chew each other up with our rotors.

The wind-whipped trees would make it hard to get people cleanly from the rooftops on the hoist. It was a close and dangerous dance, and I caught myself holding my breath for long stretches as I tried to concentrate. But the storm's destruction made me angry as well as anxious, and more determined to snatch its victims from its grasp.

Tech Sergeant Clegie "Junior" Chambers was lowered onto the hoist to the first rooftop. Junior was a guy you would want to run away from if you saw him walking toward you in an alley. He was as nice a person as there was, but he always wore a scowl. I couldn't see him under the hovering Jolly but I knew people were pressing close to him now as he strapped them into the harness in which they'd be hoisted to safety in the Jolly.

Behind me, Travis was hovering while his PJ, shorthand for pararescue jumper, was doing the same thing on another roof. Two 73-foot Jollys hovered in tandem, struggling for position in the wind, their searchlights playing weirdly over the windblown trees; the surging water; and the scrambling, desperate people.

We moved from rooftop to rooftop. The water kept taking more houses, and with them, vital hover reference points. The trees were sometimes so close we couldn't hoist people through them safely. Then before I knew it I had allowed the Jolly to drift into unseen trees. The first I knew was the sound of the rotors greedily slicing through the branches. Five whirling 28-foot scalpels cut an incision into the foliage. I was startled and scared and tried hard to not overreact. If a blade hit a trunk, the blade would have disintegrated and the helicopter would have plunged down into the floodwaters.

Travis's voice broke through on the radio. "Ed'ard, I've got nine," he said. My second PJ, Steve Humburg, gave me the same count. It was all we could carry at one time, more than the Jollys could transport in the heat and altitude back in the Philippines. Larry Brooks leaned over and stabbed his finger at a spot on the map, showing a nearby village close to Kwan Ju. We could drop them there, on higher ground, and then go back for the rest. I put the Jolly's nose down and we headed that way.

You never knew if you were getting the right people out first. You wanted to take the weakest, the sick, the very young and old, to give them extra minutes that could tip their odds in favor of survival. But in the panic it didn't always work that way. Sometimes in their rush to survive, stronger people pushed others aside. I sadly wonder who might have perished because of this confused survival triage. Sometimes the strongest are also the most cowardly.

We fought the wind, rain, low clouds, and fog to reach the higher village, where we dropped off our bedraggled human cargo into the welcoming hands of their neighbors, then went back down the mountain. It was significantly darker now, and finding the disappearing village was a problem. It was difficult to find your ass with your hands in those conditions, let alone a dark village when the landmarks on the map were now washed away.

We rescued the remaining surviving villagers on the next trip. Travis had nine, and I had eight, I thought. I looked back into the bay to see if the door was closed and everyone secure. Then I saw a woman fighting the motion of the helicopter to strap herself into a seat, while over her stood burly Junior Chambers, clinging to a gunner's belt with one hand and holding a tiny baby with the other. The baby couldn't have been more than a few weeks old, and the infant must have come up the hoist concealed and warmed under his or her mother's clothes. The baby looked impossibly fragile in Junior's massive arms. Junior wasn't scowling as fiercely as he usually did, and I had one of those surges of certainty about the rightness of things, when you feel that through it all you're managing to do some good.

"Jesus, that was close," Larry's voice muttered in my headphones. He indicated the searchlight beam. It lit the grass roof of the hut from which we'd just lifted the woman and her family. The hut had collapsed into the water, and it was now breaking up as it swirled downstream with the flood.

Again I put the Jolly's nose down and headed for high ground. As we worked our way under the low clouds to the higher village, I thought of the infant we'd rescued and my young sons. I missed them. No matter what I was doing, in the back of my mind I thought of them and their mom. I pictured Jean holding Cavan and reading to Keith.

We flew our way back out of the maze of tunnel-like valleys. On that fierce night I was reminded of the rescue service's unflinching motto: *These things we do that others may live.*

In July 1974, the trauma of Watergate was nearly at a head. The Supreme Court ruled that Nixon had to turn over his secret tapes to the special prosecutor, and the House voted three articles of impeachment. The war in Vietnam was coming to an ignominious end. South Vietnamese forces, left to fight on their own, had fallen steadily back to Saigon until they were at the city's door-step. The implacable forces of the North were doing what they would have done ten years earlier if we hadn't intervened. We'd only delayed history at the cost of almost sixty thousand American lives, deep fissures in the national fabric, and untold trauma that had only started to emerge as the troops who returned home tried to cope with what had happened to them and to their country. From Korea it was impossible to see the full extent of the divisions. But I was a military man and my every sympathy was with the men and women who had done their duty, as unpopular as it had been.

In April 1975 North Vietnamese troops were poised to take Saigon. Detachment 13 was put on alert to assist in the inevitable evacuation of the American embassy employees who still were in the embattled city, and the South Vietnamese who were American friends and employees. But the call never came. Det's HH-3Es didn't have the lifting power to contribute to Operation Eagle Pull, which was the code name for the evacuation. More capable helicopters were sent to do the job. Television and photographic images of them lifting off the roof of the U.S. embassy with people desperately scrambling for the doors and clinging to the landing gear are seared in the memory of a generation.

Soon after the last helicopter lifted off at the end of April, I received new orders and headed home with a grateful heart for a leave and my next assignment.

9

We're Going Down

A certain recluse, I know not who, once said that no bonds attached him to this life, and the only thing he would regret leaving was the sky.

—Yoshida Kenko

I arrived home in Buffalo to a different family from the one I'd left. My mother had remarried and moved to a new house, and we welcomed her new husband into the family. I had absorbed the grief of Lynne's death over the months since I'd learned about it, but coming home renewed the hole left by her absence. I had always looked forward with excitement to talking with Lynne about my latest quests for knowledge, knowing it was an enthusiasm she would share. Now I shied away from talking about the things I had learned and wanted to learn for fear of boring my listeners.

Jean shouldered the burden beautifully, giving me one more reason to rejoice in the homecoming that restored me to her embrace and to my family.

Keith and Cavan hadn't seen me for a year. I knew I had to be careful not to overwhelm Cavan with affection, because at eighteen months he barely remembered me. I took it slow so he'd get a picture of all of us together and would gradually get used to it.

Keith was a lot bigger. He did remember me, of course, and at four was becoming a real person. I was deliriously happy about reentering their lives and picking up the thread of their growing and developing again.

I'd arrived in a different country, too. Nixon had resigned the previous August. Gerald Ford, elevated from House minority leader to vice president after Spiro Agnew resigned, was serving as the first president never elected to national office. The outrage that followed his pardon of Nixon in September had subsided, but the wounds left by Vietnam and Watergate were everywhere in evidence. Evel Knievel was jumping buses on a motorcycle. Two of the top bands were Kiss and War, which said a lot about divisions in the country. Bell-bottoms and beads were in style, along with long hair and Afros, and when I wore my uniform some people looked at me with scorn.

Before I knew it, my leave was over. In May 1975, Jean and I and the two boys boarded a plane for Salt Lake City. We were headed for nearby Ogden, Utah, and Hill Air Force Base. I was a captain now and had been assigned to Hill as an instructor pilot with the 1550th Aircrew Training and Test Wing, the premier flying school in the world for mountain and high-altitude operations.

I was glad to be back at Hill. The place had changed since I had gone there for training. Vietnam was no longer eating up helicopters right and left and we had plenty to fly. The mountains around Ogden were spectacular, and I looked forward to family outings that would take advantage of the abundant natural beauty at our doorstep.

My assignment to Hill carried an additional bonus in that it reunited me with two old friends from the 31st ARRS in the Philippines. One was Rich O'Dell, under whose tutelage I had learned to fly the HH-3E. He was the wing's standardization officer, meaning he was chief instructor and evaluator pilot. Lieutenant Colonel Dick Smith, who had shown me settling with power in the demonstration I still remembered vividly, had given up the cockpit for a desk. He was hobbled with the back pain common to so many helicopter pilots. Colonel Smith had lost some of his easygoing air; every time I saw him, he was frowning over his superiors' demands for on-time takeoffs and a steady pace of graduations.

Those same demands reached me right away when I received my briefing as a newcomer instructor. The briefing officer let me know that pushing students through the school was a top priority. "We have never graduated a student late," he told me. "And we definitely frown on late takeoffs."

Our job as instructors was to take student pilots to the edge of their capabilities and give them the skills and instincts they needed to survive. This wasn't the brutal, unforgiving, and exhilarating work of operational rescue but it was difficult and demanding nevertheless.

The air force base, east of the Great Salt Lake and north of Salt Lake City at the foot of the Wasatch range of mountains, was a mile high and the training sites twice that. The mountains were snowcapped year-round. You could take off from Hill on a clear day and fly into a blizzard between the Wasatch and Bear River Mountains. The rock-walled canyons were narrow and steep. Down in the canyons, the winds could rip up one slope and down the other at 50 and 60 knots, even in the summer.

These were borderline conditions even for an experienced helicopter crew.

They also made the 1550th the outstanding unit that it was. Air rescue and special operations teams came from around the world to train there. Helicopter and tanker pilots and crews from Israel, Denmark, Sweden, Australia, Canada, and the United Kingdom were among the regular trainees; the tanker pilots were there because aerial refueling and other rescue procedures were part of the training. They mixed with air force regulars and reserves and Air National Guard fliers in training and gave the place an international feel such as you'd expect to find at the Olympics. They infused Hill students with a kind of swagger.

*　*　*

Sometimes, however, the students represented the most potent flying hazards.

Jack Baker came to Hill for training from an Air National Guard unit on Long Island. We regulars found the guard fliers a mixed group. They were mostly good, professional fliers, dedicated and efficient, even though a few showed up in pumpkin-colored flight suits that made them look like space shuttle astronauts. Then there was a very small minority in this group who acted as if they were the *National Lampoon* version of the air force. Jack was neither of these. He was, strangely, a breed apart. The first time I met him I liked him well enough aside from the fact that he smoked heavily, which in those days wasn't that unusual. He was a few years older and worked as a senior flight engineer with one of the airlines. His personality seemed tightly wound—behind his soft-spoken demeanor he was a little formal, a little too carefully courteous, and his smile was tight and fixed.

Jack's outfit had taken on a new mission; it was changing from a fighter unit to rescue. This meant that he and the unit's other fixed-wing fliers were getting their first real introduction to rotary-wing flying and were training intensely for the first time in helicopters.

One night in February 1976 I had Jack and another student, the flight engineer, scheduled to practice a standard rescue maneuver, hovering and hoisting from the surface. Jack paid careful attention in the preflight briefing, as he always did. Then we got on board and strapped in, Jack flying as copilot. In those days, before night vision goggles became part of the standard rescue kit, we often practiced night hoisting in conjunction with another helicopter. One helicopter at a time went down to practice the hoist while the other flew at 3,500 feet, following a rectangular pattern and dropping parachute flares to light the work below. Rich O'Dell was piloting the second helicopter.

I was the high ship, waiting my turn, when suddenly my helicopter lost its main transmission fluid. The sound was unmistakable even through the headphones. The gearbox started screaming in distress as the input gears, driving at 18,900 rpm, lost their lubrication and started grinding apart. I reached up and pulled the engine speed selectors back to ground idle so they would no longer power the rotors through the disintegrating input gears.

Now, without the engines driving the input gears, gearboxes, and rotors, only the pilot maintained the fine balance among airspeed, collective inputs, and cyclic inputs that would keep the rotor rpm at a sufficient energy level so we could cushion our impact. It had to be done quickly, because if the gearbox froze first, the rotor would freeze with it and the helicopter would stop gliding and fall straight down.

"Jolly 30, Jolly 30," I radioed urgently, using Rich's call sign, "I've lost gearbox lubrication and I'm autorotating. I need a landing spot."

"Wilco, Jolly," Rich replied in the affirmative.

I ordered Jack to give me readings of altitudes passing through, rate of descent, airspeed, and rotor rpm, all information that was vital to allow me to slow our descent just 25 feet before ground contact. The rpm would fluctuate drastically as I maneuvered the aircraft and moved the controls. If the rotor rpm dropped below 75 percent of cruise rpm, the main rotor blades would cone—flap up to the mechanical limits of their attachment points—and then flex even farther and snap off.

Jack didn't respond. "*Jack,*" I repeated sharply, thinking he hadn't heard me.

He still didn't answer, and I looked to my left to see him sitting there frozen, staring straight ahead. He was as still and cryptic as the Sphinx. Jesus, I thought, he's in some kind of trance. He was glued to his seat as if his brain were trapped in a force field. "*Jack!*" I yelled, louder. I needed him to snap out of it if I was going to get us down safely. The rotors swished overhead at a rate that I could only guess at.

Nothing. Jack sat frozen. A light bloomed below us, Rich's flare illuminating the flat spot he'd found where I could land. Suddenly Jack's head snapped back as he woke up to the emergency. At the same time, he started babbling hysterically. "Oh, my God! Oh, Jesus!" he cried out. "We're going down! We're going down! We're going down!" I stared at him for just an instant in what I'm sure was stark amazement. He was whimpering and pitiful if he hadn't been blocking our only possibility of surviving the descent. We were on a hot mike, the emergency intercom where the voice talking blocks out all the others. Jack kept screaming, filling my earphones with noise that prevented the flight engineer from giving me the information I needed to get us safely down.

"We're going down! We're going down! We're going down!" I had never seen such undiluted panic.

I resisted being sucked into Jack's dark place as I flew the helicopter, performing both Jack's duties and mine. Behind and between the pilot seats, the student engineer struggled with his safety harness. He got it open, shot out of the jump seat, stretched a clawing hand to Jack's microphone cord, and yanked it free. Then he started reciting from the instruments the rotor rpm and altitude.

Banking and circling, I brought the helicopter to a bumping halt on the flat spot of canyon floor that Rich's flares had lit. The rotors slowed and the helicopter shuddered as I stopped them by putting on the rotor brake.

I took my helmet off and looked at Jack. I wondered what the hell had happened. We could all have been killed, but I fended off the inclination to be angry. How can you be angry at someone who was clearly in a state of panic? I knew enough about psychology to know that he had had some kind of mental lapse that froze him and kept him from acting.

He felt my eyes on him. He took his helmet off, brushed his blond hair back off his forehead, and turned to me with a dazed smile. There was no explanation in his expression, not even an acknowledgment of what had happened. "Good job, skipper," he said. "Am I cleared out for a smoke?"

Were we on different planets? I hadn't expected him to be so deeply in denial. "What happened up there? Are you all right?" I asked.

"Never better," he said. "Why?"

The human brain was a wonderful instrument. Jack's was blocking out a piece of knowledge that he didn't want to face, a piece of knowledge about his own abilities in times of dangerous stress. It had erased his panic and allowed him now to be one of the flight crew again, with nothing to apologize for or feel bad about. He was so serene, yet so unintentionally dangerous. I looked through the windscreen to the desert sky and thanked the stars above that I wouldn't have to fly with him again—or so I thought at the time.

Changes were occurring in the military. Late the year before, Congress had approved the admission of women to the U.S. service academies. It was merely part of the accelerated rate of change that seemed to have overtaken all aspects of society, as if the residue of Vietnam and Watergate was an insistence that the past be left behind and new ways of doing things explored.

Unlikely political figures were emerging. A former governor of Georgia, Jimmy Carter, was contending for the Democratic presidential nomination, stressing such matters as human rights and energy conservation.

All the instructors at Hill had gone through extensive training in the gamut of high-risk operations, or "ops," including combat ops. In addition, before any of us were shipped overseas we all went through intense survival, escape and evasion, and resistance training, the last being techniques to use to resist interrogations during torture.

This rigorous introduction to what it might be like behind enemy lines took place in the mountains outside Fairchild Air

Force Base in Washington State. They turned us loose with sleeping bags, survival vests, two cans of C rations, a few sticks of beef jerky, and not much else. We were supposed to forage for food, but my rotation through the program came in January and there wasn't much to find. It was in the thirties and raining in the daytime, below zero at night. Capture was designed into the program, and that's when things really got rough. The trainers took away our clothes and herded us into an unheated metal storage building. They put hoods over our heads, stood us in closets, gave us coffee cans to pee in, and filled our ears with screams and curses and every manner of annoying noise, all designed to break us down. They pounded on the doors every few minutes to make sure we weren't asleep, snatched the doors open just in case we'd decided to sit down, and harassed us during simulated interrogations. The training went on for two weeks. It was a harrowing program, but a good one to introduce us to the brutal tactics that can be used to break a prisoner. At the end I was dedicated to evading capture, but I knew how to cope in case I became a prisoner of an enemy.

The other instructors and I were now to train students in many of these more intense rescue and special operations missions. The curriculum included mountain ops, emergency procedures, air refueling, low-level operations, navigation (primarily by map reading in those days), and combat maneuvers such as aerial gunnery and fighter evasion tactics.

The flight engineers and PJs served as aerial gunners. We trained the pilots to maneuver the aircraft aggressively to avoid the attacks of a jet fighter and to bring our M-60 machine guns to bear on "soft," or easily attacked, ground targets. It all added up to a picture of rescue that had become quite "toothy," as I liked to put it: we were training our people to be able to chew their way into a survivor situation and to chew their way back out again, no matter what the conditions.

Combat training brought home the harsh realities of our fragile world. We knew that America inhabited a hostile planet.

Our standing orders called on all rescue units—regular air force, reserves, and Air National Guard—to be ready to deploy anywhere in the world in less than seventy-two hours, and to carry enough ordnance and supplies for thirty days of full-scale operations. This was the performance standard we all trained to achieve.

Maintaining these rigorous standards exacted a price. About this time I learned that a friend I had flown with over the years had been killed overseas in a refueling accident. We all knew we followed a dangerous profession, but his death seemed unnecessary. He was flying an HH-53, one of the Super Jolly Green Giants that had gone into service during Vietnam. It was just a practice run on a clear day with little wind. They didn't even need the fuel.

The accident report, compiled from interviews with the tanker crew and the one surviving crewman, described the copilot as having difficulty mating the probe with the drogue. The tanker pilot said he sounded frustrated and the crew member on board described his control inputs as excessive. I could see it. He'd gotten frustrated and used force on the controls to try to force the probe into the drogue. Even a big helicopter such as an HH-3 or an HH-53 is extremely sensitive to control inputs. When you make it move, it's like a dancing elephant—it moves hard. As he slammed the controls, the helicopter lurched forward and its nose dropped.

The fuel hose is 83 feet long. Some of it remains wrapped around the reel, which means that 60 to 73 feet extends behind the tanker's wing during refueling. It can deliver 1,000 pounds of jet fuel a minute, so it's heavy, and it's tipped with a 63-pound drogue, shaped like a badminton shuttlecock, which contains the female end of the connection. The normal turbulence and vortices from the large HC-130 tanker in slow, near-stall flight causes the hose to swing even in calm weather, and the arcs can be large and menacing. The fuel probe extends just 4 feet beyond the sweep of the main rotor. The pilot has to hit an 8-inch bull's-eye with more than 480 pounds of direct force to couple in the hose.

As the HH-53's nose dipped, the rotor system slashed into the hose and drogue, disintegrating parts of the main-rotor blades.

The lone survivor on board told investigators that the helicopter immediately began to shake and pound under the damaged, out-of-balance rotor system. In the shuddering cabin, the pilots tried desperately to keep it flying. Behind them, the crew were being tossed like rag dolls against the hard sides of the cabin.

They were over water, but they decided to try an emergency landing on an island just two minutes away. Before they got there, the disintegrating metal of the aircraft failed, the tailboom and tailrotor sheared off, and the helicopter plunged nose down into the sea.

Aerial refueling was the maneuver we and the trainees practiced more than any other because it was the key to extending the helicopter's range and making every rescue site accessible in terms of distance. From then on, whenever I gave control of the aircraft to a young and inexperienced pilot, I imagined that helicopter disintegrating in the air. Then I'd preach the gospel of delicate force and I would explain the necessity of being alert to almost imperceptible cues.

The slightest increased increment of motion needs to be corrected. If the drogue twitches up, it can sail into the rotors. Too quick a motion toward the tanker may mean it's turning. The pilot can't relax when he's driven the probe home, but must instantly slow the helicopter's momentum to keep it from carrying forward into the tanker. Sparks of static electricity between the probe and the drogue, combined with even the slightest misting of jet fuel, can explode the fuel load.

I hoped this knowledge would spare the students from experiencing disaster.

*   *   *

Ogden was the first place we had lived as a family with any stability. During training, we'd been shuttled from one base to
another. The Philippines hadn't been conducive to a settled family life. Then there was Korea. Now, with my assignment at Hill
and the 1550th, Jean and I and the boys were enjoying camping
in the mountains, trout fishing in the summer, and snowshoeing
in the winter. My sister Joanne and her husband lived nearby in
the 7,000 foot-high Park City, and we visited them often. It felt
like home, at least as much as a military life makes possible.

Then in the middle of 1976 the air force moved the 1550th to
Kirtland Air Force Base outside of Albuquerque, New Mexico.

What politician lobbied for Kirtland I will never know. Albuquerque is both higher and hotter than Ogden, a combination
that was tough on the power-challenged Jollys and their crews.
We literally couldn't fly safely on a hot day. But we still had to
keep the training flights lifting off on time and to keep the graduates pouring out the far end of their training like water from a
spigot.

So we had to fly at night and in the predawn hours, when the
cooler temperatures would allow us to lift safely off the ground.

Summers were the worst. We showed up for flight preparation at one forty-five in the morning. At two-forty I'd be standing in front of a group of students who were only half awake,
instructing them for a flight briefing at three-forty. We'd take off
at five. And this was just the daytime sorties.

On the second day of the week, instructors often had to come
in for regular office duties, a shift that ran from seven-thirty in
the morning to four-thirty in the afternoon. Then the next day
most of us would swing back around to the middle of the night
again for flight training. I called it circadian abuse, a disruption of
the natural rhythms that govern our lives and keep us physically
and mentally healthy by helping us get enough sleep.

All the while, many of our immediate supervisors rarely showed their faces on the graveyard shift. I learned then how remarkably little it takes to win the hearts and minds of the men and women serving under you. They could have won our affection and respect if they'd shown up to ask how we were doing and maybe asking if we wanted a cup of coffee. As it was, their absence contributed to a deterioration of morale.

I was committed to the air force and air rescue. But the lack of support, the brutal schedule, and the demands to keep pushing out graduates got me down. I started to look for alternatives.

Nick Dawson was a major, and the commander of the same Air National Guard unit that Jack Baker belonged to. The two men couldn't have been more different. Where Jack was a coiled knot of suppressed emotions, Dawson was down-to-earth and solid. He was an experienced airline pilot and military fixed-wing aviator. Rotary-wing flying befuddled him at first but he kept at it until he mastered it.

Nick was my student and we spent a lot of time together. One day we were in the ready room on a weather hold when he described the history of his unit.

The 102nd Aerospace Rescue and Recovery Squadron on Long Island was the oldest Air National Guard flying unit in the United States. It was almost as old as the airplane itself, having been formed in 1908, just five years after the Wright brothers' first flight. Then it was the 1st Aero Company A, Signal Corps, of the New York National Guard. The company used balloons to send signals. Its first aviators were Columbia University students who took it upon themselves in 1910 to build the unit's first plane, which they crashed the same year. From these roots the unit grew into the early days of military aviation. Its long history gave the 102nd a deeper tradition than most regular air force units.

Air rescue was still new to the 102nd when I met Nick in Albuquerque in the second half of 1976. But it wouldn't be for long. The 102nd had been tagged as an air rescue unit with mission responsibilities around the world. Dawson was in charge of the upgrade.

"Ed, I'm telling you," Nick bragged, "the 102nd is going to be the best there is. You're not going to find a better rescue unit in the world."

I thought about the differences between training and rescue. Training was more structured. As an instructor pilot, I was one of the people in charge of creating "variables" that would challenge students to cope with different situations. I was pretty good at it—damned good, in fact. But real missions created variables of their own that had to be coped with in real time. That was a real challenge, adjusting to the shifting sands of a real-time operation as they formed and re-formed, demanding constant updates of command approach and strategy. That was exhilarating. And instead of the demands to push students through the program, to lift off on time and meet arbitrary graduation rates, the only demand in rescue was to bring back survivors and come back alive yourself. It was flying reduced to an essential purpose. I wanted that again, and I told Jean what I was thinking.

Of course, Jean would be a large part of my decision. I wouldn't make a move without her approval. We had bought a house northwest of town, and she was active in Albuquerque life, playing in a soccer league and sewing clothes for a specialty shop in the Old Town tourist area. But after talking it over, we agreed that a move back East, putting us closer to our families, was also something we wanted. It would be good for the boys, too; they wouldn't have to move from school to school depending on where the air force sent me.

From there, it was just a matter of time before we made a firm decision, and we progressed from talking to planning. I resigned my regular air force commission for a commission in the Air

Force Reserve, and accepted Nick's offer to join the Air National Guard as a reserve officer and part-time instructor at the 102nd.

Months remained, after we set the plan in motion. Meanwhile, the aircrews of the 102nd kept coming through our program. John Sfeir, whose career and assignments had seemed to parallel my own, was one of them. Knowing that John was at the 102nd and that Jean and I could expect to reestablish the close friendship we'd shared with John and Jacquie—they had stood up at Cavan's christening, and we'd done the same at the baptism of their twins—was another incentive for the move.

John Kleven also was with the 102nd. Kleven was a strong-willed pilot, as I learned in June 1978. He was one of two students I was instructing in a simulator course that included heavy doses of extreme weather operations. When a conversation between us turned to flying into thunderstorms, John grew intense and quite emotional.

"Ed," he said, his eyes narrowed and his face set, "I will never take the HH-3 where there are known or even forecast thunderstorms. I will never even go into the clouds when they're forecast. I'll never be caught in that situation."

"Well, sometimes you've got to," I replied. "It might be the lesser of two evils. What if the forecast predicts a 30 percent chance of thunderstorms and you have no safe options underneath? If you've got low clouds and you're in the mountains, the main thing you want to do is miss the mountains. You'd be better off taking your chance with the thunderstorm in a case like that."

"Ed, I mean never," he said in a tone that left no room for argument. He sounded as if he'd thought about it quite a bit, but I didn't ask him why he felt so strongly.

Two weeks later I put Jean on a plane to New York, where she was going to visit the Sfeirs and to check out school districts and houses in eastern Long Island. The morning she left, I was taking students through instrument training in the simulator when Major Ben Pearson, the head of the simulator section, called me out.

Pearson never called anyone out of the simulator during a session, so I knew it wasn't good. Then he asked me one of those questions you wish you hadn't heard: "Ed, isn't it the 102nd you're joining in November?"

"Yes, sir," I said.

"Didn't you tell me Jean was going up there today to see the area?"

"Yes, sir."

"They lost an aircraft today. Crashed in the Adirondacks south of Plattsburgh Air Force Base. Looks like no survivors."

I felt sick. I wondered who it was. A haunting premonition told me to expect the worst. While I tried to find out more, I called Jean's sister Ann, who was to meet her at the airport, and told her not to let Jean go out to Long Island. Even if John and Jacquie weren't affected by the crash, I knew everyone in the unit would be busy.

But all too soon, word came back that John Sfeir was one of the pilots killed in the crash. The other was John Kleven. They'd been scud running, flying low in marginal visibility trying to avoid thunderstorms that had been forecast. Witnesses said they'd missed clearing a small hill by just 2 or 3 feet.

When you hear about the loss of a close friend who died doing what you both did, you wonder why you're still alive. Maybe, I thought, I could have made a difference, or at least offered extra comfort in the wake of the disaster. John was someone I admired and trusted as a pilot. I considered him a lifelong friend. We had much work to do together. I would miss him a great deal.

Jacquie had support from the squadron and group members. Jean and I went to John's parents' home in Utica, New York, in honor of John and to support his grief-stricken parents the best we could.

The fact that John Kleven had been present in the aircraft stunned me. The emotional conversation we'd had during the simulator course came back to me in stark detail. They had crashed in just the conditions he had been so adamant about

avoiding. I had the eerie feeling that Kleven had somehow fore-
seen the conditions of his death.

Several weeks later, I learned a new dimension of the tragedy,
a dimension that made the picture clear and, at the same time,
heartbreaking. John Kleven's father had been an airline pilot.
Three years earlier, on June 24, 1975, he had been at the controls
of Eastern Airlines Flight 66 from New Orleans as it approached
Kennedy International Airport. The approach pattern took the
Boeing 727 through a field of thunderstorms. "Adverse winds"
drove the plane into the ground, where it struck approach lights,
broke up, and caught fire. One hundred and thirteen of the 124
people aboard died. At the time it was the nation's worst domes-
tic airline crash.

A meteorologist tied the crash to a phenomenon little known
at the time—severe downdrafts or wind shear associated with
thunderstorms. Study of these "microbursts," as they are called,
eventually led to the installation of Doppler radar at airports as
a safety measure.

Kleven's obsession made sense when I learned where it came
from. It was tragically ironic. It was not the thunderstorms but
his determination to avoid them—and his father's fate—that may
well have killed him.

IO

Two Emergencies
in One Day

Fear is the mind-killer. Fear is the little-death that brings total
obliteration.

—*Frank Herbert*

I reported to the New York Air National Guard's 102nd Aerospace Rescue and Recovery Squadron on November 3, 1978. It was a tumultuous, unnerving time. The nation seemed as if it was being dragged kicking and screaming into a future nobody wanted, torn by energy and water shortages, tax revolts, inflation, and staggering interest rates. We were not at war, but were fighting its "moral equivalent" in efforts to conserve energy. At least that's what Jimmy Carter told us, wrapped in a cardigan. Carter had brought Israel's Menachem Begin and Egypt's Anwar Sadat together at Camp David in September just five years after the Yom Kippur War, but rejoicing at the landmark peace accord was muted by the general tone of joylessness at home.

The squadron, the flying unit of the New York Air National Guard's 106th Rescue Group, occupied a corner of Suffolk County Airport at Westhampton Beach. The group had about twelve hundred pilots, pararescuemen, maintenance workers, and other support staff, 80 percent of them part-time volunteers. The squadron, with about two hundred of the group's personnel, flew five

77

helicopters, all Jollys, and four HC-130 tankers, call sign King. But a valuable part of the rescue experience it had possessed had been lost in the crash the previous summer. As the only flight examiner instructor pilot for helicopters and the chief of aircrew standards for both the helicopters and the tankers, I had the job of bringing the squadron up to speed.

That meant a lot of time in the cockpit, which I looked forward to. Jean had stayed behind with the boys to sell the Albuquerque house while I looked for a new one. And with only a part-time salary, I needed the extra instruction time and the pay that came with it to keep up with rising prices.

The grinding wheels of fate brought Jack Baker to my cockpit once again.

Headquarters at the 106th had slated him for a leadership position. To be appointed, he had to be qualified as an HH-3E aircraft commander. He had been, once, but curious episodes in his past had gotten him downgraded to copilot, where the lives and safety of a crew weren't under his control.

A story got back to me about an Operation Red Flag combat training exercise at Nellis Air Force Base in Nevada.

Jack had been in charge of the aircraft when the fuel ran low as it headed home to Nellis. The crew watched as gauges dropped below minimum levels, and the emergency low-fuel warning lights glared. The crew started imploring Jack to land the aircraft as they passed over several civilian airports, but he didn't acknowledge their warnings. He was fixated on reaching Nellis, still miles away, and oblivious to the warnings. The flight engineer switched on the additional fuel boost pumps to ensure that the engines would not flame out on final approach, if they made it to an approach at all.

They made Nellis, and both engines flamed out seconds after landing while he was trying to taxi off the runway. They'd avoided disaster by some thirty seconds.

I studied Jack for some clues to this behavior. He was quiet and courteous in normal circumstances. But his smile was as tight as a drumhead, he spoke through tight lips, and his words were controlled. Everything about him indicated a tightly harnessed tension. There was something coiled within him, some kind of uncertainty, which is unusual in a pilot.

When they assigned me to reevaluate Jack for an upgrade, the senior officers at headquarters didn't know that I, too, had been exposed to Jack's performance under stress.

To pass the test, Jack had to perform in-flight emergency procedures. We talked about them ahead of time. The flight profile included a healthy dose of autorotations, the same dead-stick maneuver that had caused him to panic in my aircraft at Hill.

Some months after that had happened, I received the Military Airlift Command safety award for outstanding airmanship in bringing the helicopter down safely. Now, however, Jack would have the controls. Despite our preliminary conversations, during which Jack assured me he was comfortable with the test requirements, I felt uncertain as the test drew near. I didn't bring up the earlier incident, and I didn't really expect Jack to, but I had the impression that he didn't remember it—or didn't want to.

I arrived at the air base on the morning of the training flight. A light breeze blew in off the Atlantic and the air was clear and crisp. The weather wouldn't affect the flying one way or the other, and that encouraged me that things might go well.

Tech Sergeant Tom "Smitty" Smith, the flight engineer, was sorting equipment in the ready room when I walked in. Smitty was a pro who kept his own counsel until something needed to be done, and then he didn't hesitate. He seemed a little pensive and on edge. Jack arrived all smiles, a picture of confidence in his crisp green flight suit that was new squadron issue.

We took off and climbed to 2,000 feet. The extra altitude was a safety precaution. The loss of power in a helicopter is not at all like the loss of power in an airplane. In a small airplane, a pilot can control a rate of descent at about 500 feet per minute. In a helicopter, the rate of descent after power loss can be in the thousands of feet per minute. Most routine flights don't achieve an altitude of more than 1,000 feet, so a power-loss emergency gives the crew very little time to make decisions; maintain aircraft control; and find a clear, flat area in which to try a landing.

This makes autorotation an excellent maneuver in which to judge whether a pilot can deal with complex, rapidly changing, stressful situations. If he can't, it's an excellent way to get killed.

On this brilliant November day all across eastern Long Island, late fall foliage in reds and yellows brightened the landscape. Here and there, smoke rose from burning leaf piles. The waters of Long Island Sound, Peconic Bay, and the Atlantic shone blue in the sunlight.

Following procedures, I demonstrated the first autorotation, maintaining the rotor rpm in safe limits with the collective while simultaneously maneuvering to a landing spot with the cyclic, collective, and pedals. Jack watched intently with no hint of confusion. I thought that was a good sign. Once on the ground, I went over it with Jack to make sure he wouldn't be surprised or confused when he had the controls.

"Do you think you've got it?" I asked when I finished.

"Absolutely," he said.

"The aircraft's yours, then," I said, feeling a little like a poker player with all his chips on the table and holding a pair of threes. I wouldn't say I was scared exactly, but rather alert to signs of trouble.

He took off and climbed to 2,000 feet. "Hold it here," I said. I pulled the engines off-line to a detent position, at which they no longer turned the rotors. The jet engines slowly spooled down, leaving the main sound the swishing of the rotors. I waited for Jack's next move.

Immediately, almost spasmodically, he drove the controls to extreme positions.

He pulled back on the cyclic stick, dropping the helicopter's airspeed from its minimum safe 75 knots to near zero. Simultaneously he rolled the aircraft onto its side. Now confused, he jammed the right pedal. The rotor speed slowed dangerously.

Things came unglued in a split second. It was amazing how quickly we went from relative safety to real peril. We were coming out of the sky vertically, yawing to the right and rolling over in the same direction, accelerating straight down and nearly on our side.

Then Jack froze on the controls. His left hand locked onto the collective, right hand on the cyclic, and both feet wedged on the pedals.

I gave him the standard order to release the controls. "Jack, I've got the aircraft."

He didn't respond.

"Jack, I've got the aircraft," I repeated.

We didn't have much time. The ground was rising relentlessly, and Jack was still frozen. We had perhaps twelve seconds to ground impact. I had to get the controls away from him. Time slowed as we plummeted relentlessly down.

"Jack, let go of the controls!" Now I was yelling, in a combination of fear and fury with the persistence of his unawareness.

Again, he gave no response. We had ten seconds left.

Smitty reached up from the jump seat and grabbed Jack's helmet cord. He yanked it hard, and Jack's head snapped to one side. He didn't say anything, but he loosened his death grip on the sticks and pedals. We were five seconds from crashing.

I grabbed the controls, nosed the aircraft forward, and straightened it out with pedals. Smitty jammed the engine speed selectors forward to spool up the jet turbines, which began their agonizingly slow whine back up to flying speed. I knew from practice that it took the engines a second and a half to reach sufficient speed to start driving the rotors again. Four seconds to hit. The aircraft was moaning and yawing. Smitty started calling out the rotor rpm, airspeed, and rate of descent, giving me the information I needed to keep the aircraft in the critical envelope and still keep watch outside.

Three seconds to impact. The engines screamed as they neared full power, the helicopter stopped its wild yawing, and the rotors started to arrest our fall. With maybe two seconds to go, less than 50 feet from the ground, we started flying again.

I savored the relief. The controls in my hands made me feel secure. I didn't want to let them go, but I knew I would have to.

I took the helicopter back to 2,000 feet. The landscape had never been more beautiful. I looked down to where we would have hit. The smoke plume would have drifted across Montauk Highway and probably stopped traffic. The roads were relatively clear. I imagined them with fire trucks converging on the crash site, their lights blinking in the sun. Ambulances, too, but I don't think they would have had a lot to do.

"Jack, what were you thinking back there?" I asked. I'd seen people freeze before, both in actual emergencies and during training. Everyone has difficulty during unusual, threatening events, but most don't freeze. Still, it happened, people recovered from it, and went on.

His response was a jawdropper. "I feel great, Ed," he said with a smile. "This is the best I've done. Things are going pretty good today, aren't they?"

"Jack, we wouldn't have survived that. We need to work more on these."

He looked at me with wonder, and I had the same feeling I'd had at Hill. For the few seconds in which we'd almost crashed, Jack had been somewhere else. His brain had taken him to a different place and returned him afterward with no memory of what had happened. The expression on his face said he didn't believe me.

I swiveled around to see how Smitty was reacting. His face was grim and his eyes narrowed to hard slits. He'd clearly seen enough. He was ready to stop the test right there. I felt obligated to give Jack another try, if only to have ammunition for denying his upgrade.

I explained the problems with his first autorotation and stressed that those problems had nearly killed us. "A helicopter wants a gentle hand, Jack. It's a subtle machine. Give it subtle movements and you can make it come down smoothly. You jam it, and no way you can control it coming down."

"Great, Ed. Let's do another," he responded sunnily. "I felt more comfortable with this autorotation than some in the past."

Nothing I said was getting through. My words had no effect, as if they were bouncing off his helmet. I was now concerned. I knew I'd have to watch Jack for the faintest cues of trouble, and senses heightened as I turned over control of the aircraft.

"Now, Jack, you understand what we are doing?"

"Yeah, Ed, no problem," he said.

I pulled the engines off-line. The turbines spooled back. As their whine quieted, I felt as though two good friends had left me.

Jack again snapped the large helicopter into a violent contortion. I cursed myself for giving him the controls again, even though it was my responsibility to give him several autorotations. A flash of motion outside startled me as the rotor blades flexed downward, so deeply I could see their tips outside the windows and hear them slash the air close to the cockpit roof. I knew of rotors flexing so extremely they'd cut off the top of the cockpit, even amputating the refueling probe at the level of the pilot's feet.

In the contortion we were in, the rotors slowed quickly below the rpm needed to autorotate and land safely, and the blades flexed closer to the cockpit and our heads. We plunged sideways out of the air. Once again, Jack froze.

I didn't wait this time. "Jack, I've got the controls," I said. I was afraid I wouldn't have time this time.

He sat motionless and silent.

The extreme inertial forces of our fall initially jammed me and Smitty to our seats. I looked out the side window and watched the earth rush up. It was as if we'd rolled off a 2,000 foot ledge. It astounded me all over, the speed with which control could plummet into chaos. I should have resisted letting Jack have a second try, but at least now I had double proof of his bizarre and frightening lapses. Smitty had cranked up his panic detector, too. He managed to rise from the jump seat and grab Jack's shoulder to shake him. I wrestled the controls away. Smitty got a hand on the engine speed selectors. The jets started their slow whine back up to speed.

We were again about 50 feet off the ground when I managed to recover the helicopter and get it flying again. Again the relief, and with it this time the determination not to relinquish my old friends the controls.

A third attempt was out of the question. Smitty and I had seen enough. I swung the Jolly back toward the barn. On the way in, I made another effort to get inside Jack's head.

"That's two emergencies in one day, Jack," I said, trying to keep it light. "I guess you're finding autorotating to be a little tricky."

Again, he took off down a mental side street. "I feel great and the autorotations are going tremendously," he said. "Thanks to your instruction, Ed."

We finished the flight in silence. When I looked back at Smitty, he was wearing an expression so grim it would have frightened a hit man for the mob.

Back at the barn, I huddled with Nick Dawson. "Were you watching, by any chance?" I asked.

"Yeah," he said. "It looked pretty exciting."

"Oh, yeah. You should have been there. There's no way I can certify this guy. He'll kill a crew if he's in charge."

"They'll be unhappy to hear that at the group," Nick said. But he agreed, and Jack stayed a copilot while the group promoted someone else.

I had arrived at eastern Long Island at a time of seasonal transition. The summer folk had retreated, leaving the year-round residents to resume their normal lives. The fishermen who harvested the sea and the bays between the two forks of the island that spear into the North Atlantic were gearing down for the winter ahead. Farmers piled potatoes, onions, and the rest of their late vegetables into boxes and trucked them away, leaving a few for the East End farm stands that were beginning to convert to pine garlands and other Christmas wares. The days were short and the hurricane season was dwindling.

I missed Jean and the boys. Every time I looked at a house, I thought of them. Every time I calculated a mortgage at interest rates that seemed to be climbing by the day, I hoped Jean would find a buyer for the Albuquerque house before we were priced out of the market. But I told her in one of my many phone calls that they were going to like the East End. I didn't really know what the summers were like, but the year-rounders were for the most part frank and solid, as you'd expect from people who depend for their living on the soil and the sea.

As Christmas approached, we all paused in our anticipation of the season.

Like eastern Long Island when I arrived, the 102nd was in transition. Nick was still trying to change the mind-set of some pockets of its jet-jock, weekend-warrior culture.

When Nick wasn't around, another officer at the squadron was a prime example. He carried a rubber chicken around with him. One of his favorite tricks, and he had many, was to stuff a rubber chicken into his pants and let the flesh-colored head dangle from his fly. This got him a great deal of attention that he apparently craved, but it reflected badly on the squadron majority, who were outstanding people and professionals. Under the officer's Animal House style of leadership, a small yet visible minority clung to his lead, and a frat party atmosphere was visible around the squadron. The concept of high-risk rescue operations hadn't taken root so far with this minority. To them, flying was still a part-time endeavor focused on Cold War superpower confrontations that they trusted would never materialize. But rescues would—and did—happen.

People new to rescue had to be ready to step up. Getting them ready to fly into the North Atlantic at night in deadly storms would be a difficult challenge.

The old fighter jock culture showed little sense of concern despite the loss of Sfeir and Kleven and their crew just months earlier. I was in the briefing room one morning when one of these pilots revealed a shocking combination of callousness and igno- rance. "I'm not worried," he said. "These helicopters don't fly fast enough to hurt anyone."

His comment stopped the conversation, and the other pilots turned away and busied themselves with their flight preparations, ignoring him. Most of the squadron knew better, and the aero club veneer began to crack.

"The Adirondacks crash wasn't an isolated case, you know," I said bluntly, just to keep the record straight. "More than forty-six hundred helicopters were lost in Vietnam. Thirty-five hundred crew members and pilots died. You might think they got shot down. But most of the losses were because of weather, equipment failure, pilot error, things like that. They might not fly that fast, but they can kill you in an awful lot of ways if you don't know what you're doing and even if you do." I hoped that sobered the guy.

Despite the interest rates, I found an affordable house in Cutch- ogue, a village on the North Fork that stood in the middle of potato fields. Jean found a buyer for the Albuquerque house, and she, Keith, and Cavan joined me on Long Island in time to cele- brate the new year, 1979. And by that spring, about six months into my new career at the 102nd, I became the squadron's full- time flight examiner pilot, with a salary from the Department of Defense.

Meanwhile, the strange and sad deterioration of Jack Baker's piloting skills continued at a rapid pace. He lost his qualification to fly either as a pilot or copilot and was given a staff job. But rescue calls don't always provide the luxury of assembling an ideal crew. You have to get into the air quickly. And when the Coast Guard tasked us to rescue a fisherman whose hand had been severed by a winch 200 miles out in the Atlantic, Jack was the only other man available to fly. Only in a life or death emergency could I fly with him in the copilot's seat, but I had to fly as an instructor, teaching and encouraging Jack as we attempted the rescue.

The weather was no problem. It was not night and there were no hurricanes or nor'easters, nor any ice to cling to the rotors and drag the helicopter down. It was a good day, with light winds, calm seas, and clear, blue skies. I assessed the risks and determined we'd be safe with Jack in the cockpit.

The HH-3E we drew was an old one. Its condition worried me a little. Going out to sea in a helicopter always involves some hazard. The older Jollys didn't have adequate backup emergency systems for long-range operations. Some critical backup systems were engineered to work for only thirty minutes, not enough flight time to get the crew back from that far out to sea.

But I felt comfortable that the conditions and workload were in our favor. We could get out and back again with only minimal assistance from Jack. It looked easy. Even Jack thought so, but then again, he always did.

We were about 150 miles out and I was flying the aircraft when suddenly the rotor tachometer, which displays the main-rotor rpm, pegged back to zero. Jack was supposed to be monitoring the instruments. The flight engineer, Master Sergeant Greg Couture, was in the jump seat. We were still flying. The rotors kept turning despite what the gauge showed. It was clearly an instrument problem.

Normally we would have turned back, but we were already most of the way to the boat where the fisherman was in danger of bleeding to death. Greg and I discussed the problem, Jack nodding in agreement as we talked. We could no longer measure rotor rpm, but as long as we babied the aircraft to keep the rpm steady, we'd have no problem. If we got too aggressive or if we got abrupt on the controls the rotor speed would vary an unknown amount and likely overspeed.

We decided after twenty minutes that we could continue as long as we were smooth on the controls.

Once we decided we could baby the Jolly through the mission, I gave the controls to Jack so I could enter coordinates in the Doppler Navigation System. He'd been flying for only a couple of minutes when his panicked voice erupted in the intercom, "Trouble! We've got trouble! The rotor, the rotor! We got to get down!"

He slammed the collective control down, and the helicopter nose-dived toward the ocean. The force of his abrupt input caused the rotor to decouple from the driving engines and free-wheel, spinning faster and faster.

I exploded in a curse that I couldn't contain and didn't want to. Jack had done it again, changing a flight that was under control into an emergency. This was just what Greg and I wanted to avoid, overspeed that could upset the delicately balanced forces of the rotor, and at worst cause severe damage. Now the rotors were freewheeling, their high-pitched whine was growing in our ears, and we could only sense how much the rpm were climbing. Without the tachometer, we had no idea how much we'd exceeded aircraft limits for rotor overspeed.

We had to get out of the dive first. "I've got the aircraft, let go of the controls," I told Jack sharply. Wonder of wonders, he did. I leveled the aircraft by pulling gingerly back on the cyclic. Level now, we were no longer looking straight down at the ocean but could see the sky. I adjusted the power. As I added power to the rotors, the increasing drag generated as a by-product of lift slowed the rotors down. The whine of the freewheeling rotors dropped to the deeper pitch of rotors working to keep the heli-copter airborne. It was comforting music.

Now we had to check for damage. None of the gauges indi-cated overspeed but the rotor rpm gauge wasn't working. The first sign of failure came when I added power to fly the helicopter faster than 75 or 80 knots. It began to shudder and pound. We were seriously hobbled, but at 200 miles out to sea, we continued with the rescue. The slow pace would hamper us when we wanted a flat-out run for the survivor's sake with what I was sure was a damaged helicopter.

Jack was visibly shaken. I suddenly realized that even though he'd nodded yes, Jack had neither understood nor absorbed what Greg and I had talked about earlier. Somehow Jack had just blanked it out.

I stayed at the controls, and the old helicopter held its own. Greg shifted to his hoist operator's role when we found the fishing boat. One of the PJs went down to strap the injured fisherman in, and Greg lifted them off the deck in the hoist. When they were in the bay, I turned the Jolly toward the safety of land. Three hours later, we had made it.

Mechanics checking the aircraft found that the overspeed had caused the failure of a main-rotor head damper, an important system—the main rotor had just held us in the air.

A few members of the squadron laughed at Jack and ridiculed him after these humiliations. That infuriated me and I stopped it right away.

Jack was a gentleman and he endured these occasions with a quiet grace. Jack's flying performance couldn't be ignored, but he had no power over it. Deep in the recesses of his brain was a man for whom helicopter flight was a Gordian knot of mystery, a knot he wasn't meant to solve. The only answer was to keep the controls out of his hands.

The 102nd ARRS gradually moved closer to being able to perform its new role. As the months passed, the pilots, the engineers, the PJs, the ground crews, the maintenance staff—everybody who was vital to the success of the high-risk, lifesaving operation that the 102nd was intended to become—started to hit their stride. The better they got, the more pride they developed in their very special skills. We all were bound by the knowledge that there weren't many people anywhere in the world who could do what we did. In our corner of Suffolk County Airport, where even then the sleek private planes of the rich and famous people who summered in the Hamptons vied for runway space with our dumpy, dull green rescue aircraft, we were quietly aware of the importance of our skills to the people who might need them.

My first year at the 102nd passed that November, a troubled month in which the nation and the world were transfixed by the spectacle of Americans held hostage in Iran. The Soviet Union was adventuring in Afghanistan after engineering a Communist coup there a year and a half earlier, setting off forces that would take years to come to roost. But the hostage-taking in Iran was the Western world's introduction to a level of religious fundamentalist fervor that came as a surprise. The dour visage of the exiled Ayatollah Khomeini staring down from walls and posters, the students burning American flags and chanting "Death to America," the pictures of blindfolded hostages being paraded around the U.S. embassy in Teheran—all formed a montage of a part of the world that seemed more and more foreign even as we became more familiar with it.

Less than two months later, between Christmas 1979 and New Year's 1980, a vicious storm struck the North Atlantic. It would test the squadron's competence at its new role and demand every skill at our disposal.

11

The Indifferent Sea

When I emerged on deck it seemed that the end of everything
had come. On all sides there was a rending and crashing of
wood and steel and canvas. The *Ghost* was being wrenched and
torn to fragments.

—Jack London

The call came while we were burying one of our own.

Master Sergeant Joe Gusmano had been a senior
noncommissioned officer, one of the maintenance people who kept the Jollys and Kings in the air. He'd joined the
106th after twenty-three years in the air force, then dropped dead
of a heart attack. He was well respected, and much of the base
turned out for his funeral on December 27.

The church was still hung with Christmas decorations. The
priest talked about bravery and sacrifice. When the service was
over, the officers and NCOs exited through the front door to
reassemble in funeral formation, forming two facing rows to
salute the casket as it passed between us on its way to Calverton
National Cemetery. A cold wind out of the northwest ripped at
our blue dress uniforms.

We were forming our lines when Master Sergeant Bill Hughes,
one of the PJs, rushed out a side door of the church and whis-
pered into Dawson's ear. As usual in those prebeeper days, the
squadron had the number where we'd be in case of an emergency.

As Dawson approached me, word rippled down the line that the wind that was whipping the pine garlands and red bows was causing havoc out in the North Atlantic. A small cargo ship was foundering and its crew of nine was in trouble. The ship was beyond the range of Coast Guard rescue, and they had requested our help through their Rescue Coordination Center on Governors Island in Upper New York Bay in New York City.

At the base, the officer on duty, Captain Marty Ingram, had laid out aeronautical charts in one of the planning rooms and done some plotting. The ship was 265 miles southeast of Montauk, and he figured that if we wanted to reach the survivors before dark we'd have to launch right away. We rushed from the church without waiting for the casket to come out.

When I reached the squadron, Marty was waiting. His plotting showed the ship was beyond the point of no return for a single fuel load, so it was declared a high-risk mission. He wanted to fly the mission, too, but we had full crews already preparing. Nick Dawson had assigned me as mission commander and I asked Marty, the squadron's scheduling officer, to work as ground supervisor of flying. He would file our flight plans, provide weather updates, and stand by the phones in case another emergency developed.

I didn't have a flight suit with me and there was little time for me to change clothes. Nearby, PJ Jay Jinks was wrestling into an arctic wet suit that would keep the cold at bay if he had to go into the water. Jinks, a master sergeant, was a big guy, and I asked to borrow one of his Nomex flight suits. It fit over my dress blues with room to spare. I loosened my tie and we headed for the line.

The mission called for two helicopters and a tanker. One Jolly might have done it, but we normally planned to launch two for mutual support in case of an emergency. Even in a brand-new helicopter, the odds of something bad happening are three to four times higher than in a military airplane. Our machines were fifteen years old.

Once we got into the air, details about the ship in trouble formed a fascinating picture. This was no rusty tramp steamer, but the flagship of a nostalgic revival, a ghost from the past. *John F. Leavitt* was a 97-foot, two-masted schooner modeled on vessels of a century earlier that had worked the ports of the Northeast and elsewhere, transporting loads of small cargo.

Deepwater sailors scorned these "coasters" for hugging the shoreline. One writer said they set course "by the bark of a dog." Her owner and skipper, Ned Ackerman, believed there was still a place for them in hauling small, nonperishable cargo between small ports, at no cost to the environment. He'd built *Leavitt* out of love and deep conviction, along with a showman's sense of the publicity his venture would attract.

Ackerman had little experience in this type of sailing. As Peter Spectre later wrote in *Wooden Boat*, the sum total of Ackerman's cargo-carrying experience or of skippering a boat of this size and type was a three-day maiden voyage from Thomaston, Maine, to Quincy, Massachusetts.

The voyage had gotten off to a bad start. Ackerman had run *Leavitt* aground on a mudbank a quarter of a mile from the shipbuilder's ways in Thomaston. The tide floated it free, and Ackerman sailed on to Quincy. With no engine, it took *Leavitt* three days to get around Cape Cod. When it finally reached Quincy and the Duane Company wharf, *Leavitt* took on its maiden cargo—75 tons of lumber and fifty 55-gallon drums of tanning chemicals. Then Ackerman made several fateful decisions. He violated the defining restriction of the coaster, taking it far from shore with a relatively inexperienced crew in December, when winter gales sweep the North Atlantic. *Leavitt* had been on course for Haiti with its cargo when it encountered an overwhelming series of problems. In the typically vile December North Atlantic a heavy cargo boom had broken loose and was flailing uncontrollably. The bilge pump failed. The weather worsened, and the beating boom made it impossible for the crew to manage the sails. The boom drummed against the sides of the boat, loosening its seams. *Leavitt* started taking water and with no functioning sails and unable to make headway, it lay broadside to the waves.

I was flying *Jolly 40* with Air Guard major Denny Morrell, an airline pilot transplanted from Wyoming to the Hamptons. As we flew into the teeth of the storm, he blew off nervous tension by singing square dance calls. He had a whole repertoire of them. Over the intercom it sounded like a barn dance with a hurricane going on outside. Denny was a gifted and conservative pilot, but the conditions were enough to make anybody nervous.

While Denny's "do-si-dos" and "allemande lefts" warbled through the intercom, my own thoughts were of the variables we faced. I wondered if anybody in the ship's crew was injured, if we'd be able to hoist them from the deck, if they had a lifeboat or rafts in case we couldn't. All these questions went into the scenarios I played out for the rescue ahead. The weather and the seas were the wild cards. I couldn't see what they'd be like when we reached the scene, so I put off being really nervous until later.

Captain Bob Bagshaw, a full-time pilot with the unit, shared the cockpit of the other Jolly, call sign *Jolly 78*, with a guardsman named Captain Rex Rivolo. Bagshaw was intelligent, witty, and somewhat antiestablishment. He was constantly at war with the commanders, often with good justification. Bags was a logical thinker who became frustrated by the command's "bonehead" decisions. His venom was never directed at Dawson, but Bags would level some of our Animal House officers daily. Bags seemed to be determined to go down guns blazing. Rivolo, a dark-haired, dark-eyed native of Italy, was an uncompromising guy who had flair and style. He often wore his flight jacket over his shoulders like a cape. Members of the squadron called him Doctor Rex because of his Ph.D. in astrophysics. He had served a tour in Vietnam in F-4 Phantoms and he often became impatient with the apparent frailty of the helicopters. Nevertheless, he was an aggressive flier who liked to push the machinery to its limits, and I knew Bags and I would have to hold him back.

As we sped along in the HH-3Es, with an HC-130 tanker shadowing us overhead, the winds increased to about 60 knots, Force 11 on the Beaufort scale. The next step up, Force 12, was a hurricane. Higher gusts slammed *Jolly 40* this way and that and gave us a beating. The storm's energy resonated through the aircraft and matched the rotor throb in a ceaseless, bone-jarring vibration. The storm ceiling was low and fingers of fog trailed ghostly white over the ocean surface. With no ceiling most of the time and zero visibility—"zero-zero" conditions—we had to keep from crashing into the other helicopter. And we had to stay above the ocean swells, reported at 30 to 40 feet, that would drag us down in an instant.

I was always aware of the swells. Sometimes when I lost sight of the ocean surface for a second or the radar altimeter would momentarily shut off, some instinct would make me power the helicopter a few feet higher, just to be sure. The swells had a rhythm and a presence, and I could almost feel them below the helicopter like the stir of air that signals the approach of a train through a subway tunnel.

I worried about ice. A recent storm at home had deposited ice that snapped huge towers and trees under its weight. I didn't want to be anywhere near such destruction. I knew heavy ice storms could cause a helicopter to break up. The problems started subtly. The temperature was low enough to form ice on the rotors. It added weight, and granular ice would increase surface friction and reduce lift. And unlike the HC-130, which had heating elements in its wings, we had only centrifugal force to free the rotor blades of ice. If one shed its ice and the others didn't, the imbalance could destroy the rotor system.

We caught a break halfway out. "*Jolly 40* flight, this is King," the tanker radioed. "We've got a little break in the weather up at about 7,000 feet. If you fly up here, maybe you can avoid getting your dental work knocked out."

"That's good news, King. Thanks." We were the lead aircraft in the two-helicopter formation as we climbed free of the surface turbulence that was pounding us, and both helicopters took on fuel.

The relief was temporary. We reached the rescue site just after the middle of the afternoon. Now we would have to descend through the same garbage we'd escaped, again in "zero-zero," to seas high enough to slap us down.

Keeping the helicopters from colliding with each other while still staying in formation was our biggest challenge as we dropped through the thick clouds. To do it, we had to fly the formation blind. I kept constant radio contact with Bags and Rex, both helicopters maintaining 100 knots of airspeed while descending at 500 feet per minute. We kept a minute's flight, or 500 feet, apart. It wasn't much margin, but I trusted it was enough. We went first, and when we reached the first plateau I keyed the radio. "This is *Jolly 40* at 6,500 feet."

This was Bags's signal to start down from 7,000 feet. "Thanks, Jolly," Bags responded. "We're a step behind you."

We descended by 500-foot stairsteps into deepening gloom.

We broke out of the clouds just 300 feet above the ocean surface. Wisps of cloud and fog bled into the gray-green ocean, and the wind tore water from the wave crests in sheets of flying spray and spume. Thirty- and 40-foot swells marched across the ocean. It was 4:00 P.M., late December twilight.

"There they are," said Denny on the intercom, pointing through the windscreen.

The scene was from a child's book of sea stories or a ballad. There below us in the fading winter light was a tableau from the seafaring legends of the past. A storm-tossed wooden schooner lay broadside to the swells, listing with one rail underwater, waves breaking over its deck. Its masts were bare, the sails lashed to their booms. Thickets of ropes and wires ran between the masts and the deck. Between the two masts, a long boom flailed from side to side, sweeping lethally across the deck with every wave.

From above, I felt like an intruder. Hundreds of such ships lay at the bottom of the ocean, but I doubted whether their death throes had ever been witnessed from a helicopter. It seemed almost disrespectful to see the schooner in extremis. But our mission wasn't to bemoan the ship, it was to save its crew.

Leavitt's crew huddled on the afterdeck, away from the thrashing boom. Except for their orange life preservers, incongruously bright against the gray ocean, they looked like flood refugees I'd seen in Korea and the Philippines, bedraggled, exhausted, their eyes turned up to the hope of rescue. We might have picked them up from a clear deck but there was too much rigging on this schooner. The wildly thrashing masts or any of the stays and shrouds could have snagged the hoist while it was being lowered or retrieved. I didn't want to be tethered to a sinking ship that was rising and falling on 40-foot swells. Nor did I want to entangle the survivors and PJs in the rigging; they might not survive such a ride. We were better off retrieving the crew members from life rafts in the water.

In the back of *Jolly 40*, Jinks moved to the open cargo door in his scuba and survival gear. Tech Sergeant Paul Bellissimo did the same in the back of Rex's helicopter.

We moved in first, hovering "low and slow," 10 feet above the water at about 10 knots, close to the side of the floundering boat, which was awash. That would make it easier for the PJs to board. Jinks jumped into the water, gave us a thumbs-up to let us know he was all right, and started swimming to *Leavitt*. Bellissimo followed from the other helicopter.

They reached the boat's side easily but I held my breath while they were trying to board. I remembered another rescue, when PJ Mike McManus struggled to board a sinking freighter as its hull alternately towered above him and slammed down, first threatening to crush him and then pushing him away in a surge of water. Finally a rogue wave broke over the ship's deck and washed him aboard, to materialize before the astonished crew. Timing and luck were critical that day, and Jinks and Bellissimo needed the same combination.

They got it. *Leavitt* had a low freeboard for a 97-foot boat, and with her deck awash both pararescuemen caught a high wave and simply swam aboard.

Leavitt's flailing cargo boom continued its sweep across the hull, harvesting rigging and pounding the hull. I now knew for certain that we couldn't hoist survivors through the chaos, and that we'd have to retrieve them from the water. "Denny, they're going to have to abandon ship," I said.

He looked surprised, but we radioed the PJs and told them to get the crew off the ship and into rafts. "Roger, sir, they're as good as off," Bellissimo radioed back.

Moving slowly overhead, keeping one eye out for the other helicopter and one on the ship below, I watched the two PJs shouting over the storm to convince *Leavitt*'s crew to trust themselves to the life rafts for pickup. The broken schooner didn't offer much security, but it must have seemed better than a bathtub-size piece of inflatable fabric. Jinks and Bellissimo stressed the danger of trying to hoist up through the rigging, the dying light, the need to abandon the ship *now*.

The crew understood. The PJs radioed to let us know they were going to move the sailors into rafts. *Leavitt*'s crew had already dragged two life rafts, encased in plastic pods, on deck and tied them fast to keep them from washing overboard. Jinks and Bellissimo deployed them over the side, in the relative shelter of the stern away from the wind, and cracked the seals that automatically inflated them.

The instant they inflated, the wind snatched the orange rafts and threatened to tear them from *Leavitt*. But the ropes held, and the PJs urged the crew members over the side and into the rafts. When the last person was on board, they cut the rafts free.

It was after sunset. What light we had was fading fast, painting shadows over the details of the dying *Leavitt*, the rafts, and the sea. In the gloom, the rafts seemed impossibly small and perilous, and the crew more vulnerable than they had been on *Leavitt*'s deck.

Free of the mother ship, the rafts moved swiftly, pushed by the 60-knot wind, rising and falling like lightbulbs on the foam-flecked swells. We were moving at interstate speeds, but without mile markers, trees, or exits flashing by, there was an illusion of standing still. Since I had followed blowing rafts in the past for 10 or 20 miles while a recovery was in progress, I knew we were in for a chase. I kept an eye out for *Jolly 78*, only fifty yards away, making sure to keep clear in the disappearing light as it pursued the other raft. We stayed close to the surface to minimize the amount of slack, since our speed would blow the cable out behind the helicopter. Our challenge was to fly to the raft, get down over it as it rode the swells, then sprint ahead to get the hoist cable to the PJ.

From my view in the cockpit, *Jolly 78* looked absurdly like a kid playing on a pogo stick behind a hedge, bouncing into sight, disappearing into the trough between two swells, then rising into sight again to clear the crest of the next wave.

Aboard *Jolly 40*, flight engineer Greg Couture switched to his hoist operator's role and readied the cable with the forest penetrator at the end, fitted with a flotation collar.

He deployed the hoist, and the wind caught the penetrator and blew it back. But he led the raft perfectly, and the PJ grabbed it the first time. "That's Bellissimo down there," he said with a tone of surprise. In the chase, we'd somehow followed the raft with *Jolly 78*'s PJ.

Below, Bellissimo urged two of the sailors onto the penetrator's tiny seats while he rigged a tag line, a line with a weighted end that would help him control the hoist and guide the cable when it came back down. When the sailors were straddling the penetrator on opposite sides, he harnessed them in with a single nylon strap that ran around their backs and underneath both arms and snapped to a point on the penetrator. Satisfied that they were secure, he looked up and gave a thumbs-up to Couture, who took up the slack and reeled the sailors in.

It was a good pickup. At such moments I never failed to think about the skill, strength, and courage of the PJs and flight engineers. I smiled, remembering the many times I'd tried to compliment one of these crew members for their remarkable talents. When I did, I'd receive a shrug, a small smile, and have the compliment dismissed as just a day's work. They knew they were good, but you embarrassed them if you called attention to it.

The sailors came into *Jolly 40* through the open door behind me and sprawled like wet fish on the oil-stained cargo bay floor, shivering with cold. Couture unhooked the survivors from the penetrator and pushed them unceremoniously to the back and away from the gaping open door.

If it was turbulent in the sea, it was equally turbulent in the air just above it. These two stormy masses fed on each other through surprisingly virulent currents and eddies, twisting and turning both the helicopter and the raft. There was always a danger of someone being thrown out of the open helicopter.

Couture then sent it down again as the second PJ, Mike Durante, checked them for signs of hypothermia and wrapped them in the few blankets we had. Couture unspooled the cable, and Bellissimo reeled it in using the tag line. Bellissimo put the two remaining sailors on the penetrator, and the second lift went as smoothly as the first. Two more crew members came into the bay wet and shivering, and Durante handed them blankets and urged them to huddle together for warmth. Couture sent the cable back down for Bellissimo.

In the raft, Bellissimo was seasick. He had been running on adrenaline, but now the motion of the helicopter in the air and the rocking and tossing of the raft had caught up to him, and he was leaning over the side of the raft, vomiting.

"Bring him up and let's get out of here," I said over the intercom.

"We should let him finish first," Couture said wisely. He watched Bellissimo out of the open bay door, and after a moment said, "What's he doing now?"

The PJ had finished heaving and was kneeling in the center of the raft, struggling with two boxes that looked about a couple of feet square and that were obviously heavy. He got himself onto the penetrator seat, strapped himself to the device, and jammed his hands into straps around the boxes. Then he signaled Couture to take him up.

Without the tag line to control the hoist, the penetrator swung wildly. A wave caught Bellissimo and then fell out from under him, pulling him off the seat. Dangling from the penetrator by his safety harness, he still clung to the boxes.

To Couture, he suddenly appeared limp and lifeless. "I think he's hurt bad, unconscious. He's dangling half off the penetrator," he said. That call sent a shiver through us all. Couture hoisted him up to the open door, and only then did we know he was okay. The smiling PJ clattered into the bay with a sound of scraping metal.

"What are those things?" I asked.

Couture took a minute, then said, "Sir, they've been making a documentary about the ship down there. Two of the guys we just picked up are cameramen. That's the film they shot.

"Paul says they begged him. He didn't have to make an extra trip. It's a piece of history."

The last I saw of *Leavitt*, it was still thrashing a few hundred yards behind us in the dim, fog-threaded light. Couture was right: it was a piece of history. We wouldn't see any more like her outside of floating museums. "Just make sure they get our names right," I said.

My final glimpse of *Leavitt* showed a boat with its deck fully awash, and listing so that the push of the waves exposed its keel. One sail had torn free and was dragging in the water. The sea was slowly claiming the schooner, bringing the era of the northeastern coasters, finally, to an end.

"*Jolly 40*, we've got five aboard," Rex radioed from the other Jolly.

"Four here, Jolly, and two boxes of documentary film. We're going to be movie stars."

"Roger, *Jolly 40*," Rex came back. "Guess we failed our screen test, huh?"

"It's a matter of star quality," I said with a laugh. Rex, with his Italian good looks and his flight jacket slung over his shoulders, would have been the perfect lead in a helicopter rescue flick. Maybe the documentary producers would write him into the script. I told Rex we needed to refuel. "We're getting a little thirsty. Are you?"

"Roger, Jolly," Rex replied. "I'm going to have to pull over pretty soon myself. But with one pit stop we ought to make it fine."

Refueling was always harder in the dark. We had no night vision goggles at this time, so we had to rely on the searchlight playing on the fuel drogue as we ran at it with the probe. Radioing back and forth with the tanker that had been circling overhead while we picked up *Leavitt*'s crew, we tried to find a good altitude to fly in as we headed west to land and safety—but there wasn't one. We had to fly in the narrow envelope between the ocean and the lowest clouds. The wind was behind us now, still battering the helicopters and making the aircraft yaw and shudder.

The minimum safe altitude for refueling is 1,000 feet. We couldn't get higher than 300 or 400 feet. But we had to have fuel. We had to go for it.

Denny was closing a tight circle to make contact with the drogue when suddenly the lights went out. The helicopter began to shudder uncontrollably, but not from the wind this time. The searchlight was gone, and the tanker disappeared. What the hell? I thought as Denny banked sharply away from the HC-130 to keep from hitting it.

It was black in the cabin—I couldn't see any emergency instruments, not even the altimeter to tell us whether we were descend-

ing. But most importantly, our attitude indicator (horizon reference) and the stabilization system that kept the aircraft under
some semblance of control were gone. My stomach told me we
were falling.

I called the second helicopter. "*Jolly* 78, this is *Jolly 40*. Mayday. Lost generators all electrical. No lights, no instruments, stability lost. We're flying blind. Are we descending or what?"

"You're going down fast, Jolly," Rex's voice came back.

Couture found a flashlight at last and shone it on the panel.
"Damn, look at that descent," I said as adrenaline coursed into
my system and with it, a hammering of heartbeats and a sudden
urgency. "Rex, we'll fly on your left wing. That way you keep us
level."

Rex was all we had, and we needed him close to act as our
eyes until we found our lights again. His searchlight helped us
keep away from him, and him from us. He started calling out altitude, headings, and airspeed from his gauges, a stream of information that calmed my initial fears of flying sightless. But we still
had to refuel. And so did he.

Couture ran through a systems check. "It's the generators,
sir," he said shortly. "We've got one partially working, but it's
weak. If we shut down everything except what we really need, we
can get instruments, searchlight, and stability control for a few
minutes. Enough time to refuel, maybe."

Maybe wasn't good enough. If we couldn't get fuel we'd have
to ditch, and I knew that with all of us in the water some would
be lost. *Jolly 78* was already pushing its capacity; it would be difficult to recover nine more. We had already defied the fates and
pulled off night water rescues; we didn't need to risk more. The
only bright spot was that our position would be known, but only
Bellissimo and Durante had survival gear. Without it, the rest of
us were unlikely to survive more than an hour in the cold ocean
water. We had to get that fuel.

Denny maneuvered to rejoin the tanker while I briefed its
crew on our predicament. Couture played the searchlight on the

dangling, swaying fuel hose. But as soon as he sped up to mate the probe with the drogue, the lights and stabilization shut down again.

"Shit," Denny muttered as he yanked the controls and maneuvered the aircraft away. The air swelled with tension. Couture went back to work and brought the lights and stability control back online. It was now my try, and I didn't wait for the lights to go out another time. As soon as the searchlight found the drogue, I zeroed in. I was scared. We all knew this was the last chance. We luckily hit it on the first pass, and as it coupled in and the fuel flowed, I felt a kind of joy for the fact that I wasn't going to feel the cold water invading my flight suit and robbing me of warmth and life.

Now it was Rex's turn. He had forty minutes of fuel when he started, not much of a margin for such problems. But Rex's probe wouldn't lock into the drogue. We watched from below and behind as he hit it perfectly, but it kept falling out, and without it locking, he couldn't take fuel. He kept running at it, trying to make solid contact. Finally he charged at it and hit it with such a jolt that I saw, in the light of the searchlight, sine waves run up the length of the hose to the tanker's wing. Then he banked left to avoid chopping into the tanker's wing, climbed a little above it, and then banked back right before he tore off the hose.

Then the probe dropped out again. *Jolly 78*'s refueling window was down to about five minutes.

Denny and I started talking about night water hoists and how we were going to get Rex and Bags and their crew and their survivors up into our helicopter without being dragged down by the waves. It was academic. There were still too many of us for one helicopter, but we would give it our best shot. In our cargo compartment, Couture started rounding up flares. Bellissimo and Durante zipped up their wet suits and got ready to jump into the water in case the other helicopter had to ditch.

Rex ran at the drogue again, ramming the probe into it another time. It held in place, but the helicopter and tanker had seemed joined before. I kept waiting for it to drop out, staring at the point of union in the waving searchlight and willing it not to. After what seemed like several minutes, I heard Rex exhale on the radio. He was locked in. "Sweet elixir," he said. The fuel was running.

We heard him again when his tank was full. "*Jolly 40*, this is *Jolly 78*. Sorry about that little delay back there. It was one of those blind dates where you have trouble connecting. But we're loaded now and ready to head home."

"Roger, Jolly. We're on the way."

We all breathed deeply for the first time since we started picking up the survivors. The storm wasn't any better. If anything, it was a little worse, but we were headed home with enough fuel in our bellies to get there. Denny fought the bucking helicopter as the generator kicked offline and killed the lights and stabilization again. There's no blackness like the impenetrable dark over the ocean in a storm at night. Your instincts beg you to trust them and not the instruments. I shut out the dark and the ocean and the storm and stared at the gauges in the glare of Couture's flashlight as he tried to get the generator back on-line. What will it be next? I thought with exasperation. It was as if when we were flying to *Leavitt* we'd reached back into the past and now unseen forces didn't want to let us back into the fully functioning present.

Couture got the generator working well enough to run the stability control and instruments, but not the lights to read them. "King," I radioed the tanker, "we need some headlights. Think we could follow you back home?"

"Sure, Jolly. Climb aboard. Just don't tailgate."

"And don't you slam on the brakes."

I radioed *Jolly 78* that we were going to fly formation next to the HC-130's left wingtip back to the base. This way their wing would be our attitude indicator and altimeter and their lights would guide us as we penetrated the blackness. Then we fell in behind the four-engine tanker, staying low just in case, and we nursed the weakening aircraft through the remainder of the flight. Back in the cold, oil-slick bay, I imagined the snores of the exhausted sailors. Finally, we descended and broke through the low clouds to the welcome sight of Suffolk County Airport's runway lights.

The wind still rocked and buffeted the helicopters even when they were tied down on the landing pad. The silence with the engines off and the rotors stilled was a blessing, as much of a blessing as reaching the barn safely with all the survivors of *Leavitt* alive.

On the ground, squadron members had been trying to prepare for the arrival of the ship's survivors. They were learning that a rescue unit had dual responsibilities. Saving people from the ocean wasn't the last of it. They needed food and blankets when we got them back to land. Some maintenance people had gone out and scrounged blankets and begged a spread of sandwiches from a local deli.

A storm of media awaited as we and the survivors crawled out of the helicopters. The maiden voyage of *Leavitt* had attracted much publicity—Ackerman had seen to that. The quixotic nostalgia of his dream was red meat to the news teams. Throw in the appeal of the boat's namesake, sailor and artist John F. Leavitt, whose book *The Wake of the Coasters* now seemed prophetic, and you had a genuine media event. I hadn't seen so many reporters since a rescue back in the Philippines when the PJs delivered a baby in the back of the helicopter over the South China Sea.

The media focused on Ackerman. The bearded, shaggy-haired skipper in his fisherman's sweater couldn't have looked more different from the uniformed rescuers. He faced the cameras and microphones and told the reporters he would salvage the ship and try again. I couldn't tell which he thought was more important, delivering the cargo or finishing the documentary, because every time someone from the squadron asked about the ship and its voyage, Ackerman said, "Wait for the movie."

The next morning I picked up the phone receiver at the squadron. It was a producer from NBC's *Today* show, calling to invite any member of the rescue crew to come to the studios in New York City and be on the show. I'd had all the stardom I wanted in my brief exchange with Rex about the film. The attention just didn't appeal to me that much. Denny Morrell, on the other hand, enjoyed a moment in the spotlight. I put the phone on hold and told Denny, "It's for you." Jean and I and Keith and Cavan watched from home as Denny described the rescue to a national television audience.

A few months later, on a summer day off the south shore of Long Island, we reenacted the rescue for the concluding chapter of the documentary that Paul Bellissimo had saved. It wasn't quite the same.

Nor had the rescue been the same experience to all the people who had been a part of it. When we were on the ground and *Leavitt*'s crew was getting ready to step out to face the waiting television cameras, Cynthia Slater, the ship's cook, stopped to thank me. "You guys are really thoughtful," she said earnestly.

"Oh, why's that?" I asked.

"Well, you turned the lights out on the way back in so we could sleep. We needed it. That was really thoughtful."

I reflected for a moment on how crises pan out for their different participants. For the crew of the doomed schooner, crunch time came when the cargo boom broke and *Leavitt* started taking on water without a working pump. For us, it was the moment that the lights went out. By then, to the mind of the sailors, they had been rescued and were safe, while we faced a sudden and dire emergency. I wouldn't have traded places with her. I don't think she would have traded places, either.

My dog-tired face summoned up a smile. "Thanks. We try to be," I said.

12

New Realities

Training is everything.

—Mark Twain

The 1970s ended with the United States facing a disturbing set of new realities. Governments we supported had fallen to popular revolts, not just in Iran but also in Nicaragua. OPEC had spurred inflation to levels not seen since the end of World War II by doubling oil prices. The Soviet Union invaded Afghanistan in December 1979 with fifty thousand troops. The invasion wiped away the tentative goodwill that had followed the signing of the SALT II arms limitation treaty six months earlier. As the 1980s dawned, we were back in full confrontation mode with the Soviets, sending arms to China, embargoing wheat and high-tech equipment sales, and threatening to boycott the Olympic Summer Games in Moscow.

The signal event remained the hostage-taking in Iran. It burned and rankled. It wasn't just the students at the U.S. embassy burning flags and chanting anti-American slogans, which was shown over and over on TV along with shots of the blindfolded hostages.

For those of us who flew military helicopters and knew their capacities and limitations, the biggest moment was the April 1980 rescue attempt that had come to grief in the Iranian desert. Three marine helicopters had failed in the desert conditions and a fourth crashed into a tanker at a rendezvous point when its rotor-wash stirred up a blinding, vertigo-inducing dust storm. The crash killed most of the helicopter crew and five crew members of the tanker.

Americans felt a hunger to move on. Jimmy Carter delivered his famous "malaise" speech in July. He described a "crisis of the American spirit" in a nation that had turned from sacrifice to self-indulgence. Many citizens agreed with him. But Ronald Reagan's promise of "a new morning in America" caught the mood of the people better than Carter's doleful take on things, and Reagan swept to victory in November, making Carter a one-term president.

The squadron had come of age as a rescue unit with the *Leavitt* mission. But the new global realities introduced by the hostage crisis and various civil wars and revolutions around the world opened military planners' eyes to the need for rapid response and special operations forces. The Air National Guard expanded its operational emphasis, and the rescue units were a part of this new order. We trained to deploy on combat rescue missions anywhere in the world within seventy-two hours. The Air National Guard was evolving into a key component of the regular air force, and similar units there met the same rigorous standard.

Early in the 1980s, technology advanced to the point where night vision goggles (NVG) became part of the rescue and combat arsenal for pilots. These devices work by capturing the photons of visible light energy in extremely low-light conditions and converting them to electrons that then provide an amplified image of the reflected energy on a phosphorescent screen. The electrons excite the phosphors on the screen, which give off the green image characteristic of night vision devices.

The first goggles we used were designated PVS-5s. They covered your whole face, with the result that a pilot could see outside the aircraft at night for the first time without a searchlight. But when the goggles—two separately adjustable binocular tubes—were focused for distance, the instrument panel was a blur. Focusing them separately, one for distance and the other to scan the instruments, was a disaster. A number of helicopter pilots experienced disorientation, dizziness, mental confusion, and worse.

The army's Task Force 160, the Special Operations Aviation Regiment, crashed four aircraft between March and October 1983 while they worked on goggle procedures. During the marines' initial checkout of goggles, they crashed eleven helicopters.

Test pilots tried cutting away the bottom of the face mask. This allowed pilots to peek under the goggles to see the instruments directly. It worked, but serious challenges remained to making the goggles really usable.

They were too heavy. A counterweight to balance the weight between the front and the back of the helmet made them heavier. Reports of strange helicopter crew deaths started to filter into our safety office. Fatalities occurred in relatively minor accidents that crew members should have survived. Instead, they were dying with their necks snapped. Research eventually determined that the combined weight of helmet, NVGs, and the counterweight was to blame.

This was hard for me as an instructor training pilot. But for all of their problems, I thought the goggles were a safer alternative to spiraling down a narrow gorge between steep mountains with a spotlight that lit nothing farther than 250 feet in front of you. What was harder was the squadron's unfilled job slots. The squadron never had its complement of three full-time helicopter instructors, and the burden fell on me, as I was often the only one. This meant frequent bone-crushing hours.

A normal flying day consisting of meetings, training, and flight planning started at about eight in the morning. I also often flew maintenance test flights. They could go on most of the day, as it became more difficult to keep the aging Jolly Green Giant flying. The flights took a lot of concentration to analyze what was going wrong with the helicopter and to discuss possible solutions with maintenance. Then I'd move into a night-flying schedule with no break. I'd still be flying at ten at night, but now training an inexperienced pilot in hazardous night maneuvers. Somehow, when they were finally trained to be full-time instructors, they would move on and I'd have to start over again with someone new.

Having to spend so much time flying and at the squadron ate into the time I had with Jean and the boys. Keith and Cavan were growing up, and I was frustrated to lose time with them as they were growing and developing.

My absences were offset by Cutchogue itself. The village on the North Fork was a wonderful environment in which to raise two sons. In those days it was still a small agricultural community near such historic fishing villages as Orient and Greenport. The schools were good and not too crowded, and the educational advantages were matched by a wealth of recreational opportunities. Water was everywhere around us—Long Island Sound to the north, Peconic Bay a short distance away, and the Atlantic Ocean farther south. The boys developed early into good and confident swimmers, and eventually expanded their outdoor activities to windsurfing, hiking, camping, and biking.

Jean, too, thrived in the stability of life in one community. She became very involved in school affairs. The fertile soil of the North Fork gave us a productive garden, and she made jam and put up vegetables. Word got around about her sewing talent, and she soon had a busy practice making curtains, slipcovers, and even wedding dresses.

When we managed to spend time together, one of the things we treasured was just walking on the beach along Peconic Bay. The sound of the waves and the smell of salt water restored me. Later, we stole time away, and with family and friends we built a log cabin in the north of Vermont, and that place became my mental retreat.

The year 1986 began with the horrific explosion of the space shuttle *Challenger* on liftoff over Florida, a disaster that many

Americans saw on live television and many millions more watched over and over again in replays. The tragedy was heightened by the presence on board of a schoolteacher, Christa McAuliffe. The high school social studies teacher from New Hampshire was to have been the first civilian in space. She had been chosen because of an extraordinary record and because President Reagan believed that a teacher could best communicate the wonder and excitement of space travel.

Jean and I watched the coverage along with the rest of the nation, and it was hard to hold back tears. Keith was just entering high school, and Cavan was three years behind him. We knew how important teachers are, and how the disaster would shake kids and teachers in classrooms across the country.

In high school, both boys developed into good soccer players. I did my part by coaching and helping their teams with conditioning. On days with good weather, I often biked the 22 miles from Cutchogue to the air base, and I'd run at lunch with some of the PJs and pilots. Jean and I played tennis, and I gave tennis lessons when I could squeeze them in with my busy flying schedule. When I could, I helped her in the garden.

We all took up sea kayaking. Keith was a sophomore when he and I got caught in six-foot breaking waves past the tip of the North Fork at Orient Point, where Long Island Sound and the bay give way to open ocean. The waves were breaking over the tops of the kayaks, and it was hard to keep them upright in the seas. I felt stupid for having my young son out there. I knew the sea from a rescuer's perspective and I knew I could get in, but I wasn't going to leave him. Of course he showed no concern and got back to shore just fine.

Later that year, he and Cavan went hiking and camping on Slide Mountain, the highest peak in the Catskills, in late December. The temperature dropped to 4 degrees Fahrenheit in Cutchogue as a wicked cold front came through. Jean and I worried, knowing that 4,000 feet up on Slide Mountain it would be 10 below or worse—dangerous temperatures. Once again, however, they breezed in the next day and were surprised—but grateful—that it had crossed our minds to worry about them.

Both boys were artistic. They painted, sketched, and did charcoal drawings, which I had started doing with them when they were both much younger. Keith's artistic side took another form of expression as he advanced through high school. His light blond hair underwent many transformations—he spiked it, grew it long, and shaved his head entirely. And on the day he graduated from Mattituck High School in 1989, as we searched the stage for someone we recognized when we heard his name announced, we were amazed to see Keith accept his diploma with his hair dyed jet black.

That was an artistic avenue Cavan never explored. He kept the same haircut and hair color throughout high school.

At the squadron we prepared not only for combat rescue and heavy weather rescue far out at sea or in the mountains, but also for the kinds of special operations that the new warfare scenarios predicted.

As the eighties continued, it became ever clearer that Americans and especially the military faced terrorism in foreign cities. Late in the decade, when I had become commander of the 102nd, we joined Special Agent Bob Aldrich and his FBI SWAT instructors while training U.S. Marines in Aldrich's TRUE program. The initials stood for Training in an Urban Environment—high-risk operations conducted in densely populated city space. Aldrich, a lean former Green Beret, initiated this program well ahead of its time to increase the capabilities of the marine expeditionary forces.

Helicopter ops were a big part of these missions, and they utilized tactics our squadron was already skilled in. The marines were training to rescue hostages and to attack hostage takers, warlords, guerrillas, and private militias. The marines flew in low off the ocean, from over the horizon, and under the cover of night and foul weather. These were things we did as well as anybody. The marines also needed rescue support in case any of their helicopters went down. I was glad we were able to join the intense marine training. If this was the way the world was going to be, I wanted to be prepared to deal with it.

Among the final images of the decade of the 1980s were two that stood in stark contrast. In June 1989, Chinese troops fired on students demonstrating for greater democracy in Beijing's Tienanmen Square, killing hundreds. The Tienanmen Square massacre, as it was called, returned Communist hard-liners to power. But that fall in Berlin, citizens spontaneously began the brick-by-brick dismantling of the wall that had divided their city for almost thirty years. President Reagan's military escalations had driven the Soviet Union to the point of bankruptcy, and suddenly the assumptions of the Cold War flew right out the window. It was a triumphant moment for the West.

Keith (left), Cavan, and myself reading
a book in our home at Hill AFB,
Utah.

My dad in uniform just before
shipping out to the Pacific.

My younger sister,
Lynne.

A 102 Rescue Squadron pilot shows the extremely cramped conditions of the MH-60 cockpit. The helicopter was not engineered for more than two-hour flights.

I am learning to fly the venerable HH-3E Jolly Green Giant high over Luzon in the Philippines, near the extinct volcano Mt. Arayat. Known as Huk Hill by U.S. service members, it was a location infamous for insurgent activity.

Junior Chambers (left) and myself hamming it up after the flood mission in Korea, 1974.

Moving in close to an HC-130 for fuel during a daylight air refueling mission.

Hoisting PJs down to a survivor from the HH-3E Jolly Green Giant.

An MH-60 formation passing Montauk Lighthouse.

An MH-60 in a high hover with pararescue jumper rappelling to a simulated survivor.

John F. Leavitt leaving Boston Harbor.

A pararescue jumper being lowered to the boat. Sail and rigging are blowing dangerously close to the rotors.

Jean, myself, Alex, Keith, and Cavan outside church.

Col. Jassim (left), Major Abdullah (right), and I relax after discussing logistics support issues for my command, the 4412 (Provisional) Squadron, Kuwait.

Jolly and King checking probes and hoses before going feet wet out to sea. Montauk Lighthouse in the background is often the last sight of land before many arduous miles over the North Atlantic.

Some of the crewmembers who flew on the *Salvador Allende* mission. From left: Rich Davin, Darryl Carrick, Dennis Diggett, myself, Kevin Metz, Jim Dougherty, Graham Buschor, and John Krulder.

Alexander Taranov, one of only two survivors from the *Salvador Allende* sinking, meets with two of his rescuers, Chris Baur and Rich Davin.

Taranov showing gratitude toward pararescue jumper Jim "Doc" Dougherty.

Col. Rob Landsiedel, a unit HC-130 pilot, demonstrates the newer and lighter night vision goggles.

An LC-130 demonstrating a jet-assisted takeoff, used primarily in deep snow in the Arctic and Antarctic. The location of this demonstration was Stratton ANGB, Schenectady, New York.

Lt. Col. Bill Mathews, senior pilot at the 109 Airlift Wing. He is an expert on polar operations and was one of my primary advisers while planning the South Pole medevac.

Dr. Jerri Nielsen signing copies of her #1 best-selling book, *Ice Bound.*

Col. Tony German, a highly trusted officer, selected at my direction as the Deployed Mission Commander. We maintained close contact throughout the South Pole medevac.

An LC-130 performing a takeoff on a resupply mission to a Distant Early Warning (DEW) site, seen in the background.

An injured survivor being hoisted in a litter from a small fishing boat.

13

A Killing Machine

Pleased with the danger, when the waves went high he sought the storms.

—*John Dryden*

As the 1990s began, the world-changing events continued. The Soviet Union slid toward dissolution. The end of Communist domination over Eastern Europe unleashed a Pandora's box of mischief as stability gave way to nationalism. Yugoslavia began to splinter at the seams. But then Saddam Hussein, a dictator we had supported when he went to war against Iran, brought the world's attention back to the Middle East with his invasion of Kuwait and the takeover of its oil fields.

President George Bush responded with Operation Desert Shield, a blockade of Iraqi oil exports and all imports except food. Then he assembled a coalition that massed troops in Saudi Arabia and the Persian Gulf, and in January 1991 he launched Operation Desert Storm. The U.S.-led battle force flushed Hussein's troops from Kuwait in days. The Iraqis retreated, leaving torched oil fields and a litter of destruction in their wake, and the coalition ceased hostilities before the retreating columns reached Baghdad, with Hussein still in power.

Back on Long Island, I was pursuing a campaign of my own. The air force, no longer able to ignore the HH-3E's design age and maintenance problems, had acquired newer helicopters. The new

MH-60 Pave Hawks, made by Sikorsky like the machines they replaced, were designed for day or night rescue missions in all conditions, including combat. The sleek MH-60s had many advantages over their bulkier predecessors. The MH-60s had more power, flew 50 knots faster, and were more nimble. They responded beautifully to the lightest touch on the controls. I loved flying them.

The Pave Hawks had disadvantages as well: they carried fewer people and their control array included no altitude hold, which meant that for a pilot, they required a higher measure of concentration and just harder physical work to fly them. That could make a difference over a long mission.

But one disadvantage was more significant than the others, and was potentially dangerous. The version of the MH-60 the air force sent to Air National Guard units had the fuel capacity to fly for only two hours at a stretch. This was because the Air Guard machines lacked auxiliary internal fuel tanks.

The 102nd was consistently improving its aerial refueling skills. But with our aircraft often fighting gale force and stronger winds and marginal visibility, it made a lot more sense to have more fuel in the helicopter in the first place than trying to get it from a hose whipping behind another aircraft. The Coast Guard's rescue helicopters had the auxiliaries and they had demonstrated time and again that it's safer to flip a switch and transfer fuel internally than finding, catching, and connecting a probe to a hose on an HC-130.

I thought a configuration with two internal tanks, one more than the air force version, made sense. This would give us a 4,800-pound fuel load and allow us to fly for 500 miles, or about four hours, without having to refuel. Our range with 2,200 pounds of fuel was less than half of that. As the squadron commander, I aggressively lobbied to get our helicopters retrofitted with auxiliary tanks. In the fall of 1991, the dust from Desert Storm had settled, and the services could focus again on other things. Air force general Ace Hearon, who carried weight as a senior officer at our depot at Warner Robins Air Force Base in Georgia, scheduled a visit to the 106th Rescue Wing to hear my case. He arrived at the base on October 30.

The weather had been wild and rough for several days. Out in the Atlantic, Hurricane Grace had wandered north since forming three days earlier over the warm waters of the Gulf Stream southwest of Bermuda. A cold Canadian high had moved east, where it encountered a swirling low-pressure system off the eastern coast of Nova Scotia. Those two systems joined to form a typical nor'easter that battered the coast of New England with high waves. On October 28, when the warm, humid flow of Hurricane Grace met the drier, colder air of the nor'easter, the result was anything but typical.

The massive energy of the dying hurricane was absorbed by the nor'easter, transforming it into a monster storm. National Weather Service computer models caused meteorologist Bob Case in the Boston forecast office to call the coalescing fronts, joining at just the right time in their development, "the perfect storm." It turned the ocean into a killing machine.

Towering waves, piled up as the water absorbed energy generated by high winds over thousands of miles of open ocean, began streaking toward the New England coast. They sank the *Andrea Gail*, a swordfishing boat out of Gloucester, Massachusetts, that was fishing on the Georges Bank off of Nova Scotia. The fate of the *Andrea Gail* and its six-man crew would become the focus of Sebastian Junger's book *The Perfect Storm*.

But as of the morning of October 30, the storm's fringes had only touched Long Island.

The day dawned warm and windy. The early-morning sky was torn and turbulent when I left the house to drive to work. Halloween pumpkins, goblins, and skeletons decorated front windows and doors in the eastern Long Island neighborhoods I drove through. Black and white cumulus clouds with wind-torn edges raced overhead, revealing blue sky and brilliant sunshine in their breaks.

It was a romantic kind of storminess that alternated threat and promise. I imagined the waves on the southern shore of Long Island, tempting surfers with their offshore curls and falling on the sand with a sound like thunder and a jolt you could feel through your shoes. The thought made me want to walk on the beach with Jean.

I reckoned that the wind gusts were about 45 knots. When I got to the base, the morning weather briefing predicted an improvement. The storm, moving west to east, was laboring out to sea. My experience with weather told me the same thing.

The massive seas caused by the storm had battered the North Atlantic coast up into Canada. The worst of it was farther north of us, off New England. Radio traffic told us the Coast Guard was working overtime. Midway through the morning, the Rescue Coordination Center's Boston office tasked us to search for a man missing off Narragansett, Rhode Island. The briefing said he was either a surfer or a surf caster. Both were the kind of obsessive sportsman who would defy the heaviest waves. But these waves were too heavy; he'd been caught and dragged out to sea.

We scrambled and headed out in one of the MH-60s, call sign *Jolly 10*, following a vector toward Point Judith. As we crossed the land to water over the bluffs on the northern shore, the water of Long Island Sound was lashed with white.

I was anxious as I worked the controls on the trip out. It hadn't been that long since our son Keith had been windsurfing with some friends in Peconic Bay when some serious thunderstorms rolled in. Jean and I had gone down to the beach under a purple and black sky, watching the horizon and praying that the fingers of lightning ripping toward the water wouldn't find one of the small masts. Now, as the winds buffeted *Jolly 10*, I hoped another set of parents would see their son arrive home safely.

Jolly 10 was skittish in the turbulence. The body of the MH-60 swayed and fidgeted in all directions while the rotor moved doggedly on course. At the front of the cockpit, it felt as if we were in a gimbaled cradle suspended underneath a gyroscope and somebody was pummeling the cradle like a punching bag. We hit potholes of air that dropped us 100 or 200 feet in a twisting, gut-wrenching second. The engineer and PJs in the rear strapped in and fought airsickness. I held on to the jerking controls and wondered about the weather that was supposed to be drifting out to sea.

Off Point Judith we started searching in our usual expanding square. We were flying just above the wavetops and I kept one eye on our altitude. The water looked as if it was on full boil. High, steep swells broke into crashing breakers that exploded and sent towers of spray hundreds of feet into the air. Wind-streaked foam stretched as far as I could see. The spray glazed *Jolly 10*'s windscreens with a glaze that made it harder to spot anything or anybody in the waves. It wasn't that late in the year, but the fall air was cold, and the ocean water would have been cold enough for hypothermia to set in fairly quickly. We searched until our fuel ran low; then a Coast Guard helicopter took our place as we headed back to base.

Flying through the increasing turbulence, I felt regret that we'd failed to find the missing man. I imagined him as young, before his time of dying. I thought of parents like myself and Jean and the agony that went with waiting for a missing child.

Nobody talked on the flight home. A failure can do that. Some like to describe rescue in macho terms, but I don't feel that way. Any attempt to rescue a person is a human endeavor. And when the opposite of success is not only failure but sometimes also death, you wonder if you did everything humanly possible. Would one more turn have done it? Did we look hard enough through the clouds of spray? The cabin smelled of jet fuel, oil, salt air, and airsickness, and I felt cold and sad. Gusts kept slamming at us until we set down at the base.

When I opened the cockpit door, I thought the wind would snatch it off. A cold gust clawed at my flight suit and sent me reeling a few steps when I hit the ground. Back in the Operations Dispatch Center, I checked to see if the Coast Guard would need us again. They didn't anticipate it.

I headed from Ops straight to the Headquarters Building for my meeting with General Hearon. Flags stood at attention, whipping straight out, with their halyards drumming in a nervous, agitated chatter against the metal flagpoles. The patches of blue sky I'd seen earlier in the day were gone. The clouds had filled in and darkened—thick, cumulus clouds bunched all together. They loomed over the air base like a mugger in an alley.

General Hearon and Colonel David B. Hill, the commanding officer of the 106th Rescue Wing, were waiting for me. Squadron and wing administrative staff also were there, seated around tables in the briefing room. I felt a growing unease about the day, but I knew that each gust of wind would add backing to my argument.

I took my place at the front of the briefing room and started talking. "It'll happen in a high-risk mission, out of reach of land, probably at night, and most likely in a storm," I said. "Some rescue unit somewhere will lose a helicopter and crew when they fail to plug into the tanker's hose and take fuel. I know the arguments. I know air refueling systems are already in place. I know we've got the tankers. But it's false economy when you're talking about lives.

"We could cut our refuelings and our risk in half or better with auxiliary tanks. You know it, sir. Fuel already in our belly is better than fuel through the hose out of an HC-130 wing. We need the air force's support for our request."

General Hearon wrote notes and asked questions. He had a sympathetic face and when he looked up I thought he was receptive. He'd been a pilot long enough to know what happened when aircraft ran out of fuel. The sky outside continued to darken.

Suddenly a phone rang, breaking into the discussion. I waited for somebody to take a message, but the clerk who took the call hit the hold button and said, "Colonel Fleming." It was a mission call, the only kind that would interrupt a briefing with an air force general. I excused myself and picked up the receiver.

Captain Graham Buschor, one of the squadron pilots, was on the line. He sounded excited. The Coast Guard had tasked us to respond to a Mayday call from a Japanese sailor, Mikado Tomizawa, 270 miles out to sea in a 35-foot sailboat. The Coast Guard already had dispatched a C-130 search plane. One of their cutters was in the area, but they didn't know if it could reach the boat in time. And it was too far out for their helicopters, despite the auxiliary fuel tanks. *Jolly 10* had been refueled, and Graham was ready to launch.

I felt the quickening of excitement that came with any mission, whether I was flying it or not. "Who is the crew?" I asked.

Graham rattled off the names. "Me, Dave Ruvola, Mioli, Smith, and Mickey."

Staff Sergeant Jim Mioli was fairly new to the unit. He was a flight engineer and hoist man. Tech Sergeants Rick Smith and John Spillane were the PJs; Smith preferred Rick to his real first name, Arden, and it didn't matter what Spillane preferred, everybody in the unit called him Mickey after the tough-guy detective writer. He was part-time with the guard, and a full-time scuba diver with the New York Police Department, while Smith was a full-time PJ. Ruvola, a captain like Graham and an experienced pilot, had been a PJ himself as an enlisted man and was the squadron's standardization officer on the MH-60.

I knew Graham better than the others. He was one of thirteen kids from a closely knit Long Island family and a former officer in the merchant marine. An aggressive, boisterous young officer who kept his crews laughing with wisecracks, I always assumed he got his sense of humor from being one of the trail ships in a large formation of kids. His father had been a helicopter pilot in the Army Reserve, but when I interviewed Graham after he applied to the 102nd he said he saw piloting a helicopter as one step toward the cockpit of an F-16. I gave him points for candor. He also said that he wanted to be with us because he thought it was an honorable thing to serve one's fellow citizens. That put him in my camp. And I knew that if he'd graduated from the Merchant Marine Academy, he knew the power of the sea.

"Do you have safe enough weather?"

"Yeah, boss."

"Can you do it in daylight?"

"If we launch now. We just need you and Colonel Hill to approve. Because it is high-risk, Hill needs to say yes as well." Graham knew his regulations.

"Who's in the tanker?" I continued.

"No problem there, boss, we got the best." He named the names.

"Okay, I'll talk to Colonel Hill," I said. "Do you need me down there?"

"No, sir. Finish briefing General Hearon." Every helicopter crew member in the squadron was pulling for me to get those auxiliary tanks.

I described the scenario to Colonel Hill. As Hearon listened in, Hill asked the identical questions of me that I had asked of Graham. We agreed that the crews were highly experienced and that the risk was manageable. The latest weather fax from McGuire Air Force Base at Wrightstown, New Jersey, where by air force regulation the 102nd gets its weather forecasts, predicted moderate to severe turbulence. A prediction of severe turbulence alone would have scrubbed the mission. My search in *Jolly 10* had encountered steady moderate turbulence, and by the afternoon the worst of the storm had supposedly passed. There was no longer any forecast for severe weather, unless something extremely unusual were to happen.

I got back on the phone. "Okay, Graham, you're clear to launch. But Graham, it has to be a day recovery because of the high seas."

"Roger, boss," came the confident reply.

With the mission settled, I returned to briefing General Hearon. The briefing room was full but I still spoke straight to him. "General, *Jolly 10*, accompanied by one of our HC-130s, will be heading southeast out over the Atlantic. They're going 270 miles out. With auxiliaries they could get there and back with possibly one refueling. As it is, they'll need at least four and maybe five. You see the weather. We fly these missions frequently enough that crews need the extra protection of additional fuel. Sir, can you help us?"

"Colonel Fleming, I'll do what I can," General Hearon said, and I returned to my office to clear up some paperwork at the end of a blustery fall day. I felt as if I had done what I could.

Jolly 10, Ruvola at the controls and Graham as copilot, launched at about 3:10 P.M. and set a course to the southeast. They didn't know what they were heading into—none of us did.

The nor'easter, we'd been briefed, that was heading out to sea had turned around and was coming back again. Weather normally moves from west to east, but the storm's counterclockwise cyclonic shape was pushing south and west, creating the conditions for yet another storm of hurricane proportions.

Jolly 10 hit the HC-130 twice for fuel on the way out, the last time just before the helicopter reached the coordinates where the Coast Guard C-130 was circling over Tomizawa's flailing boat. It was twilight, nearing the cutoff time for a hoist pickup. The winds had increased and when Ruvola switched on the searchlight his crew looked down at the sailboat rising and falling on boiling swells that appeared to be well over 50 feet from peak to trough.

As Mioli saw it, it was just about impossible. The helicopter was shuddering and yawing in 80-mile-per-hour gusts, and when he lowered the hoist, the forest penetrator blew almost straight back at the end of its cable. To put it onto the plunging sailboat would be difficult, if not impossible. The boat was rolling in a 60-degree arc and the penetrator could easily snag in the rigging. If the hoist cable snapped and flew up from that trailing position, it could destroy the tail rotor.

Putting Smith or Spillane in the water was another problem. The swells were too high. A mistimed slide down the braided fast rope and the PJ could be snatched off by the walls of water or left dangling 100 feet above the waves. And once one of them was in the water and needed to be picked up, along with the survivor, Mioli doubted if the hoist could retrieve the 200-foot hoist cable fast enough to outrun the rising swells.

The rescue team stayed on the scene for almost an hour. It was ironic that as the aircraft struggled, the sloop rode high in the water and seemed in no real danger of sinking despite the massive seas. Everyone in the helicopter judged the sailor to be relatively secure.

Finally Dave radioed the tanker that a helicopter rescue was impossible and that the forty-five-year-old Tomizawa would be better off waiting for rescue by a surface ship. He asked the HC-130 to drop the sailor a life raft and survival gear, and both the helicopter and the tanker turned for home. The drop took another hour. All the while *Jolly 10* burned fuel and the weather closed in behind.

It was now fully dark. Ruvola and Graham put on NVGs to pilot the narrow space between the heaving sea and low, black clouds. Dave climbed to 5,000 feet and hooked up with the tanker for the first of two homeward-bound refuelings. *Jolly 10* took on 1,800 pounds of fuel. They'd need another hit. To make sure they wouldn't need a third, Dave decided a little after seven to put the next air refueling off as long as possible, to a twenty-minute window between 7:40 P.M. and 8:00 P.M.

The weather was still rough but manageable as the refueling time approached. But as *Jolly 10* closed with *King 88* at the 5,000-foot refueling altitude, *Jolly 10* hit a wall of turbulence more violent than anything anybody in the crew had seen before. A razor edge of windshear slammed the helicopter 300 feet straight down, with no warning. Dave fought to keep the aircraft steady. Graham bent over and threw up. Mioli and the PJs, strapped into jump seats in the rear, held on for dear life. The turbulence mocked Dave's control inputs, and it felt like it would snatch the sticks out of his hands. Headwinds jumped to eighty knots, leaving *Jolly 10* nearly running in place.

"We were getting the shit beat out of us," Mioli said. That was putting it mildly. Nobody back at the base knew what they were going through. Only afterward when the weather picture became clear in retrospect did the full horror of the conditions they experienced emerge.

They had hit the edge of the re-forming weather system, which was spawning an unnamed hurricane. An impenetrable band of rain and wind had swung across their path. Visibility dropped to almost nothing, and the air seemed alive. Not a man on either crew had seen conditions even vaguely like this. Positioned behind the tanker's left wing, Dave watched the refueling drogue dance at the end of its 83-foot hose, took a shot at it, missed, and broke off while the aircraft tried to find some smoother air.

Until they hit the violent weather wall, Graham and Dave and the tanker pilots had been interested mainly in weather forecasts for the air base for their time of arrival. Now Lieutenant Colonel Tom Parks, who as the HC-130 pilot normally initiated calls for weather information, radioed the base to find out where they could go to get clear air.

Captain Jim MacDougall, the squadron's supervisor of flying, frantically worked the phones in the 102nd Operations Center trying to get the information the two aircraft needed. But McGuire's weather station was short-staffed at night and its priority response list was stacked up with requests from air force flights departing from the base. Frustrated by busy signals at McGuire and then being put on hold when he did get through, MacDougall started calling the Federal Aviation Administration's weather office at Islip, Long Island. But neither of the forecast centers could provide what the crew of *Jolly 10* really needed—a ceiling and visibility prediction for a low-altitude point over the ocean. The clouds showed up on radar, but there was no way to judge the current visibility or turbulence at their low altitudes.

As happens too often on rescues, *Jolly 10* and *King 88* were on their own.

* * *

They flew farther into the tempest as they tried to line up for refueling. Farther west, they might have broken free. But what Graham called "the sucker factor" lured them on. The pilots and crew were motivated to head in the direction of home base. Given normal weather movement, they would have felt that they would break out of it at any second.

But there were no soft spots in the weather, and the massive storm was in retrograde—moving the wrong way. The wind kept tearing at the helicopter. Dave had no choice but to try to take fuel anyway. He lined up with the tanker and went at the drogue with the fuel probe, hit it but didn't lock in, went at it again. Graham, through his night vision goggles, watched the drogue shimmy and jerk. He could barely see it in the rain, but he flinched involuntarily each time it whipped up toward the main rotor. That would have taken them down like a rock. Dave got very close at times to hitting the 27-inch drogue, but the 8-inch sweet spot at the center eluded the probe. Dave offered Graham the controls, but Graham declined. The way he saw it, Dave could do it if anybody could, and the pilot wasn't the problem, anyway.

Suddenly Parks radioed from the HC-130 that he'd lost oil pressure in the number one engine. Dave had to hold off while the King's pilots and flight engineer shut it down. That cost more time and fuel. When he went at the drogue again, it was too battered to take the coupling. He had to switch to the drogue trailing the tanker's right wing. The aircraft turbulence was greater on that side, and the right-hand placement of the fuel probe meant the helicopter was flying closer to the tanker, too close. Every time he overshot the drogue or got slammed by a wind gust, it increased the chance of a collision.

Several refueling attempts turned into more than two dozen. Every unsuccessful run at the drogue reduced the pilot's options as the fuel ran low.

Dave finally faced a harrowing decision. Should he spend the MH-60's last minutes of fuel trying for a contact that had eluded him during forty-five minutes of superhuman concentration or use what was left to make a controlled ditch in the ocean? The swells were six stories high, and the wind-driven foam was coming off the wavetops with enough velocity to drown a swimmer. But ditching was better than running out of fuel and falling a mile into that same ocean.

Graham radioed a Mayday as Dave took *Jolly 10* from 5,000 feet down toward the waves. The distress calls reached the King and the Coast Guard cutter *Tamaroa* more than 15 miles away. *Tamaroa*, headed home after picking up three sailors from a dismasted yacht 75 miles off Nantucket, changed course and radioed the airmen to hold on.

A short time earlier, both aircraft had reported operations normal, and were presumably safely en route to home base. Before I left for home they had called in that all was well.

I was at home when the phone rang. It was MacDougall in the Operations Center. "*Jolly 10* can't refuel. They've got to ditch," he said.

"What?" My blood froze. The previous refuelings had been problem-free. "What happened?" I asked anxiously. I looked at the clock on the wall of our den. It was about 9:15 P.M.

"They ran into more weather." Nobody knew exactly what had happened, MacDougall said. The weather had all at once gone crazy, and Ruvola had decided to ditch while he could still control the helicopter. Jim sounded nervous.

Auxiliary tanks, I thought as I sped to the base.

I arrived at an Ops Center that was thick with tension. Mac-Dougall swiveled between a bank of phones and radios and a muted television tuned to the Weather Channel. The announcer was pointing to a radar view of the eastern seaboard. It showed the storm extending in a long curl that blanketed the coast of

North America from Newfoundland to New Jersey. The curl tightened near the center, looking suspiciously like a hurricane. Anxious members of the ground and flying operations crews filled the remaining swivel chairs. They bent over their work, but every ear was alert to incoming messages that would give some hint about the fate of *Jolly 10*. Forgotten cups of coffee and half-eaten sandwiches lay among the papers scattered over the counters and desktops.

A horizontal window looked from the Ops Center onto the hall outside. The hall was busy, with people pausing to look into the center and study the flight scheduling board on the far wall. It wasn't the flight schedule that concerned them; they were looking for clues about the fate of the crew from the body language inside the room. Seeing nothing but frantic, head-down activity, they drifted into the main briefing room and waited.

By then *Jolly 10* was confirmed down in the Atlantic some 60 miles south of the base. I struggled with frustration and anger as I got on the phone and started assembling search crews. They were so damned close, and I irrationally hated the air force bean counters for making us beg for the auxiliary tanks instead of giving them to us in the first place.

There was no shortage of volunteers. Pilots, engineers, and PJs rushed through the stormy night from their homes all over eastern Long Island. In no time we had several rescue crews standing by, eager to launch. Saving lives was their business, but if anything could motivate them more than they were in the first place, it was fellow rescue crews in mortal danger.

The Coast Guard was already airborne. The Coast Guard called the shots on all overwater search and rescue operations. Their on-scene commander decided that with a small search area and hardly any visibility, there already were too many aircraft in the area. They had us stand down until morning, when the risk of a midair collision would be less.

That made the frustration worse. I could see it on every crew member's face when I gave them the word. We all felt helpless to be standing by when we could be out looking. Doing something, anything, no matter how dangerous, seemed better than just waiting. It was agony. But I knew the Coast Guard was as committed to saving lives as we were and that they'd give the search everything they had.

The worst duty fell to me as the commander of the squadron. I had to call the families of the missing crew. I braced myself to make the calls when another PJ, John Brehm, volunteered to notify Spillane and Smith's families. Both men were married, and Smith had three small daughters. It was hard to call the wives and families, knowing that we didn't have the answers to their questions, only that the Coast Guard was doing everything it could and that we'd be moving at first light to assist them. I was grateful for Brehm's help.

I went into the training office and sat at Graham's desk to make the remaining calls. My head was throbbing. Pictures of his two children stood next to the phone. I made myself punch in the numbers. His wife, Anne, answered. She knew when she heard my voice that it wouldn't be good news. She had questions that I couldn't answer, and my assurances that I was sure the crew would be found and rescued sounded hollow.

Next I called Dave Ruvola's wife, and Jim Mioli's parents. We had so little information that there wasn't much I could tell them either. I tried to sound confident, telling them that the crews were well trained for these situations, that the two pararescuemen on board were among the world's experts in survival. I said we'd call again as soon as we knew more.

I was on the phone when MacDougall handed me a note. It was a rundown on the storm conditions, and I saw for the first time just how bad this Halloween monster had become. Wave heights were 50 to 60 feet, winds were 70 knots, turbulence was still building. It was the end of October, and I knew the ocean temperatures were cold. My God, I thought, how is anybody going to survive this? I had a bleak feeling of events spinning out of control, of helplessness in the face of the sheer fury of the weather. The overwhelming power of nature filled me with humility and fear for the lives it still had in its grasp.

Graham was in the water by himself. He'd heard the left engine sputter out from lack of fuel and Ruvola's order "Get out! We lost number one." He watched the altimeter as Dave held *Jolly 10* in its final hover. The readings bounced from 10 to 90 feet. That meant, figuring in the helicopter bouncing up and down 20 feet or so, that the waves were averaging 60 feet high, and that if he mistimed his jump he could have a potentially fatal fall. He had switched on his night vision goggles as he stood in the helicopter's door, spied a wave racing under the helicopter, and jumped.

Behind him, without the benefit of goggles, Smith and Spillane jumped at almost the same time. Mioli had pushed a life raft out the door. Theoretically, it would inflate when it hit the water, and sea anchors would keep it from being blown away. But when he watched it disappear into the darkness, Mioli made up his mind to stay with the helicopter until it hit the water. When Dave cut the power to the final engine and it hit the waves, a surge of cold water carried Mioli out a rear door of the aircraft, and Dave struggled out the right-side pilot's door. The helicopter sank from under them.

They came up close together. Dave wore a survival suit, which provided some protection from the cold water and had inflatable bladders under the arms. Mioli should have had the suit on for the entire flight, but didn't. Dave gave him gloves and the hood from his suit and tied Mioli to him with a parachute cord, telling the engineer to wrap his legs around him to retain body heat.

Spillane was nearby, floating in his survival suit and assessing the damage to his body. He'd fallen, he later guessed, maybe 100 feet after he and Rick Smith jumped from the helicopter. Spillane had hit the water hard, and he felt like half the bones in his body were broken. But he could move and he had trained to function in spite of injury. He saw the life raft and swam toward it. He caught it and hauled himself aboard. Then the wind caught it and flipped it, and he was in the water again. He struggled to hang onto it, but the wind blew it away. Then a swell lifted him, and through the spray whipping in his face he saw strobe lights blinking in the ocean. He started to fight his way through the towering waves to Ruvola and Mioli.

Graham, who also had seen the helicopter sink, didn't see the other strobe lights, and he choked and gagged as the rollers submerged him time and again. His own strobe blinked steadily, a solitary beacon in the darkness.

Late that evening I got a call from the guard at the air base gate. I was dismayed to hear that Graham's parents were there and wanted to come in. We still had no word on the search, and I had no idea what to tell them. I was worried about how they'd take the lack of information. Worse, what if we got word that bodies had been found?

But I understood their impulse. It was better to be with those who shared the passion their son felt and the risks he had accepted. Here at the base, at least they'd feel the buoyancy and shared concern of kindred spirits. I told the guard by all means to let them in.

When they arrived at the Ops Center, Mrs. Buschor looked worried, but her voice was calm and steady. "Colonel Fleming," she said, "we don't know what to think, and we know you can't tell us Graham is safe. We know you're all doing the best you can and that the situation's out of your control. But we needed to be here. We won't get in your way. All of you have work to do."

I led the anxious parents into my office and made them as comfortable as possible. Colonel Hill's wife, Anne, was there as well. Everybody connected with the squadron in any way wanted to be there, as if their collective presence could guide the Coast Guard to those strobe lights blinking in the storm. I left Anne and the Buschors together and went back to the tension-filled Ops Center.

As his parents worried and waited and I checked off the crews who would spell the Coast Guard searchers in the morning, Graham was retching seawater and thinking about his family. He was feeling irritated with himself. Here he was, twenty-nine years old, father of two, a healthy, vital guy who could make other people laugh, and he'd thought until an hour or so ago that he was pretty much invulnerable. Now he was alone in freezing cold water 60 miles at sea, with 8-story waves washing over him and submerging him for 30 seconds at a time, and he was so fucking tiny and inconsequential.

"I was pissed," he said. "I'd gotten myself into a situation that was totally out of my control."

He started thinking that he'd let his family down, and he grew madder still. They need me, he thought. He wondered who was going to take Alex and Mary trick-or-treating and what they'd wear. He wondered if Anne knew where his life insurance policy was filed.

In my office, Graham's mother also was wondering what would happen to the children. "I don't know what they'd do if they were to lose their father," she confided when I checked in to see how they were doing. "It would be too quiet," she added thoughtfully. "Nobody would laugh."

At 9:48 P.M., *Tamaroa* radioed that it was nearing the area where *Jolly 10* had ditched, but the monstrous seas were slowing her progress. The cutter was a brute, a 205-foot, 1,731-ton salvage tug originally commissioned by the navy during World War II, but it was taking a beating. Also zeroing in on the coordinates Graham had given in his Mayday were a Coast Guard HU-25

Falcon, a small, twin-engine jet used for search and surveillance, and a Coast Guard HH-3 Pelican, one of the original Jollys, out of Cape Cod, Massachusetts. The Falcon reached the scene at about 11:00 P.M. and started a low-altitude search pattern.

Forty-five minutes later, the Falcon picked up the radio signal from the emergency transmitter in one of the life vests. The jet homed in on the location where the signal was strongest. The pilot spotted a single strobe, then three other strobes grouped about a mile away. The Falcon passed overhead and radioed the sighting to the Coast Guard mission commander.

The news reached the Ops Center, and I felt elated. But it was only momentary, until I realized four strobes were accounted for, not five. But it was better than if none had been spotted, and I rushed in to tell the Buschors. I didn't add the disquieting news that one strobe hadn't yet been spotted. There was no reason to force the Buschors to play mental roulette with the missing strobe, hoping for their son's life against another's.

"I know Graham," his mother said. "What will happen will happen, but I feel things are going to work out."

Mr. Buschor took her hand and spoke for the first time. "Whatever happens," he said, "we know he'll never give up."

The father's voice was so similar to Graham's that it sent a chill through me. "I know he won't," I said.

At midnight, the Coast Guard HH-3 found the three bunched strobes. Mioli was sinking close to fatal hypothermia despite being lashed to Ruvola. Spillane, who had managed to reach the other two despite his injuries, was trying to preserve his strength and wondering how he'd manage being hoisted.

The Pelican hovered over them, dodging the huge swells that tried to claw it into the sea. Its searchlight found the cluster of survivors. But when the crew dropped the hoist basket, it blew straight back toward the tail rotor and the operator quickly reeled it in again. The HH-3 faced the same problem that had made Mioli decide against dropping the hoist to Tomizawa. The

80-mile-per-hour winds were too strong to get the hoist down to a moving target.

Working at it, the Pelican's crew managed to get the hoist basket to the water. Now the problem was the waves. The basket floated for a few seconds, but then the swells rolled out from under it. Then it tumbled to the end of the cable and jerked taut before another swell rolled in to pick it up again.

Watching from the water, Ruvola and his crewmates knew exactly what the problem was. They'd have to get into the basket in seconds, then take the chance that the cable could hold all three of their watersoaked weight. With Mioli tied to Ruvola and barely hanging on and Spillane injured, they couldn't do it. But things didn't get any better when the Pelican, low on fuel after an hour of hovering, turned to head for shore. Its search-light disappeared, and they were alone again in the surging ocean. Mioli was reaching the point where he wouldn't recover from the cold.

Graham hadn't seen the helicopter, but he'd seen the jet pass overhead. That told him his strobe had been spotted, and he started looking around for more aircraft. What he saw, when the wave crests lifted him, were searchlights stabbing through the darkness, and then the rolling, plunging bulk of *Tamaroa*. He swam toward the cutter as hard as he could.

Captain Larry Brudnicki, aboard *Tamaroa*, had decided against putting swimmers or boats in the water. He would maneuver the ship broadside to the waves and let it drift down to the survivors. If his crew could lower rope netting without being washed over-board themselves, and if the survivors could hold on, the *Tam's* crew could drag them aboard.

Graham watched the ship's spotlight arc wildly, lighting the spume slashing off the wavetops. Then it found him and he heard the crew screaming, "Swim! Swim!" The huge hull loomed over him. First he saw its bottom almost to the keel, then it rolled until he saw its deck and superstructure, and he thought the ship was going to fall on top of him. He had no idea how he was going to get aboard, but he swam anyway.

There was nothing to grab on to when he reached the cutter's hull. Then a surge pushed him toward the bow, pulled him under, and up the other side. Now the wind pinned him against the ship. Finally the crew on deck got a cargo net over the side that he could reach. He clamped his fingers around the ropes and held them like a prayer while the crewmen hauled him up the side of the boat and over the rail.

He flopped exhausted and retching on the deck. Through his ringing ears, as if from a great distance, he heard an excited voice on the ship's loudspeaker, "Survivor recovered," and then voices joining in a cheer. Then arms raised him and helped him stumble belowdecks, where he was wrapped in blankets.

Dave Ruvola had seen the ship's spotlights and sent up pen flares. *Tamaroa*'s helmsman saw the flares and churned toward them. But this time the survivors couldn't swim to the ship as Graham had. Mioli was too cold, Spillane too badly hurt, and Ruvola refused to leave them. The ship would have to come to them.

Slowly *Tamaroa* drifted down, rolling wildly. The three grabbed the net, and the deck crew hauled. They had the men halfway up the side when Mioli lost his grip and fell back, pulling Ruvola with him. Spillane managed to hold on, and made it onto the deck. The Coast Guard crew watched in horror as the seas carried Ruvola and Mioli toward *Tamaroa*'s stern and its big propeller. Somebody called the bridge to take it out of gear.

Dave figured that the next chance was the last one they'd get. He screamed at Mioli to break through his cold-induced delirium: "This time don't let go. You understand?" The net came within reach, and Dave grabbed it. He boosted the pair of them against the netting, twisted his hands into the strands, clamped his fingers over Jim's, and got a purchase with his feet. *Tamaroa*'s crew pulled them slowly up the riveted metal of the hull, over the rail, and onto the deck.

* * *

We got the news at about three in the morning. The Coast Guard called from the Boston Rescue Coordination Center to let us know that *Tamaroa* had picked up four of our men. Mac-Dougall told me, and I had to clamp down an explosion of relief and joy, because what I heard was cause for celebration and agony at the same time. The fifth man was still missing, and we didn't have names.

For the Buschors waiting in my office and the other families waiting at home, knowing one man was still out there and not knowing who it was was torture that none of them deserved. I resisted the impulse to rush in and tell Graham's parents until we had ID on the survivors.

Within the hour, the Coast Guard's official confirmation of the names of the men aboard *Tamaroa* gave us the green light. When I told the Buschors that Graham and three of his four crewmates were safe aboard a Coast Guard cutter, Mrs. Buschor reacted in a way that's typical of rescue families. Her face showed relief that her son was rescued and alive. Then immediately her concern shifted to the missing man, Rick Smith, and Rick's family.

None of us doubted that Rick was still alive. Logic said that with four of *Jolly 10*'s crew recovered, Rick would have survived the ditching, too. Something had happened to his strobe, but he was out there in an Arctic wet suit and a one-man life raft that was part of his gear, and he was trained to be able to survive for as long as a week. Doc Dougherty, who trained with him, was one of the PJs standing by, waiting for daylight. We were going with every crew at our disposal. Even in the horrendous storm conditions, with the light to see and additional search crews, he'd be located in no time.

Rick and his wife, Marianne, had three young daughters. The thought of them would keep him fighting.

Preparations to put our crews into the air at first light stood ready. There was a lull in the normally chaotic Operations Center when I felt a presence at my elbow. I looked up to find General Hearon standing next to me.

I was surprised to see the general. The Ops Center wall clock showed four-thirty, too early for breakfast or a morning run, even if the wind wasn't still shrieking outside and drumming rain against the windows.

General Hearon wasn't a big or an imposing man, but the two stars on his shoulders indicated a life of dedication to the air force and its personnel, and I saw sympathy and understanding in his tired, red-rimmed eyes. He pressed his lips together and nodded. He'd obviously been thinking about what he was about to say.

When he spoke, his words were measured. "Colonel Fleming," he said, "you told me at our meeting yesterday that your most critical need here at the squadron was auxiliary tanks for your helicopters. I thought they'd be useful but not critical. I was having dinner with Colonel Hill when we learned about the ditching. It's haunting me that the unit lost a helicopter and might lose a crew member this very night due to lack of fuel. I couldn't sleep. I had to come in." He paused and dropped the formal title. "It's the strangest thing, this chain of events, Ed. How did you sense it coming?"

"I didn't, sir," I said. "I just sensed a lot of small cues adding up to a hazard. I felt the odds for a mishap were mounting."

That a once-in-a-century storm would occur on the same day as my briefing of the general was a freak of timing. The storm had more than amply illustrated the need for auxiliary fuel tanks in our helicopters. But as I stood there with the general, I would have given anything for a fine fall day without any wind at all that would have guaranteed the safe return of every member of every crew we had sent out over the water.

The days that followed were painfully long for families, for crews, for everyone involved. Tomizawa, the Japanese yachtsman whose distress call triggered *Jolly 10*'s mission, was picked up by a freighter on Halloween day. Spillane was airlifted from *Tamaroa* to a hospital in Atlantic City, where he was rushed into intensive care. Doctors discovered four cracked ribs, two fractured wrists, a cracked bone in one leg, a bruised pancreas, and a nearly burst kidney that had swollen to the size of a football. Graham, Ruvola, and Mioli, whose temperature was down to 90.4 degrees when he was hauled from the ocean, stayed with the ship as it joined the search for Rick.

Finally, after three days with no sighting, Captain Brudnicki turned his ship toward home to rest his tired crew. For six more days our remaining helicopters, HC-130s, Coast Guard aircraft, and other surface ships continued to scour the area. The search covered 33,000 square miles. Nobody wanted to give up. Rick Smith was one man in a vast ocean, but he was a strong man, even among the strong.

The search produced moments of false hope. Floating life rafts, a patch of marker dye—but no sign of Rick. Spillane's grievous injuries—he was in intensive care for a week—hinted that Rick might have died when he hit the water after jumping out of *Jolly 10*. When the Coast Guard called off the search after nine days, the squadron and Rick's family tried to find a source of healing. We all, especially Marianne, knew the risks of Rick's profession. But knowing the risks didn't prepare you for the reality of loss.

I thought that the mystery of Rick's whereabouts was solved when the Coast Guard reported a body washed up on a New Jersey beach. It was a grisly find, a torso without head or limbs in a black diving suit, and when I heard about it I suddenly was sickened by the reality of death at sea. I thought that the news at least would give Rick's family closure. But when the Coast Guard caller said the torso had been covered with tattoos, I realized it wasn't Rick. The electricity jolting through the squadron as we had prepared to contact his family faded and we settled into our business of preparing for the next emergency call.

We held a memorial service for Rick in a hangar at the squadron. Marianne didn't bring their daughters because the news media were there. It was a misty dark gray afternoon that meshed perfectly with the lamenting wail of bagpipes. The squadron turned out in dress blues and the Coast Guard attended to show respect to a fine warrior. It gave a form of closure, the best we could do under the circumstances.

Then, one strange November day two weeks after the search was halted, Colonel Hill ordered us to start it up again. The wing commander was an enigmatic man who had a way of keeping us off balance. This time, he'd heard from a Westhampton Beach, Long Island, psychic who claimed he'd seen mental images of Rick, still alive but just holding on. He said he could assist in finding him. Marianne Smith had already rejected the man's overtures, but Colonel Hill had met with him and was convinced of his powers.

He brought the psychic into the Operations Room for a seancelike exercise. The psychic suspended his hands over a map of the North Atlantic, closed his eyes, and received vibrations from some unknown source that moved his hands. Where they traveled determined instructions to the HC-130 crews who had been sent back out at Colonel Hill's order. The thought of reviving hope on the slim thread provided by the psychic was very painful to me. To my mind, paranormal powers didn't match the efforts of hundreds of men and dozens of aircraft and boats over an extended period. Reality said to let it go.

The surreal search continued for a few days over thousands of square miles, with the crews calling in sightings of debris and oil slicks. Finally, when I called Colonel Hill at home one day to tell him the search still had discovered nothing, even the CO, the commanding officer, decided we were wasting time and resources. He told me to call it off. The psychic was still sitting there, his hands trembling over the map. I ordered the HC-130 to return to base.

The tanker was winging its way home when the crew radioed that they'd sighted a pod of whales. The psychic looked up, his eyes glazed. "That is very significant," he said. "They must resume their search at that location. I have seen Rick among whales and dolphins."

I looked at the psychic, then at Master Sergeant Bob Hampton standing by the radio, waiting to reply to the HC-130 crew. Hampton looked the way I felt, in complete disbelief. The whole thing was a mockery of the way we went about our business. Hampton didn't want to continue the charade and neither did I.

"It's time. Bring them home," I said.

Ace Hearon was as good as his word. About three weeks after the Halloween storm, technicians from Warner Robins Air Force Base arrived at the base and began installing auxiliary fuel tanks in the squadron's five remaining Jollys.

About a month after Colonel Hill finally called off the psychic-inspired second search for Rick Smith, he and I were called to Washington. We had to answer for the loss of a highly trained pararescueman and a helicopter that would cost $12 million to replace. General Philip G. Killey, director of the Air National Guard for the United States, presided. He looked like he wanted to eat us for lunch.

We sat at a table in the hearing room as the accident investigator from the 16th Special Operations Wing at Hurlbert Field in Florida made his report. Next, the meteorologist from McGuire clicked through slides and satellite images projected on a 15-foot-high white wall. They showed clear and crisp images of the Halloween storm in all its coiled and turbulent fury.

The briefing took a lot of hindsight and work to prepare and left an impression that they were sure what was happening the day of the storm. They hadn't been. In fact, it had been a once-in-a-century surprise—a hurricane that the National Weather Service hadn't named for fear of frightening coastal residents. When the last image clicked off, General Killey thrust forward in his chair and said, "What do you have to say for yourselves, sending men out in that?"

Developed in hindsight, the picture the maps painted wasn't pretty. The counterclockwise motion of the storm had formed a comma the tail of which curved past Long Island. The edge of the weather system had been perilously close. The eye of the unnamed hurricane showed clearly. It looked, from the evidence submitted, as if we should have seen the danger.

Colonel Hill was silent. I opened my briefcase and brought out the weather information we'd been operating on that afternoon and night. "That's not the weather we got, General," I said. I pushed the faxed report and the satellite image we had received down the table toward the general.

He picked it up, looked at it, and made a sound of disgust. "This is shit," he said. Then he came to a decision. "It wasn't your fault," he continued. "This was a battle, and this was a combat loss."

No trace of Rick Smith was ever found. In time, the squadron returned to a semblance of normality. Slowly, Graham Buschor's joke-cracking boisterousness returned. Dave Ruvola kept flying. John Spillane recovered and took on a job as a New York City fireman in addition to his part-time PJ duties. Dave Mioli settled in and became a long-term member of the squadron.

But I think we all looked even more fondly on our wives and children after losing Rick Smith, one more comrade among many in the rescue community. We took more care to express love. We looked differently at one another, too. The trust in one another, the vital union that bound our rescue teams, grew deeper. We faced stormy weather almost with defiance, as if to say, *We're not going to let you do it to us this time.*

14

All Scorpions
All the Time

Wild, dark times are rumbling toward us, and the prophet who wishes to write a new apocalypse will have to invent entirely new beasts.

—Heinrich Heine

The memory of the Halloween Storm of 1991 faded quickly, except among the people who had seen it at close hand and lost or feared for loved ones. It would be revived later as the Perfect Storm of Sebastian Junger's remarkable book and the movie that followed. But in the world at large, attention turned to other things.

It was hard to believe how quickly the Soviet Union had come undone. The enemy we had learned to fear from a childhood of air raid drills and fallout shelters had lost the gravity to hold its satellites. The first to spin away were the Baltic states of Estonia, Latvia, and Lithuania. Others followed in a rush to independence. In Poland, the pope and the unions of Solidarity had already brought the end of communism. But the news about the Soviet Union's breakup and the fall of East European communism was not all good. Slobodan Milosevic was tearing open old wounds in the Balkans as he whipped up furies of religious nationalism.

At home, four policemen in Los Angeles were indicted, and the nation once again was transfixed by a blurry videotape that showed them beating and kicking an African American motorist named Rodney King. As the election year of 1992 got under way, recession and unemployment were eating into the popularity President George Bush had enjoyed after the Persian Gulf War. The governor of Arkansas, Bill Clinton, started piling up delegates on his way to the Democratic presidential nomination.

Jean and I were empty nesters now. Keith was in college at Wesleyan University in Middletown, Connecticut, majoring in psychology. Cavan was studying chemistry at Swarthmore in Pennsylvania. But with me working long hours at the base and Jean's sewing business thriving, it seemed that we were always too busy to enjoy each other's company as much as we wanted to. Then I volunteered for another overseas assignment.

In the aftermath of the Persian Gulf War, Iraq's minorities had been encouraged to revolt. Saddam Hussein had put them down with brutal force, moving against Kurds in the north and Shiite Muslims in the south. He accelerated the systematic destruction of the five-thousand-year-old culture of Shiite Arabs who lived in the wetlands where the Tigris and Euphrates Rivers come together. The United Nations passed a resolution condemning the repression and slaughter. Acting on the strength of that resolution, the United States, England, and France, the principal Allied nations in the Gulf War, took to the skies to enforce a ban on all Iraqi fixed-wing and helicopter flights below the thirty-third parallel of latitude and above the thirty-sixth parallel. The patrols were an air occupation that would both eliminate Iraqi overflights and prevent Saddam from hurling masses of troops against the minorities.

Iraqi missile batteries tracked the Allied fighters on patrol. They regularly locked on and periodically launched. A hit and a downed fighter crew was an ever-present possibility, and combat rescue and special-ops-capable aircraft and crews needed to be ready in case someone needed the service. The air force's 20th Special Operations Squadron (SOS), flying MH-53s, provided special operations and rescue coverage for the combat air patrols. But conditions in the gulf were taking a toll and the air force looked to Air Force Reserve and Air National Guard rescue units to provide needed relief.

Early in 1992, the Air Guard reorganized the 106th Rescue Wing to create the 106th Operations Group. I was named its commander. In many ways it was the same job I'd had as commander of the 102nd Rescue Squadron, only now the squadron had a new commander under me, and I had an additional squadron to manage as well. The 106th Operations Group Support Squadron, combining maintenance, administration, life support, weapons, and tactics—as well as a large intelligence section—provided essential mission support.

With this new position I became even more involved with expanding the mission of the 102nd RS and the new 106th Operations Group. I was never happy sitting still.

That fall, Headquarters Rescue at Scott Air Force Base in Illinois convened a series of meetings to study whether the Air National Guard and the Air Force Reserves were capable of relieving the active rescue unit in the gulf. After Christmas I represented the Air Guard on an advance team that traveled to the gulf to look things over.

A dozen or so of us flew on the regular military 747 rotator out of Philadelphia. We flew to Dhahran, Saudi Arabia, where the 4404th Composite Wing was headquartered. The 4404th was headquarters for the 4412th Squadron, which was made up of personnel from the 20th Special Operations Squadron, the active squadron we were to relieve. This is the squadron I would command. Briefings in Dhahran described the dangers and austere state of the Arab Middle East for American servicemen and -women. They covered the pervasive danger from land mines, unexploded bombs, and other military ordnance, the threat of terrorism from Islamic radicals, and Muslim strictures regarding women, alcohol, and display of the body.

The briefings paled next to the actual conditions. The advance team flew from Dhahran to Kuwait City, where we saw many destroyed areas. An army Special Forces NCO met us and escorted us through an unsparing panorama. Kuwait remained a hostile fire zone torn with the aftermath of Saddam's vengeance in defeat. Some of the oil fires his retreating troops had set still burned. Oily smoke salted with blowing sand tinged the sky an ugly brownish-gray and seemed to trap the smothering heat day and night. Blasted, burned-out tanks littered the roadsides, their shattered hulks lying side by side with Mercedes sedans and high-end SUVs that had suffered accidents and been abandoned where they crashed. Near Kuwait Bay and the Persian Gulf, great flocks of seabirds had been reduced to a few stragglers after the Iraqis discharged man-made oil spills into the sea. From the air you could see the veneer of oil that blanketed the gulf. The empty windows of ruined buildings stared from the streets of Kuwait City. In the desert, lines of Pakistanis walked abreast across minefields labeled in Arabic and English, probing with long poles to locate land mines for removal.

Kuwait's desert was a lifeless, lunar image without a hint of trees, cactus, or any kind of small plants that could find a foothold in the desert, just mounds of gutted tanks and blowing sand. Bedouin camps remained, but now instead of using camels for transportation, they used expensive four-wheel-drive vehicles.

On the ground the temperatures hovered at about 100 degrees Fahrenheit, and the wind sanded everything down day and night. It was the middle of the winter. I couldn't imagine what the summer would be like.

What I saw made me very sad, and it raised a question I was never successful answering: Why had we only driven Saddam back to Baghdad and left him alone to lick his wounds? The destruction he brought was extraordinary, horrifying. And for what?

No reason that I could see other than the evils of vengeance, greed, and lust for power.

While we were there we observed a week of air strikes in the southern no-fly zone. Some of us flew with the 20th SOS as observers, and saw the cat-and-mouse night combat operations firsthand from one of their HC-130s. The tanker refueled the massive shadows that we knew were the Super Jollys, the MH-53 Pave Low special operations helicopters. The pros of the 20th were very impressive and carried out their tasks without a hitch, but I saw that they also were suffering from the operations tempo.

The ten-day visit convinced me that the Air Guard and reserves could step up and remove some workload from the 20th. I reported back to the Air Guard Bureau, in Washington, that I felt we could perform the mission.

Be careful what you wish for, somebody once said.

Once the air force decided to send guard and reserve rescue units to the gulf, the question became, who and when? I had two choices, winter or summer. Neither was good. If I chose to take a guard rescue squadron to Kuwait in the winter, that meant that my crew would be away from home and their families during the year-end holidays. The winter brought the kind of storms that wrecked ships in the Atlantic, and while the 102nd would remain at operational strength, pilots like Dave Ruvola and Graham Buschor were among the gulf volunteers, and I didn't want to shortchange the rescue operation. And for the part-timers, juggling their jobs would be harder than during the summer, when people were expected to take vacations. Summer seemed the better choice.

The 4412th Rescue Squadron (Provisional), comprising Air Guard members and reservists who had volunteered for duty in the gulf, assembled for deployment to Kuwait in June 1993 for a three-month tour. About 40 percent of the squadron's 150 members belonged to the 102nd Rescue Squadron.

The Long Island volunteers gathered at the 106th Rescue Group headquarters to begin the journey. Buses idled as I briefed the troops on what to expect, and what items local customs prohibited that they might want to pull out of their luggage now. Then we slung our duffel bags into the undercarriage holds and we said good-bye to our families for the summer. Keith and Cavan had both come home from school for the occasion. I was proud that they'd showed up with Jean to see me off and I boarded my bus for Philadelphia grateful that my family was strong and intact despite my absences.

As the 747 took off from Philadelphia a few hours later, we left behind a nation that seemed torn and increasingly troubled. A new kind of hate was on the rise, and for the first time it had expressed itself inside the borders of the United States. Its targets, once military and official, now were any and all things American, in this case a symbol of America's global financial dominance. The deadly car bomb set off in the parking garage of the World Trade Center in lower Manhattan was tied to Muslim extremists. Seven people died and about a thousand were injured. More Muslim extremists were building bombs in a Brooklyn garage and plotting mass murder and political assassinations. All were under the influence of a blind sheik who preached hatred of America from a mosque in Brooklyn. The very freedoms that America guaranteed were being turned against it. And in Texas, a mad religious cult led by a man named Koresh barricaded itself inside its Waco compound after killing four FBI agents in a gun battle and after a long standoff set fire to the place, killing the leader and eighty-six others, including a number of children.

The gulf between cultures was apparent as soon as we landed in Saudi Arabia. No briefing was adequate to prepare our crew for the Saudi customs agents in Dhahran. They went through every piece of luggage looking for just two things: magazines and alcohol. In the strict Wahabbi version of Islam practiced by the

Saudi royal family, a body-building or even a tennis magazine was off-limits, let alone the *Sports Illustrated* swimsuit issue or *Cosmopolitan*. And the ban on alcohol wasn't limited to beverages. The Saudi customs men confiscated rubbing alcohol and after-shave lotion.

After Saudi customs had inspected our luggage, we boarded an HC-130 for the short leg to Kuwait International Airport south of Kuwait City. The sky seemed to thicken on the way with the haze from oil fires. We landed in daylight obscured by a scrim of blowing smoke and sand. Behind it, the sun seemed to have enlarged until it took up half the sky. I got off the plane, and the heat hit me like a hammer. It was easily thirty degrees hotter than during my winter visit. The haze formed a dome that trapped the heat. I hadn't seen at the time how it could have gotten that much hotter. Now I had a taste of summer in the earth's oven.

Army Special Forces met us at the plane. They would act as our escorts. While our equipment was being unloaded, they drove me and the squadron's other senior officers into Kuwait City to the U.S. embassy for a series of classified situational briefings. The briefings included the threat to U.S. forces, procedures for safe passage through Iraqi airspace, our air defenses, and our over-all mission. Then we were taken to our new home, a pinprick huddled between the airport and the desert.

It was a short drive. The bus skirted the airport perimeter and pulled up at a one-story building at its edge.

A trim, athletic guy wearing the silver oak leaf of a lieutenant colonel came out as we were getting off the bus and approached me with a handshake and a grin. His name was Bob Weed. He was a member of the Portland-based 304th Rescue Squadron of the Air Force Reserve, the unit that had taken over for the 20th SOS in March. Now he was commander of the 4412th Provisional Squadron, the most forward-located and isolated air force squadron in the gulf—and my future command. Weed eyed my sweat-soaked camo uniform and said, "Welcome to the Desert Inn and Spa. Let me show you around."

The one-story structure had thick walls, and he explained that our quarters were an old Kuwaiti prison. A moat of frothy gray water stood around the entrance. This puzzled me. This was a land where water was in such short supply that some desert tribes were said to wash their hair in camel urine.

Weed followed my eyes. "Oh, that," he said. "You'll get used to it. It's the plumbing system." The Middle East was often an awkward blend of old ways and modern technology, and the plumbing system here was one example. We had the modern amenity of hot and cold running water systems, but on closer inspection it became clear that both the hot and the cold systems fed from superheated metal tanks on the roof of the prison. If you turned on either hot or cold, you got painful 140-degree water.

I stepped around the water and followed him through a pair of metal doors into a tiny foyer stuffed with tattered furniture. A few dog-eared magazines were scattered on a table. I picked up an L.L. Bean catalog and saw that the pages picturing Bean's modestly presented lingerie had been inked out. The rest were automotive magazines.

The stone walls sucked up light and left dingy layers of shadow. The gray haze outside fought unsuccessfully to make its way through tiny windows. A couple of groaning air conditioners waged a losing battle with the heat.

Farther into the bowels of the old prison, Weed paused before a glass enclosure. "Here's the menagerie," he said. I peered through the glass into a terrarium that contained sand, rocks, and sticks. I suddenly realized that the box was writhing with scorpions ranging in size from a knuckle's length to a good three inches.

"These suckers are everywhere," he said. "Tell your troops to shake their boots and clothes out every morning and to shake their sheets out every night before they go to bed. These babies are one thing you don't want next to your short-and-curlies. We put this here as a reminder." He gave an easy grin. "It works."

I stared at the terrarium. Over the weeks ahead, we'd all be fascinated by it. We found our share of scorpions in bedding and clothing, and as the collection grew, people would sit and gaze at them, as if it were our single-program nature channel: "All Scorpions All the Time!" It helped divert us from the heat and grime.

The colonel, continuing the tour, pointed out large hooks anchored high on the walls of several of the cells-turned-rooms. He said his contacts in the Kuwaiti Air Force had told him the hooks had been used for shackling prisoners. When I shook my head in disgust, he said, "You'll see a wall outside where people were lined up and shot. But I suppose it's better than what Saddam's doing to his people. Around Basra they say there used to be green marshes there, with people living on the islands. It's like a strip mine now. No people, no marsh, all the water poisoned."

We started settling in. I had one roommate, a copilot from the 129th Rescue Squadron at Moffett Field in California. Most of the crew lived three or four to a room in the dark cubicles, which stayed grim no matter how hard we worked to clean them. One of our pilots decided not to fight it. He added decorative dark humor by drawing the outline of a human figure stretched between the hooks in his room.

Weed took me up to give me a taste of the desert flying conditions. He tried to warn me in advance. "This'll sound crazy," he said, "but we have to fly with the cockpit windows closed."

I thought he was kidding. The preflight briefing officer had said the temperature on the desert floor was 136 degrees.

Weed continued with an explanation. "Flying an open aircraft, you're getting blasted with air at 130 to 140 degrees. No way it cools you down. And the sand will take your skin off. It gets in everything. If it gets in your nose, it'll take a drill to get it out. If it gets in your eyes, it can blind you. Believe me, you're better off in a 140-degree pocket of dead air."

Before we started the flight, Weed and every member of the crew went to a freezer and started pulling out frozen water bottles that they stuffed into their flight bags. The bottles were big, two liters, and each crew member took six or eight. "Take some," Weed said. "You'll need them."

Our operation occupied a corner of Kuwait International, and the squadron's four MH-60s were tied down outside, on the airport's military ramp. When I got to the aircraft, I reached for the door handle, but my predecessor grabbed my hand. "Put your gloves on. You'll burn yourself," he said.

The air inside the aircraft seared my nose and throat down into my lungs. Then I made the mistake of touching a toggle switch on the control panel with my bare hand, and yanked my hand away in pain. After that, I kept my flight gloves on.

The fact that we were wearing combat gear—Kevlar helmets, flight suits, heavy boots, survival vests, and flak jackets—and carrying pistols intensified the heat. It was hard to concentrate even on the start-up checklists. I found myself breathing faster and faster. Soon I was almost panting. I had the feeling that my brain was boiling like an egg in the shell of the helmet. I was on the verge of hyperventilating. My body instinctively tried to cool down.

I took the controls. We lifted off and headed for the Iraqi border, flying fast and low. I'd flown Jollys effectively for hours at a time, but now the heat was a major distraction. It cauterized my thoughts into a jumbled blur and there was no way to escape it. After five minutes I turned control of the aircraft over to Weed and sucked down ice water.

Not really believing that the suffocating heat was better than a little air, I snuck my window open. That was a mistake. I stuck my gloved fingers out through the small opening and was rewarded with a painful sting as thousands of sharp-edged particles of sand dug away the fabric. It felt like I'd been struck by a load of buckshot.

Weed turned the controls back to me after a few minutes and attacked the first of his water bottles, which were no longer frozen. Switching control of the aircraft was the only way to maintain concentration. Each of us could attend to the tasks required for about five minutes at the most. We swapped back and forth, taking turns flying and gulping water to the point where we could concentrate again.

Can I do this? I wondered. This was definitely a younger person's game. I had never felt so close to the edge of both human and aircraft performance. I had to concentrate furiously when I had the aircraft and then was mildly delirious and confused each time when I turned it over. I felt vulnerable, at the brink of a meltdown. It worried me, because I knew that if a missile battery locked on while we were flying a mission, I'd have to take rapid and violent evasive action and I wasn't sure I'd be capable of doing it.

As a special operations-capable squadron, we serviced customers as varied as the army Special Forces and navy admirals, ferrying them in and out of hostile and desolate areas. Many of our flights were classified. We flew during the day when we had to. The rest of the time we flew at night.

The blackness during night operations was as profound as a stormy night over the ocean. There were no ground lights, few villages, often no hint of sky because of blowing sand and smoke. It was a confusing black coal sack—and we were in it.

The heat turned our schedules upside down. At one in the morning, it was still 118 degrees. We'd go out to run at three-thirty, when it had cooled another ten degrees. We'd shoot hoops at four.

The heat and the sand took a toll on the equipment. The MH-60s leaked oil as a matter of course, but in the extreme heat they leaked more, turning the back cabin of the aircraft into a slippery grease pit. Handholds were precious but too hot to grasp. The searing temperatures cracked and warped the helicopters' windscreens, and the daily sandblasting rendered them opaque. The maintenance crews had to replace them nearly every day.

The rotors suffered sand erosion. Like many airplane wings, the leading edges of the rotary wings were made of a titanium spar with a skin covering of composite materials. You could see the sand eating them away from one day to the next, first as pitting that compromised the aerodynamic qualities, then quickly on to more serious structural erosion. They lasted only a hundred or so hours before they had to be replaced, down from three thousand hours in normal conditions.

The engines also weakened rapidly. Instead of clean air, they sucked in sand and grit, which eroded and degraded the engine compressors and caused serious power loss.

And desert flight seemed to heighten a strange and deadly illusion called vection, which I'd also seen trying to hover in a snowstorm or at night over water. The helicopter's 80-mile-per-hour downwash produced clouds of sand that streamed and spiraled in a mesmerizing kaleidoscope. The disorientation it caused was among the many downfalls of Operation Eagle Claw, the hostage rescue effort that failed in the Iranian desert.

I saw it on one of my first flights—sand streaming back past the cockpit made me think I was moving forward when I had thought the helicopter was in a stationary hover. Instantly the sand flow changed direction, unaccountably rising past the cockpit. My first reaction was that we were falling. I knew I was rapidly losing the ability to tell whether we were moving right or left, up or down, or even if we were spinning like a top. The false movement cues came at me from all directions. I couldn't rely on the instruments because you can't hover a helicopter without visual reference points. It took enormous concentration not to respond to the false and potentially fatal cues. I had to pull maximum power and climb straight out of it, and after that we tried to plan operations not to hover at all, because we faced the same conditions every day and night.

Major Abdullah was my Kuwaiti liaison. He was warm and friendly except on one topic. He brought it up when we first met.

"Colonel Fleming, you know you have a female problem," he said.

"A female problem, Major?"

"I have been looking over the roster of your personnel. Your flight surgeon, I believe, is a woman." He waited for my confirmation.

There were four or five women in the squadron. They were quartered behind a walled-off partition in our barracks. One was the flight surgeon and one of the others was the chief of maintenance.

"Yes, I believe so," I said.

He shook his head and waved a hand in the air like a man shooing a fly. "Your squadron is predominantly men. It is not right that a woman should have this knowledge. It is an offense. It is my duty to tell you she must be reassigned."

This didn't come entirely as a surprise. But the squadron had been carefully constructed and it wasn't easy to find a competent flight surgeon. Ours was a fine doctor and an excellent officer, and she had volunteered to come halfway around the world. I couldn't have replaced her if I'd wanted to. But I also had to acknowledge Major Abdullah's religious sensibilities, so I hedged.

"Well, we can't do without a flight surgeon, so she's going to have to stay for now. But I'll request the air force to give us a replacement. A man," I said.

The major nodded sharply. "Excellent," he said and resumed his warm, almost courtly demeanor.

The maintenance officer, like the blond flight surgeon, stood out even in her desert camouflage. She didn't make a point of being noticed, but with red hair and freckles she didn't have to. The first time she accompanied the water tanker crew to the desalinization plant depot 15 miles away where we got our water, the Kuwaiti work crew refused to fill the truck as long as she was there.

Major Abdullah did not like the fact that the squadron's women lived under the same roof, though a partition separated them from the men. This time, however, the cultural bias worked to our advantage. A couple of weeks after we arrived, trucks arrived pulling two new house trailers. After the trailers were positioned to one side of our quarters, Major Abdullah arrived with the news that these were for the women.

The women were delighted to be exiled from the dingy prison to new facilities with air conditioners that actually worked, and one of the trailers had a washer and dryer that we kept running constantly.

I was reviewing the daily air tasking order in the operations room a month after we arrived when our intelligence, or "intel," officer entered and sat down. He was a jovial guy from the Moffett Air National Guard base, but the look on his freckled face was serious. He said he'd just returned from the daily intelligence briefing at the U.S. embassy in Kuwait City. Intel normally consisted of briefings on the air order of battle, so we would know who was in the box in case we had to get them out, the previous night's Iraqi lock-ons, occasional missile and small arms firing, and the customers to be airlifted in our special operations role. We incorporated what we learned into our flight plans and kept on with the work.

Today, however, intel had had a different and more sobering message.

I listened with growing concern as he described the threat situation. A group of twenty-four to thirty terrorists were training at a remote desert site in southern Iraq. Apparently they were training for an attack on helicopters. Satellite and spy plane photos showed that they had assembled helicopter mockups, or abandoned shells, that they were assaulting and zapping with explosives. It looked like we were in their gunsights.

In our forward operating location, we were more exposed, less protected, and closer to hostile territory than any other air force unit. The prison, with the trailers alongside, was wide open to the desert on three sides. We had no real physical security, nor did we have security patrols by our own forces or any of the Kuwaiti military or police.

On top of that, our helicopters were exposed. I wondered what it would take for terrorists to plant explosives in or near our helicopters or for them to get close enough to fire missiles or grenades at a helicopter being worked on or just taking off. I knew that the aim of terrorists was to kill. They wouldn't want just to blow up helicopters. I was determined to make sure the squadron was protected.

The personnel of the 4412th were well trained in force protection and the use of arms. They had enough to do with all their other duties, but we had to take some action. We were on our own, and I wasn't going to let us be sitting ducks in the desert. Our first sergeant, Frank Guerra, was a thirty-year veteran of the New York Police Department bomb squad. Colonel Paul Mercready, the operations officer, served with the Suffolk County Police Department Special Services Force, a role that gave him extensive knowledge of terrorist tactics and security. Senior Master Sergeant Paul Bellissimo, of the *Leavitt* rescue, was the pararescue chief. He knew combat rescue and special operations tactics. Even with this kind of experience, we could never make ourselves a hard target. But if we weren't fully hardened, we'd have teeth.

I directed a team that included Mercready and John Flanagan, another Suffolk County police officer and a marine vet; Guerra; Bellissimo and his PJs; and Dave Ruvola. Together we worked out a plan modeled on the doctrine and procedures in the air force's Threatcon system.

The plan incorporated a giant voice warning system for the compound, in which a loudspeaker could warn everyone simultaneously of an attack. We chose a rally location, a single place where all personnel would go in case of an alarm, marked a standoff distance from our compound into which no one we didn't recognize could come unchallenged, and posted sentries. I ordered that all crew members on duty carry weapons.

We began to vary our daily routines so our activities and locations would not be as predictable. This included the routes and times that we sent trucks for water and supplies. Despite the heat, we carried chem gear with us at all times. Chem gear, shorthand for the "battledress overgarment" designed to protect against a chemical attack, included heavy trousers and jacket lined with charcoal-impregnated cloth, a full face respirator and hood, bulky impermeable gloves, and rubber overboots. We would flirt with heat stroke to survive a chemical attack.

At home, I'd had the 102nd crew members train in detecting mail bombs. We used this training under Chief Guerra to screen mail and packages. And finally, we mapped out escape routes and methods.

Guerra and I both knew that no matter what we did, a well-trained terrorist group could get to us. But a commander's inaction is a morale killer. And I also was concerned about defending ourselves against random acts of political violence from anti-American fanatics who would act if they saw an opportunity.

My decision worked its way upstairs. I learned about it one day when I picked up the phone to find one of the top generals in Dhahran on the line and angry. He started chewing me out good.

"What are you doing out there, Colonel?" he demanded. "You unilaterally declared a higher Threatcon level than the rest of the entire Persian Gulf. You can't change the Threatcon level. You don't have the authority to do that. I don't have the authority to do that. Only the Pentagon has the authority to do that."

I responded with a lot of "Yes, sirs." And I had to admit that I hadn't known Threatcon levels were set in Washington. But I wasn't going to reverse my decision and take away the protections we had put in place. I simply was not going to sit idly by while terrorists targeted my squadron. The threat had been described. My men and women had volunteered to come to this desolate place to perform special operations and to be ready in case jet crews needed rescue. I had to act on their behalf. I reminded the general of the intel briefing and the surveillance photos of terrorists training to blow up helicopters.

Yes, the general said, he was aware of the terrorist threat to our isolated force, but he did not have security forces to commit to us. A formal change in Threatcon—the threat conditions— would have mandated those forces.

I didn't want to end up on the wrong side of the general, but I was the highest-ranking air force officer inside Kuwait. I wasn't sitting behind a desk far from the troops. I was working with them every day. We endured the heat and sparse conditions all together. I was damned if I was going to leave my hardworking squadron vulnerable to terrorist attack and I wasn't going to let the general convince me otherwise. I said, "Sir, part of my responsibility is force protection. I needed a starting point from which to build a plan and we used the Threatcon procedures as a guide for our own actions."

"Hmm," I heard him musing on the phone.

"Sir, would it have been better if I did nothing to protect my squadron from this threat?"

He paused for just a moment. Then he barked, "No, Colonel Fleming, you did the right thing. You needed to take action. Good job."

He hung up the receiver. I breathed a sigh of relief that I wasn't getting reprimanded or worse, but I also felt a surge of sat- isfaction that my argument had convinced the general. More than anything, I felt gratified that we'd be getting some help to pre- vent an attack against our personnel. The air force was going to look out for us, and that meant that they recognized our contri- butions. And that made me feel proud.

Soon afterward, two dozen air force Special Police arrived and began regular security patrols with bomb-sniffing dogs. Despite the friends I'd made among my Kuwaiti military con- tacts, it was hard to look at people in the street without being on guard for any possible hint of an attack.

As the August heat intensified the already brutal conditions in the desert, our tour was winding down. I had flown thirty-four com- bat or combat support missions, feeling like a lobster boiling in the pot on every one. One day word arrived from wing head-quarters in Dhahran that two of the pararescuemen there had died. These PJs had flown with the 4412th, but they primarily flew with the rescue tankers from the squadron of HC-130s out of Dhahran. They had died of heat stroke after doing some heavy work and going right into physical training.

For one, let alone two, of the superbly conditioned PJs to die of heat stroke was another reminder of how dangerous the desert heat could be. In my three months of Kuwait duty I had learned to both respect and fear the desert.

I was due to shuttle to Dhahran for the regular commanders' meeting. I'd been asked to brief the group there on the force pro-tection plan I'd launched and the beefed-up security provided by the air force. Now I had a memorial service to attend as well.

I flew into Dhahran on an HC-130 the afternoon before the briefing and the service. American military personnel stayed at the Khobar Towers, a complex of eight-story buildings near the Saudis' King Abdul Aziz Air Base. I hadn't been in Dhahran since we'd increased our security, and I had a new appreciation for the chain-link fencing, razor wire, and armed patrol vehicles that guarded the perimeter. My escort driver had to steer between cement barriers through dogleg turns, and at several checkpoints air force Special Police checked my ID under the watchful eyes of troops manning heavy machine guns.

Building 131 of the towers housed the rescue and special operations crews of the 4404th Air Wing, to which our squadron belonged. The escort showed me to my room and left. Soon some of the HC-130 crew members from the 102nd showed up and invited me up to their "hooch" on another floor. The rooms had balconies that looked across the Saudi desert, and we sat out-side and talked. I chatted with a close friend, SMS Tom Elefete-rion, an HC-130 loadmaster, as night fell over the desert.

As we talked, I idly watched a dark car pull up and stop out side the security fence about 100 feet away. Two men got out and walked away. I didn't think about it. Tom and I kept talking, and the desert sky turned black and filled with stars. I slept soundly that night. When I woke up I gave little thought to the unattended car, still parked where it had been left the night before.

I gave my briefing the next morning and attended the memorial service for the PJs in the afternoon. A few days later, I turned over the prison and its menagerie of scorpions to the next commander and prepared to head for home.

Back on Long Island, I had no cause to think about that night at the Khobar Towers, the other rescue units, or the stress of desert operations for several years.

There was enough to think about starting that October with the horror of the bodies of American soldiers being dragged through the streets of Mogadishu, Somalia. The deaths were terrible. The soldiers were there as humanitarians, assigned to keep warlords from stealing food sent to the country's starving population. But on a mission to capture aides of a chief warlord, 120 U.S. Rangers and Delta Force commandos rappelled into an ambush that downed two UH-60 Black Hawk helicopters, killed 18 soldiers, and wounded 73 more. The spectacle was sickening in its physical brutality and its disregard for the dignity of life. Its celebration of anti-Americanism brought a knot to my stomach and a burn of anger that was as irrational as the behavior that had caused it. The result was good for the warlords, but not for the starving millions at their mercy. American forces ended their role in policing the delivery of humanitarian aid.

Everywhere you looked, the dogs of war were in full cry, defying efforts to bring order to a world of cruelty and chaos. Another de facto warlord, this one in the Balkans, laid siege to Sarajevo, a city celebrated for its tolerance that only ten years earlier had hosted the Olympic Winter Games. Serbs shelled the city from the surrounding mountains, aimed sniper fire at playing children and shoppers in the market, and used rape as well as murder in a campaign of "ethnic cleansing" meant to rid Bosnia and Herzegovina of Muslims and Croats.

Then one day I turned on the morning news and heard with horror that a massive truck bomb had exploded outside the Khobar Towers, killing 19 servicemen and injuring 515. I watched, numb, as television pictures showed the damage. The bomb, about 5,000 pounds of plastic explosives, had blasted a crater 50 feet wide and 16 feet deep and had ripped the front off of Building 131. A reporter described where the truck had been. I recognized it all too well. It was precisely where I'd seen the car park that night at the towers. The reporter said that air force Security Police had seen the truck and started an immediate evacuation. Otherwise, the damage and death would have been far worse.

My first thought was anger at the people who had done it. Then I thought of the friends I might have lost. Finally I thought grimly how exposed we had been in our prison in Kuwait between the airport and the desert and what the increased security we had put in place might have prevented.

Another piece of news drew the circle tighter. The 66th Rescue Squadron out of Nellis Air Force Base, preparing for another deployment to the gulf, was training overtime. The crews, according to the *Air Force Times*, were being "worked to death." Two MH-60s were on a night formation training flight when they collided over the desert. *Jolly 38*, the number two aircraft in the formation, sliced into the cockpit of *Jolly 39*, the formation lead, with its rotor blades. Both aircraft rolled over while still in the air, crashed into the ground, and exploded, killing all twelve crew members.

The *Air Force Times* reported the disaster in terms that made me want to cry. It said wreckage was scattered over a quarter mile of desert, and "Molten aluminum flowed like water along a trench made by a rotor blade, turning solid at the far end as it cooled."

When I reflected on these events, I was reminded of what a machine the helicopter is, how capable and dangerous all at once. I was reminded of the remarkable commitment rescue personnel make to save the lives of others, not only their fellows in the military services but also civilians with whom they have no direct connection.

And I was reminded of and sobered by the sheer heroism that our military people put into their jobs. I didn't feel like a hero in any way. But I felt that way about many of the others around me. I had learned to appreciate—"love" is not too strong a word—the way the men and women I worked with shouldered obligations that others would shrug off. It was just a part of them, an indelible part of who they were, to accept risk without fanfare. To work and walk and talk with them made me feel better about myself. The choice I'd made so long ago seemed far less random now, far more gratifying and fulfilling.

15

The Grave
of *Salvador Allende*

Whoever destroys a single life is as guilty as though he had destroyed the entire world; and whoever rescues a single life earns as much merit as though he had rescued the entire world.

—*The Talmud*

In December 1994 I was thinking of another profession. It had been fifteen months since I'd returned from Kuwait with the memory of the desert heat baked into my brain. I was forty-six, not old but not young either, and flying helicopters had begun to take its toll. The vibration followed me when I left the cockpit and I heard the rotors and engines in my sleep. I didn't concentrate as well as I used to, and not concentrating is a good way to get people killed. I'd been flying Jollys for twenty-four years. The stress never let up, never diminished, and its effects on people fascinated me. I wanted to study how stress affected performance, and at what point it led to failure. I was ready to go back to school.

My career was under strain as well. I had thrived when Colonel John H. Fenimore commanded the 106th Rescue Wing. He was succeeded, however, by Colonel Hill, who promoted a man for whom I had little respect. To add insult to injury, I now reported to him. Many on the base were amazed by this turn of events, which blocked any chance for my advancement. The antagonism built until I was removed as commander of the 106th Operations Group.

I was shocked at first, to say nothing of embarrassed by the sudden turn in my fortunes. Slowly, when I thought about it and talked it over with Jean, I was able to see the new opportunities that the reduction in my flying duties would allow. Thus I was feeling no strain on this particular December morning. The world's problems seemed relatively minor, unless you were a baseball fan who had been deprived of the World Series by the players' strike, a Democrat in Congress reeling from the blustery ascension of Newt Gingrich in the conservative Republican sweep of the elections, or O. J. Simpson about to go on trial for the murder of his wife and a friend. From day one, the Simpson case had been a fevered, lurid dream, from the brutal, blood-splashed murders, to the television shots from helicopters tracking Simpson's white Bronco on its slow chase around the freeways of Los Angeles, to the parade of weird and exposure-hungry players who promised to appear front and center at the trial. It seemed as if America's fascination with celebrity had warped into full-scale addiction.

I was on the road early, at 6:00 A.M., heading for the air base with the Celtic sounds of Clannad in the tape deck and the first slivers of sunlight rising over the vineyards and potato fields of the North Fork. Celtic music, with its combination of lament and liveliness, spoke deeply to me for the same reason I liked Russian composers.

The day promised to be beautiful, clear, and crisp, with enough bite to let you know you were alive. The road meandered through old farm and fishing villages along Great Peconic Bay: Cutchogue, Mattituck, Laurel, and Riverhead. At Riverhead, it left the bay to cut across the undernourished-looking Pine Barrens and on to the South Fork and the base, renamed a few years earlier for Colonel Francis S. Gabreskie, a World War II and Korean War air ace and former base commander.

The day's training schedule called for an assault formation on the aerial gunnery range. I was the instructor pilot in the lead aircraft. Graham Buschor, a major now, was to pilot aircraft number two. By seven o'clock I was surrounded by navigation maps and charts in the flight planning room, drinking coffee as I looked over the weather forecast and the flight plan for the gunnery range off Martha's Vineyard. I signed off on the flight orders and for the three thousand rounds of ammunition that were being loaded into the aircraft. When Graham came in, I expected he wanted to talk over the training exercise. But he seemed agitated.

"Colonel, did you hear about the ship that sank last night?" he asked without preamble.

"No. What ship?" I asked.

"Freighter called *Salvador Allende*. Crew of thirty-one. It happened more than twelve hours ago. The helicopter section and the PJs are upset. Nobody contacted us."

The Coast Guard would have handled a rescue within the range of their helicopters. If it was farther out, they might have asked us for assistance, unless it was so far out they thought a response was out of the question.

"How far out?" I asked.

"Twelve hundred miles. We sent *King 46* to join the search this morning. They report survivors, fifteen or twenty, hanging on a lifeboat, but the weather and the seas are bad." *King 46* was at the moment our only operational tanker. "What do you think?"

It was a loaded question. Graham had guts. He had survived the ditching of *Jolly 10* three years earlier, and the Persian Gulf, and still had a taste for a tough operation. He was learning to make decisions on his feet as a mission unfolded when you're faced with ambiguous decisions and your choices aren't black or white but gray. What we were discussing was very much in the gray. It was on the ragged edge of capability.

I did some quick calculations in my head and decided it would take three tankers to get two helicopters there and back. If the

Coast Guard wasn't asking, we would have to volunteer. I didn't know if a helicopter rescue that long had ever been attempted, but I knew our guys and I thought we'd have some takers.

There were daunting hazards. The first was that it was December, one of the worst months over the North Atlantic. The second was a storm that had been bad enough to sink a good-sized cargo vessel.

"Graham, why don't you see if we've got volunteers. And get Mike Noyes to coordinate tankers. I bet we'll need three." Noyes, a major, was the supervisor of flying.

"Got it, boss." Buschor retreated to the telephones.

No one from the newly reshuffled command structure was on base. Master Sergeant Bob Hampton, the Dispatch Center chief, had started to track down the officers who needed to be notified. I felt the frustration of being out of the command loop, but I still had the authority to launch a mission using volunteers. Its duration and danger were immaterial. I was the senior officer, and could invoke the concept of "hot pursuit" to launch as a moral imperative. It was a life-or-death emergency, and the hard reality was that people were likely to die if we didn't make a rescue attempt—now. It's a choice not many officers are willing to make because it's usually not good for their careers. But I'd had nearly twenty-five years in rescue, and I was comfortable with making decisions on the fly. If Hill didn't approve, he could order us back.

Graham quickly assembled volunteers. I told the crew members who gathered that I was willing to make the decision and attempt the rescue. I had been their commander for years and shared a bond of trust with them. They were ready to go, and we had lost too much time already.

At about eight the night before, when Jean was loading the supper dishes in the washer and I was bringing the dog back from his walk, a nor'easter resulting from the typical collision of a cold

Canadian high and a warmer low over the ocean had had an all-too-typical result. Wave heights had built with the wind and steepened, and two successive rogue waves had pushed the 450-foot Ukraine-registered freighter into a fatal starboard roll. *Salvador Allende* had gone down southeast of Nova Scotia, leaving some of its crew of 31 fighting for their lives in 30-foot seas roiled by 60-mile-an-hour winds.

Our Coast Guard and Canadian Search and Rescue had sent planes. They had located the scene, dropped rafts and survival gear, and diverted shipping to the area, all usual first steps in a midocean rescue. A Panamanian container ship, *Giovanna*, was a few miles away but so far had been prevented by the storm from reaching the survivors. The captain was unsure if he could perform any rescues in the extreme seas even if he got there. Another merchant ship was steaming at full power but was fighting the seas and making little headway toward the scene.

A picture of what needed to be done emerged quickly. I calculated that reaching *Allende* would take upward of fifteen and perhaps even twenty hours of nonstop, low-altitude flying. The helicopters would have to refuel not three or four times, but ten or twelve. The MH-60's mechanical systems were designed for only 10 hours of flight before requiring extensive maintenance checks and reservicing. Their emergency backup systems were designed for an additional 30 minutes.

None of the facts pointed to a helicopter operation. That didn't mean it was impossible, but clearly, a helicopter mission hadn't even been considered.

I could see the elements assembling. It was way out there on the edge but it could be done. I cursed to myself. We still could make a difference, even a small one. But we had already lost 12 precious hours.

Graham reappeared with the news that an air force HC-130 was on the base. One tanker ready to go, if the air force would agree to support a rescue effort. Captain Kevin Metz, one of the tanker pilots, made the calls, and they agreed. Meanwhile, Noyes had called the Marine Reserves at Stewart International Airport, in New Windsor, New York, near Newburgh. His contact, a decisive young captain named Jon Omey, assured us he could get a tanker crew to volunteer. If maintenance could get one of our own broken tankers fixed and ready, we'd have the three we needed. But there was none to spare, so the margin of error for fuel would be very small. If one of the three broke, we knew we would not return to land.

Major Hadj Thomas, Metz, and Noyes were the pros I trusted to make this third HC-130 happen. Soon they were in the flight planning room poring over maps and charts, sketching out schedules, launch times, and fuel loads to support two helicopters. If they were on the case I was willing to launch with just two tankers guaranteed. The third could catch up to the slower helicopters. If it didn't because it wasn't fixed in time and the helicopters had reached the point of no return, we could divert to Halifax, Nova Scotia, and wait.

Now was the time in mission planning when you looked down the barrel of the gun, the risk acceptance stage when you weighed the odds and either did it or not. If we were going, we needed to accept the risk and go. The planning wasn't complete, but it can't ever be in an emergency.

My philosophy differed from Colonel Hill's. He drew a distinction between an immediate response and one he preferred to think of as appropriate. But that provided a rationale for delay. This morning, the appropriate response had to be immediate. Someone had to pull the trigger. Pretty graphs and charts and crossed "*t*'s" and dotted "*i*'s" don't save lives. Rapid and decisive action does.

I wanted to get the helicopters moving. The planners could refine the plans. The tankers could catch up. We had the essentials covered well enough and I believed that we could deal with new developments as we proceeded.

* * *

It was still early. Hampton reported that the necessary approvals were still being worked on and he hadn't located Colonel Hill yet. A maintenance crew was working on it furiously.

In the next half hour, the helicopters were fueled and towed out to the launch pad and the machine gun ammunition belts were unloaded. The PJs got their gear from their lockers, first-aid kits and Mylar blankets to wrap survivors suffering from hypothermia, and suited up in their quarter-inch Arctic wet suits. I pulled on the version of the Mustang survival suit the pilots and flight engineers wore, with pleats behind the knee to make it possible to use the foot controls. I was sorry for the coffee I'd consumed. We'd be in the air for who knew how long, and there's no bathroom on an MH-60.

We launched at 7:50 A.M. I was in command of the formation in the lead aircraft. Graham flew as my wingman. There were clouds on the horizon far out to the east ahead of us. Below, the forked tip of Long Island passed from view, and we headed over open water. *Yankee 03*, the tanker from the Marine Reserve base at New Windsor, joined our route and trailed us in a three-ship formation.

We were flying past Block Island when my radio squawked. "*Jolly 14* flight, this is Operations Control. You and your wingman are ordered to return to base. Repeat, return to base."

I couldn't believe what I was hearing. "By whose order?" I demanded, although I knew that only Colonel Hill would call us back.

"Wing commander's order."

I felt a surge of frustration. Colonel Hill liked missions "planned to the nth degree," to use his words. He didn't like to launch before all aspects were nailed down. The crews in the air all sensed that he didn't want a piece of this risky mission.

"I need to talk to the colonel," I radioed back.

"He'll talk to you when you get back, sir," the dispatcher replied.

My hands tightened on the controls. No talk, no discussion. For a moment I thought, To hell with him. What if we just went anyway? But I knew he controlled the availability of the third tanker.

My voice tense, I radioed Graham in *Jolly 08*. "Yeah, I heard," he said, his voice also reflecting frustration. The marine tanker crew wondered what the hell was going on, but were polite enough not to say too much about it. All three aircraft banked around and headed back to the Suffolk County base.

Colonel Hill was waiting in my office, his face carved from stone. We nodded at each other, and I sat down at my desk. He moved from his seat in the corner, sat down across from me, and started to lecture me on the dangers of such a long, nonstop helicopter rescue. He said he'd been asked the night before about a heli-copter operation and rejected it. I looked at the pictures of my family on my desk and thought that he should have known I wouldn't take unnecessary chances.

I resisted the impulse to question him for not consulting me when he got the call. I throttled back my frustration and tried to talk my way back into the mission. "Colonel," I said, "what you know at the beginning of a mission is never the reality. The 'map' always changes, and your plan changes for contingencies. Between the crews at home and in the air, you can choreograph a mission on the fly. At least then you're moving toward possible survivors and you always have a fail-safe point. But you can never get back time you've lost already. There are people in the water out there."

He never liked to hear that. He asked to see the paperwork, charts, and computations for the operation. I gave him my paper-work from earlier that morning. He went over it, slowly and methodically, as my blood pressure rose to bursting.

We debated the sanity of the mission. It became apparent he hadn't changed his mind from the night before, that he didn't want it at all. I was frustrated, thinking we would never launch. About an hour and a half into the face-to-face, I mentioned that since we'd launched already, there was now an expectation up the chain of command that we would make a rescue attempt. He looked as if a lightning bolt had hit him. Command expectations were something the colonel understood.

Then my phone rang, and maintenance told me our out-of-service HC-130 would be up and running by 1:00 P.M.

Moments later, the colonel called the crews to assemble in the auditoriumlike main briefing room. The marines, air force, and our Air Guard crews filed in, not knowing what they were going to hear, but happy to be hearing anything rather than sitting around waiting.

The colonel laid out the plan as I'd mapped it earlier, the two helicopters supported by three tankers acting as a tag team rotating onto the scene to provide both fuel and emergency support. He spent a lot of time talking about the dangers of hoisting survivors after dark. One P.M. came and went and the real issue became the fact that we had sent our only flyable tanker on the search early that morning. It couldn't get back in time to escort us. And the third tanker was the broken one that wasn't fixed yet.

As I sat in the auditorium, the magnitude of the mission started to sink in. I couldn't remember a rescue of this proposed duration, ever. With the adrenaline of flight subsided, I began to feel frustration changing to a sense of deep emotional and physical exhaustion. At the same time, my thoughts turned to men who might be clinging to wreckage in the high seas off Nova Scotia in December, and I was eager to launch that day.

Some deadline passed that nobody voiced but everyone recognized. The air of expectation went out of the room, and disappointment took its place. The tanker wasn't going to get fixed in time for us to launch a daylight mission. The commanders decided that we would fly to Halifax, rest, and finalize plans before leaving the next morning.

*   *   *

Halifax was 500 miles away, but it seemed farther. The two helicopters flew in formation. The marine tanker shadowed us overhead. The Air Guard and air force tankers would come later. The route took us over Block Island, Martha's Vineyard, and Cape Cod, then over open ocean. Nobody talked much. I and I guess the rest of my crew—copilot Chris Baur, engineer Rich Davin, and PJ James "Doc" Dougherty—were occupied with thoughts of tomorrow's mission. The bright sky faded as we flew east and north. Wind gusts joggled the helicopter like somebody shaking a sleeper by the shoulder, as if to wake us to worse weather over the horizon.

The flight took five hours. We landed at the Canadian air base at Shearwater in drifting, cold fog with a hint of sleet and fitful, gusting winds.

I didn't know that Hill had decided to send a planning staff to map out refueling rendezvous points and fuel loads. They were still on their way when Graham and I huddled in my hotel room with Captain Jon Omey, the marine tanker pilot who would fly *Yankee 03* on the first leg in the morning. We heard reports that narrowed the number of survivors to fifteen to seventeen, in a lifeboat and life rafts. Canadian rescue and U.S. Coast Guard planes were circling, keeping their location fixed until rescue ships could reach them. Not fully aware of our pending rescue attempt, they were treating it as a typical midocean rescue, with ships diverted to the scene. But the seas were getting worse, not better, and the ships they had vectored to the area had been unable to reach the survivors. When I went to bed at one in the morning, our informal planning pointed to a direct flight to a pinpointed location, a rescue, and a direct flight back. It would take ten hours of nonstop flying.

The wake-up call came at two-thirty in the morning. I was already awake after half an hour's troubled half sleep and an hour of tossing before that. I was worried about the poor people in the water.

I was worried about my crews, who put trust in my judgment. They were good and they wouldn't let me or the survivors down, but I kept anticipating being pummeled by the storm with not enough guaranteed fuel to get to safety. A line from Yeats had clawed its way into my brain and I couldn't get it out: "the blood-dimmed tide is loosed. . . ." I connected it with the survivors, and with the crews I would lead into the storm, coming together on the wings of an uncertain risk.

Despite the tossing and the nagging, apocalyptic line, I was surprised to feel serene and confident when I got out of bed. The paperwork and details finally were behind us and we were ready to concentrate on the business all of us in rescue held paramount: reaching the survivors and getting us and them back safely.

None of us had a change of clothes or shaving gear. I splashed water on my face, pulled on my olive drab Mustang suit, and went down to the hotel lobby.

From the lobby, the planners and the crews of the five aircraft boarded a bus to take us back to Shearwater. All three HC-130s were on line now. It was a quiet ride. The length of the mission had begun to sink in, to everyone.

I thought about what lay ahead. After almost a quarter-century in the cockpit, it probably would be one of the last rescues in my career. It would certainly be the longest and most exhausting. If it went right, other rescue crews would study it and know the names of the people who had done it. And if it went wrong, they'd still study it, looking for the flaws of judgment and planning that had made us overreach and try something we had no business trying. I felt worn down from lack of sleep and many years of these operations. Risk is harder to embrace as you get older. For this one, I wished I were twenty-five again.

A breakfast table was set up in the back of the mission briefing room at Shearwater. I needed something to eat, but my stomach recoiled at the sight of fried eggs, coffee, Canadian bacon, sausages, and breads. While the tanker and planning crews chowed down, the Jolly crews only looked on. There would be no large meals for us. The tankers had bathrooms, bunk beds, and room to stretch and move around the aircraft. In the helicopters, designed for two-hour operations, we had no facilities, not even relief tubes, and the pilots would be strapped into their seats for the duration of the flight. I looked longingly at the coffee urn, then caught Graham's eye. He was thinking about it, too. But we each blurted out, "Naaah!" at the same time and turned away.

I took a piece of dry bread to curb the immediate hunger pangs and carried a bottle of ice tea for the flight.

Rob Landsiedel, who headed the planning staff that had come up after we arrived, repeated the survivor estimate at seventeen. He brought out a rough map of their locations, to which we would be vectored by the airplanes on scene. This was heartening news. We left the briefing encouraged that we weren't too late.

Sleet and cold rain peppered the windshield of the bus that took us out to the flight line. I knew that ice was a potential problem for rotors and engines alike. The clouds were only 400 feet off the deck, and that's where the base weather station said icing was likely to be worst. We could avoid the clouds as long as *Yankee 03* didn't mind refueling us in the narrow envelope between the sea and the clouds. Normally we never refueled below 1,000 feet. The altitude meant more time to react to an emergency before you crashed. But today wasn't normal. I'd refuel scraping the wavetops if I had to.

Adrenaline kicked in as Rich Davin cleared his throat and said, "Sir, are you ready to begin the checklist?" The checklist covered more than a hundred systems checks and actions needed before the helicopter was ready to fly.

"Yes."

"Crew and passenger briefing."

"Completed."

"Aft console."

"Set."

"Pilot's stations."

"Set."

"Ground wire."

"Removed."

"Caution and advisory and warning panels."

"Checked."

System check after system check, Chris, Rich, and I moved switches, set dials, checked gauges, and the PJs confirmed the state of their equipment. It was a rote exercise, performed with attention to detail and without emotion. Moving my head to each side and overhead to toggle the various switches and observe systems, I felt dizzy and light-headed. The feeling passed but I wondered how I'd hold up for the duration of the mission. At the end of the check I powered on the 1,600-horsepower engines, the jets rose to a low whine, the 54-foot rotor system turned overhead. I felt the familiar vibrations in the core of my body. The blades lost the sag of their weight and began to cone upward as they strained to lift the 11-ton helicopter into the air.

"Two ship, are you ready?"

"Roger, ready for takeoff," Graham responded.

"Let's go."

The noses tilted down, the aircraft lifted forward, and in a moment we had left the runway and the city and the channel lights for the blackness of the ocean. I had the sense that I was leaving the whole world behind.

We flew in darkness, on instruments, staying at about 200 feet, where there was less ice between the sea and the bottoms of the clouds. Sixty-knot tailwinds gave us a ground speed of about 200 knots. The turbulence lifted us out of our seats and slammed us back down every few seconds in a prelude of the hours to come.

We neared Sable Island, and my superstitious Irish mind began to send jolts of foreboding down my spine.

Sable Island is a worm-shaped curve of land about 25 miles long west to east and about 150 miles east and a little south of Halifax. Sailors call it "the graveyard of the Atlantic," but it bristles with hazards for low-flying aviators, too. Lighthouses at each end and a radio tower all rise 100 feet or more above the water and an oil rig offshore also poked into the sky. I could sense their presence, but I resisted looking for them in the darkness. That was a sure route to disorientation caused by the lack of a visual horizon. I breathed a sigh of relief when our global positioning and inertial navigation systems finally showed us past the island.

Flying in darkness, there was eerily no sense of forward motion whatsoever. It felt strange, like free-floating in a vibrating piece of metal. Instruments told me we were making nearly 200 knots, but despite the aircraft noise and vibration, there was no way to sense this. I needed to be able to see something outside, the visual textures of waves passing underneath and clouds overhead. Only then would we physically feel that we were moving toward the grave of *Salvador Allende*.

The first threads of daylight restored my sense of forward motion. The light brought *Yankee 03* out of the clouds. The tanker loomed overhead and just in front, hoses out and ready to give us our first refueling. I wanted the formation to hit the tankers for fuel as often as we could. That would give us a margin for error if the weather worsened.

Jolly 14 and then *Jolly 08* took on fuel. After we unhooked, the marine tanker retracted its hoses and stayed low with us as we worked toward the coordinates of *Allende*'s sinking. Below us, wind-driven spume tore from the wavetops. The ocean was dark and gray-green under the clouds, and the swells looked to be 30 or 40 feet high, cutting into our narrow envelope of safety. We were flying fast, with the wind behind us. We'd have to fight it heading home, but for now it was our friend.

We hit the debris line after about five hours. It appeared as a floating archipelago of human artifacts—chairs, wooden pallets, clothing, squares of what looked like writing paper, sneakers, a soccer ball, lifting and falling as the huge swells marched under them. Diesel fuel spread a rainbow pastel smear as far as the horizon. Rafts the search planes had dropped the day before floated with the debris. There were dozens of them, all empty.

I radioed the on-scene commander, a U.S. Coast Guard officer searching in a C-130, to let him know we had arrived. His response made me feel like a guest who's arrived on the wrong night for a party.

"*Jolly 14* flight, what type of aircraft are you?"

"We're a flight of two MH-60-G helicopters escorted by *Yankee 03*, a KC-130." The KC-130 was a four-engine Hercules like the other tankers, but the K identified it as a marine aircraft.

"*Helicopters!*" The Coast Guardsman's voice added an exclamation point of incredulity. "Well, Jolly, we have no survivors located, and I was told you can't search, so I am going to orbit you off-scene until we locate someone."

"We were told there were survivors located."

"That's negative."

I felt disappointment, closely followed by a stab of dread. No matter what it meant for the survivors, if there were any at this point, for us it meant extending the mission beyond the ragged edge of human and machine endurance. How had the initial reports been so drastically wrong? Either the survivors the first search planes had seen had drifted during the night to the point where the planes on scene had lost them, or the sea had gotten to them. It made no sense for us to be there just circling around. We could search more closely than the airplanes.

I radioed back to the commander, "We don't normally launch for a search this far at sea. But we're already here and the risk is the same whether we orbit or search. We request all airspace 500 feet and below, and will commence searching the debris line."

"That's approved, then, Jolly. Where will *Yankee 03* be?"

"They'll be holding hands with us below 500 feet for now."

"*Below 500 feet!*" More incredulity, since the on-scene commander knew that was a very low altitude for a tanker to sustain extended operations. Their fuel burn would be tremendous. More ominously, if they got down to about 100 feet with us, any steep turn could catch a wing in the huge seas.

"Roger," I responded, hoping that the Coast Guard commander would be willing to let the on-scene reality dictate a change from the plans laid out far from the chaos of the scene below us.

I was grateful to hear his transmission in return: "Roger, approved."

So much for the morning briefing, I thought as the two helicopters nosed along the debris line. Disappointment was thick in the vibrating air of the cabin. I could feel it in the silence from Chris, Rich, and Doc. We'd gone to the limits of the MH-60's design capability with a 10-hour round-trip flight—now we were going beyond them. And the search was working us still farther out to sea.

The width of the debris line was remarkably coherent but the winds had spread it out for many miles in length. It was the energy of the wind that had piled up the towering seas and it was the wind, not the seas, that moved the debris along the surface. It had been almost thirty-six hours since *Allende* had gone down, and we were probably 50 miles from where it had happened, but the flotsam had stayed together in a single snaking line. We moved along the line as if we were walking down a railroad track, keeping our eyes down, slowing into downwind and crosswind hovers, closely surveying rafts or anything that might be a head just above the water. I could tell from the writing stenciled on the sides of the life rafts whether they'd been dropped by Canadian SAR or the U.S. Coast Guard. The swells lifted suitcases and a Coleman cooler. They made the arms of a drifting shirt wave and a pair of pants kick out one leg. The shirt and pants, and many orange life vests, were all empty. After about eighty such maneuvers down between the swells, we'd still found no survivors.

The clouds stayed low, pushing us into an envelope between sea and sky that sometimes was incredibly narrow—100 feet or less. The swells marching under us rose 30 and 40 feet. That meant we had 60 feet of air to fly in, with 50- and 60-knot winds punching us around. Periodically the clouds would lift, allowing us to gain some altitude, and then they'd force us down again. Salt spray blinded us as it crusted on the windshield. I worried about this for upcoming hoist operations and refueling. The jet engines sucked in the spray, causing them to start to run hot and bog down. These were warning conditions just before they stall. If we lost much more power, we wouldn't be able to get out of the way of the seas or catch up to the tanker to refuel.

I kept one eye out for any breaking rogue wave that could take us down. They could be double the size of the 40-foot swells that furrowed the sea below us, and they tended to come along too often in a storm like this. I knew the awe and fear that comes with pulling power to clear a 40-foot wave and seeing an 80- or 90-footer right behind it. Once you've seen it you don't want to see it again. With the engines weakening, I didn't want to fly in these conditions for hundreds more miles.

About 8 hours into the flight, I directed Graham in *Jolly 08* to rejoin in formation and fly on our wing. We'd separated so he could check out some sightings in another part of the debris line. Moments later, *Jolly 08* loomed out of the spray and rain, directly ahead of us. Chris and I were watching the head-on approach and getting ready to rejoin in formation when Rich Davin suddenly, urgently, called, "Break right! *Break right!*"

Seated by the spotter's window on the right side of the aircraft, Rich had seen something. His voice rose in nervous excitement. "Continue around," he urged.

"Chris, punch me off the radios," I ordered. I was excited and wanted to concentrate on getting to what Rich had seen. Uninterrupted communication between us was absolutely vital. If he'd spotted a survivor in the trackless ocean, then lost the sighting, we might never find him again. Sighting him in the first place would have been a miracle. Now every passing wave threatened to erase that miracle.

"Continue around. Do you see it?" Rich was worried. He knew I hadn't spotted the survivor yet—if it was a survivor. I hoped it was. I wanted it to be.

"Not yet, Rich. Don't lose sight of it." My voice choked with nervousness and the fear of disappointment that we'd not spotted anything. The waves were blocking the view.

"It looks like a person waving. My God, it *is* a person waving! He's in the water. I can't believe it!" Rich's call captured the excitement and surprise we all felt. We expected survivors in boats, but no one, we thought, could survive in the erupting mountains of water in December in the North Atlantic.

"You're at 150 feet and descending." Chris was backing me up with instrument readings to ensure that we wouldn't pancake into a breaker while I searched the waves.

"Put a smoke out to mark the location in case we lose sight of him," I ordered. Then at least we'd know the general area.

"Already done, sir. Bring it around, harder. Bend it around as hard as you can. Roll out. Do you see him now?" He was urging me to see him, knowing that if I didn't, the rescue attempt might be over.

Below us, the storm was doing its best to keep its victim. I strained to see through the spray-glazed windshield. Then I saw him, too.

"Roger. I got the survivor in sight. Unbelievable! Just a small head bobbing above the water! Good going, Rich," I called out. My emotions soared. But we still had to get him out of the water.

The man in the water looked amazingly alive. Sometimes a corpse will move just by wave action. This wasn't the case. I lost sight of the survivor again as he passed under the belly of the aircraft. At that point Davin became my eyes again.

"Lower, sir. Slower. Go lower if you can. Fly the seas, and stay 10 feet above. Watch out for that wave, sir. It's a monster."

"No problem," I assured him. Bobbing up and down to dodge the seas was making me queasy. I cranked up my concentration level and ignored the feeling.

We hung in the trough of a 30- or 40-foot wave, just 8 or 10 feet above the water, looking up at the next crest. As I powered the helicopter to follow the rise of the next swell, I stared straight ahead at an endless procession of swells, each the height of a three-story building, moving toward us, ready to strike. If the rotors hit the water, they would disintegrate as if they'd hit a concrete wall.

Rich kept talking to me. I moved the helicopter based only on his words. "Stop down, hold. He appears to be alive. He is moving, at least. Maybe the rotor wash is blowing him. Move left 10, stop down, left 5, stop left. Hold your hover!"

I knew we were now close to being directly over the man in the water. Rich kept me there, calling directions as he looked out of the helicopter's open cargo door through exploding salt spray from the waves and the fog of water generated by the whirling rotors. I pushed our altitude down to 5 feet. "You're drifting back," Rich called. "Stop back . . . move forward 10 feet . . . stop down . . . stop forward . . . you've drifted slightly right . . . move left. Looking good, don't descend any more."

At this point Doc jumped into the water. I always hated to see the PJs leave the relative safety of the aircraft for the stormy uncertainty of the sea. Of course they were as at home there as any man could be. "Looking good. Doc's away," Rich kept up his running commentary. "Doc's okay. Giving a thumbs up. He's swimming to the survivor."

In the water, Doc's arrival startled the man. He'd seen us initially and waved, then lost sight of us, and with the salt in his eyes and the noise of the storm, hadn't found us again, even when we were directly overhead. He was still looking when Doc swam up behind him and tapped him on the shoulder. When he realized the tap came from another human being, he hugged Doc and wouldn't let him go.

Rich lowered the penetrator with its flotation collar into the water and said, "Hold what you got, sir. I'm working with the slack." Too much hoist cable submerged underneath the PJ and survivor could snag them. If that happened while they were in a wave crest, when they dropped into the trough it could turn into a noose.

"Survivor appears conscious," Rich reported. "Hold your hover, looking good. Doc's strapping him on the penetrator. He's giving thumbs up for retrieval." He put the hoist into gear, and seconds later a wet, exhausted figure sprawled into the cargo bay. I was thrilled.

"Any others?" I asked.

Chris's voice broke in with a note of urgency. "Do you hear the other Jolly calling?"

"No." I'd been off the radio to focus on Rich's calls.

"They've spotted sharks. They appear to be feeding on bodies in the water."

My heart sank with dread. "Where?"

"Not far. At ten o'clock." He pointed, directing my eye to *Jolly 08* less than 100 yards away.

"Let's get Doc," I said.

"Roger, sir," Rich answered. "Let's get him."

Now there was more urgency. Doc was in the water oblivious to the feeding sharks just yards away. He was another survivor and I had to get him out. I listened to Rich's directions as I tried to balance the helicopter over Doc. At the same time, Major Gene Sengstacken and Tech Sergeant John Krulder, *Jolly 08*'s copilot and engineer, were calling out the locations of the sharks. Their PJ, Tech Sergeant Mike Moore, was also ready to go into the water if need be. In our ship, Rich worked the hoist feverishly, trying to make sure Doc didn't get snarled in the slack of the cable.

Suddenly Doc disappeared. "He's gone!" Rich cried out.

My stomach clenched as if somebody had punched me in the solar plexus. I'd put him in the water, and he was my responsibility. "I don't have him," Chris called out on the intercom. The radio calls from Sengstacken in *Jolly 08* became more urgent. They were about 150 feet above us, with a panoramic view. Sengstacken thought he'd seen a living man being attacked by the sharks. A sickening flash of Doc and bodies in the water blended in my anguished mind.

Then Doc popped up. "There he is, at twelve o'clock," Rich called. I nervously positioned the bucking helicopter right on top of him. I wanted to see him as we pulled him out of danger. We got him.

Doc was aboard, and *Jolly 08* was still calling about a man being attacked. I instinctively wheeled the helicopter around and sped to the area. We weren't going to leave any living person in the water, feeding sharks or not.

Through the sea spray and rotor wash, I could see human forms, their lifeless, blue-gray skin tones almost translucent in appearance. Some were entangled in ropes in groups of two or three, but most floated suspended just below the surface. A few were face-up, as if searching for help that never arrived.

I never got used to the spectacle of death.

Rich had the hoist ready, and Doc was set to jump back into the boiling swells. I wouldn't have cleared him with the sharks. He said that when he'd disappeared he'd just been looking around for more survivors. We kept seeking signs of life in a grim procession of flying down into the troughs and powering to stay clear of the crests.

I couldn't force myself to believe that there was no one else alive. Then Sengstacken on *Jolly 08* called out a moving body.

We were the closest to it. I dropped the helicopter 30 or 40 feet down the backside of a wave to get closer. The body seemingly lurched forward, twisting as if using one last, powerful stroke to reach the surface. The motion stunned us all and gave us a spurt of energy and hope.

We wheeled around, ready to recover the survivor. Rich got the hoist ready. But as we neared the body, I was sickened to see that the violent motion was not a sign of life. It was the mark of a large feeding shark, hitting and twisting the remains.

Sharks most often feed at depths, but they are dangerous when attracted to the surface. These were in an orgy of feeding. I had learned in survival training that sharks are drawn to a commotion in the water. Humans struggling for survival make commotion. They also discharge streams of waste, urine, and vomit that attract and increase the sharks' initial interest. Those who want to survive must remain calm and swim away from these body fluids. As people weaken, this becomes less possible. It is also less possible to defend against a shark by punching it in the snout, another lesson taught in survival training. In the darkness of night, facing a swift predator that hunts from underneath the surface, it is almost impossible.

Sharks drawn to people or animals or fish struggling in the water stalk and circle. Then they bump their intended prey. If instinct tells them resistance is weak, they start to bite and then tear into the victim. Such deep ocean attacks are typical after shipwrecks. The most famous occurred in August 1945, weeks from the end of World War II. The cruiser USS *Indianapolis* had delivered the components of an atomic bomb to Tinian Atoll and was steaming from Guam to Leyte when Japanese torpedoes sank it in the Philippine Sea. An estimated 850 men of the crew of 1,200 survived the torpedo attack, but sharks preyed over several days, and when rescuers arrived, only 317 were still alive.

Minutes passed. I couldn't give it up. I expected the sharks to swim away from a helicopter flown close on top of them. I'd done it before, making rescues while getting on top of the sharks and literally beating them down with the force of the downwash and the noise and vibration. But that was in nearly calm seas.

From their slightly higher altitude, *Jolly 08*'s crew could follow the torpedo-shaped silhouettes as they hit and tore at the remains of *Allende*'s crew. More minutes passed in the vibrating air under the thundering rotors. None of us wanted to give up the hope of getting another survivor. We kept looking, but there was only death and the sleek aggression of the sharks. It was horrible.

"We're getting low on fuel, Colonel," Chris's voice broke in. I looked at the gauge, then checked with Graham in *Jolly 08*. Both helicopters needed to refuel. Our tanker was now the air force's *Rescue 852*, with a young crew out of Patrick Air Force Base in Florida. *Yankee 03* had bingoed, aviation talk for the point when they had just enough to return to base and land with the required twenty minutes of fuel reserves.

I radioed Graham with a feeling of urgency. "We need to get the refueling done quickly and then we'll keep on searching until we can't anymore."

"I was hoping you would say that, Colonel." Graham's voice was noticeably weary.

We had been airborne for more than 8 hours, a very long time in a helicopter. Most of us now had been without sleep for just over 30 hours. Our mouths were sticky cotton—you could hear it in the way we talked, as if we were eating taffy. What water we had left would go to the survivor. Everyone was subdued, feeling the physical and mental strain. Hope is what gives the crew the energy to keep searching. The sighting of bodies, with no more survivors, brought our alertness down a notch. Fatigue, frustration, disappointment, sadness all blended into a numb blur as we stared at the gray waves.

We refueled and kept searching. At about 12:20 P.M., we sighted a lifeboat. It was floating upright, high in the water. The briefers had told us that morning that *Allende*'s crew had managed to launch one lifeboat successfully and that it contained eleven sailors. This lifeboat was disconcertingly empty. I began to feel weak and tired as stark reality replaced the short rush of adrenaline.

I had trouble accepting that I saw no one. We had searched for that lifeboat and survivors for hundreds of miles. We got down to within 5 feet of it, looking to see if someone was clutching to the side. The rotor wash of the helicopter began to spin the boat dizzily. We viewed it from every possible angle. There was no sign of life.

As we were surveying the lifeboat, *Jolly 08* received a radio call. "*Jolly 14* flight, this is air force *Rescue 852*. We are bingo fuel and departing."

I didn't really hear the call. Hours of rotor and engine noise had mostly robbed my hearing. But I did hear when all hell broke loose over the intercom. Graham's tone conveyed his shock. "Say again, air force *852*. I must have misunderstood what you said."

"These were the instructions that were briefed to us, Jolly," came back a crew member from the air force tanker.

I asked Chris what instructions they were talking about.

Chris hid his aggravation and responded coolly, "The air force tanker thinks its planned departure time of twelve-thirty is mandatory. It's now twelve-thirty. They have no more fuel they can spare to give us, and no more time they can remain on the scene."

I'd been in situations like this before. One escort doesn't leave until the next is on scene, and takes over holding hands with the helicopters. That's the procedure that I knew. The third tanker was apparently far from the scene and we needed fuel.

Chris waved a wadded sheet of paper. "The mission plan says for them to leave the scene at twelve-thirty. It *is* twelve-thirty, sir, and they are leaving."

"No, they won't," I said, and spoke into the primary communications radio. "Air force *852*, this is *Jolly 14*," I transmitted.

"Go ahead, Jolly. We are heading back. This is our planned bingo time to return to base."

"*Eight five two*, forget your planning paperwork in front of you for a second and tell me you are actually at bingo fuel where you have to return," I said.

"Pretty close, Jolly. We'll check to see when the next tanker will be out to fuel you."

"Then can you please note our coordinates and pass them along to the next HC-130 pilot. I think it's Kevin Metz. That's where we will be when we run out of fuel and crash into the water."

There was a period of silence on the radio that seemed to stretch to several minutes. Then, "*Jolly 14* flight, we have recalculated our fuel. We aren't bingo yet, and can stay with you for another hour. We can also give you 2,500 pounds of fuel apiece."

"Thanks, *852*. Glad to have you around," I said, hugely relieved.

"Turning around, Jolly. No problem."

We wouldn't have survived without the air force crew finally ignoring the plan and looking at the reality of our situation before deciding to hang in with us.

Each helicopter refueled and we continued searching the debris line. An hour later, the Air Guard tanker arrived and took over on-scene and escort duties. At 3:20 P.M., after 33 hours with little sleep or rest, we left the remains of *Salvador Allende* and turned toward shore.

The long flight back became a fight against fatigue and dehydration. The noise, vibration, lack of food and water, and the posture I'd been frozen in for hours began to take a physical toll. I no longer was able to hear well. I had to ask that messages be repeated several times before I could make them out. I didn't know how I was going to lead an air refueling or any formation operation if I couldn't hear information passed from my crew or the other aircraft. I would have given anything to stand up and get out of the pilot's seat, to be able to straighten my legs, to be able to release the controls of the aircraft.

All of us slipped into silence. Fatigue causes you to shut down and in its worst case not to care any longer. We were on the brink.

At the 13-hour mark of the flight, we hit the heart of the storm again. Sixty-knot headwinds rattled the helicopter with new fury. It reared and bucked, the nose pitching up 25 degrees, then down 20. Rain drove against the cockpit glass with thunderous ferocity. The helicopter's airspeed and the wind produced 200-mile-per-hour projectiles of rain, and they found and invaded the weak points in the windscreen seals. Water streamed inside the cockpit, seeking out sensitive avionics control boxes, radios, and circuit breakers. A cold clamminess settled in my Mustang suit. I didn't know whether I was shivering or if it was the helicopter's vibrations.

It was night again, the second night of this single flight. Now that it was dark, my body remembered that it had been 37 hours without sleep. Each Jolly had done nine aerial refuelings. We thought the ninth would be the last, but the storm's headwinds dictated one more.

Chris had done the previous refueling. My left leg had been frozen with a bout of sciatica and I couldn't work that pedal. The last one would be mine. The weariness I felt convinced me it would be the last of my career.

Since we were now 3 hours beyond the 10-hour maintenance checkpoint, I started hearing sounds of gear and engine failure. Despite the din and my near deafness, I was convinced that the engine whine was changing pitch or that the gearboxes groaned from lack of lubrication. In my exhaustion the rotors sounded different, too, and I imagined them loading up with ice. And we were still 2 hours out to sea. I was scared. Everything just needed to keep running.

"Chris, take the controls," I told him. "I've got to freshen up a bit."

I got an 800-milligram ibuprofen from Doc and popped it dry. We hadn't had water to drink in the past 5 or 6 hours. The last of it had gone to the survivor, whose name, we'd learned, was Alexander Taranov. He spoke a little English and although he was exhausted from his long ordeal in the water, Doc had had to restrain him from trying to move around in the cabin and hug everybody. He said the water had been warm. Doc had confirmed it. The warm water and the sharks told us he'd drifted into the Gulf Stream. It had saved him, and if not for the sharks, it would have saved the others, too. Now Taranov had fallen into a sound sleep.

After another 30 minutes of flying, with each member of the crew withdrawn into his own thoughts, we and *Jolly 08* had to make our last fuel hits. I radioed the King, and heard instead a now-familiar voice. "*Jolly 14* flight, this is *Yankee 03*." Captain Jon Omey and his marine crew had refueled and come back out to give us whatever assistance they could. *Yankee 03* was back in the thick of it. Between the King and Yankee, their presence gave me a shot of confidence.

"Yankee or King. Can you come down to us?"

"No, Jolly. Once you get in it, you'll see why. Just maintaining aircraft control is a trick. Jolly, we're up at 12,000. No chance you can get up here for a one-time plug?"

"Say again, Yankee?"

"Can you make a 12,000-foot refueling?"

"No, we can't fly at those altitudes, let alone catch up with you guys and refuel."

The storm had split the Jollys from the two tankers. The tankers had encountered severe turbulence, freezing rain, and sleet, and had climbed out of it. We couldn't get that high, and we didn't have the speed or fuel to search for better weather. One of them had to find a soft spot in the weather so we could take on fuel. I knew that Kevin Metz and Phil Rodgers in the Air Guard HC-130 and Omey and crew in the marine tanker would find a way to do it.

We were starting to get beat up again, especially at 500 feet of altitude. The aircraft was bucking nose up and nose down some 40 and 50 degrees from level. Over and over again it pitched forward and slammed back, driving me out of my seat against the shoulder harness and then driving my spine down into the seat. The rain kept finding new ways into the cabin. I tried to tense and relax my leg muscles to keep from shifting in the seat, but my legs were shaking uncontrollably. Hitting the end of a refueling hose would be a crapshoot at best in this condition. We had to get out of the storm, or at least out of the worst of it.

"King and Yankee, this is *Jolly 14* flight. See if you can split up and find a soft spot in the weather. A crack in it anywhere where we can fit the four aircraft for refueling."

My mind wandered, snapped back. Nearly 25 years in rescue and now 36 hours of chaos. I wanted to get through it. I was really worried, but I knew better than to show it. We all needed to suck it up for one more effort. I needed to hold the helicopter steady right beside the HC-130. We can't bob when the storm makes them weave. There are only a few feet to spare. I was lined up with a moving hose and couldn't remember getting there. It was like driving at night in a daze and not remembering the last several towns you passed through.

The radio snapped me out of it. Air Guard captain Kevin Metz said, "*Jolly 14*, this is King. We found an area 30 miles north of your position at about 7,000 feet."

I led the formation in that direction.

Metz transmitted firmly, "We show you closing on our position, Jolly."

In this storm, I knew we weren't going to sight the tanker until the last moment. I slipped down the night vision goggles. "Kevin, what's it like where you are?" I asked.

"Rocky, but better. We might all fit. We've got you 3 miles and closing fast, Jolly. Do you have us in sight?"

"Not yet." There was only blackness through the windscreen.

"Two miles, Jolly. Got a tally on us?" Metz asked.

"No."

"We show you 1 mile. Do you have us?"

"Negative, Kev."

We should pick them up visually by 1 mile or break it off. That's what the book says. But the authors weren't there, and we needed fuel desperately. We had no choice but to press in. The book has instructions for the tanker, too. If we came within 1 mile without visual contact, he should put power to his engines and pull away out of danger. But Kevin knew that this might be our only chance.

"Confirm your altitude, Jolly."

"Sixty-eight hundred feet. You should be 200 above."

"Roger, Jolly, we're holding 7,000."

If the King was just 100 feet low, and the Jolly 100 feet high— not unusual in such turbulence—we could meet at 6,900 feet in a fiery explosion. I strained for a sign of the tanker.

"Half a mile, Jolly. You got us yet? You should have us by now."

"No. Just a little closer, King. Give us a couple more seconds."

It took courage for the tanker crew to allow us to close in on them blind. I willed the tanker to materialize. Our closure rate was chewing up any separation we had left.

"You got us yet, Jolly?" Metz sounded anxious.

"Negative. Just give us a little more, King, we're hurting on fuel." Hang in there, King, I repeated to myself. Hang in there. Don't pull away.

"Got his engine exhaust," Baur said, his voice full of relief.

"They're out to one side. Not a good angle. You probably can't see them," Rich Davin said from the jump seat.

At last I caught it. The rainy swirl of prop wash from the tanker's four engines showed up like a jet stream in the night vision goggles. Then I saw the tanker's ghostlike silhouette among the boiling clouds. I let him know I had him in sight. "Tallyho, King."

"Roger, Jolly." Metz's voice sounded as relieved as I felt. "Cleared wet contact. Three thousand pounds of fuel for each."

"Thanks, Kevin. We owe you one," I said, full of gratitude that the tanker crew had held its position during our blind approach.

I'd convinced myself over the 1,500 miles and now almost 14 hours of this flight that this would be my last aerial refueling. I don't know to this day why I felt that, but I did. I approached it with anticipation and regret. And in the exhaustion and dehydration and muscle cramps, I knew that my last would have to be one of my best. I coaxed myself as I had so many times with students. Take a moment to get your breathing under control. Slow it down. Don't let adrenaline screw up the feel.

My career in rescue was in twilight. It came down to this moment, this need to marry a refueling probe with the tiny latching mechanism inside a drogue twitching at the end of an 83 foot whip. Watch the drogue's swing and the wing at the same time. Easy . . . the probe is a little high of center. . . . Kiss just a little left pedal. . . . Don't cut toward the tanker. . . . Watch the wing. . . . Don't get up under the wing. . . . The probe enters just 6 inches of the drogue's center. It takes 480 pounds of force to lock it in.

"*Contact!*" I said, elated.

"Roger, Jolly. Contact. Hang on to my wing. You're cleared for 3,000 pounds of fuel."

We took our hit, Graham took 3,000 pounds in *Jolly 08*, and we dipped low again to head for Halifax and the Shearwater base below the sleet and snow higher up.

A set of landing lights never looked so pretty as when we cleared the coast and slowed to land. The only emotion I felt at the end was relief.

After we landed and taxied and I shut the engines down, I sat for several minutes, not wanting to move, letting the silence and gratitude wash over me. I'd been in the seat for 15 hours at that point. My survival suit stuck uncomfortably to my body. I was hungry and thirsty and I smelled of hours of stress and sweat. We'd exceeded every norm for a helicopter rescue, taken the machines beyond their design capacity and the crews beyond safe levels of endurance. The reason for it all, one bearlike sailor, was being bundled from the helicopter into a waiting ambulance, to be checked at a Halifax hospital. Thank God his life was spared.

I felt numb, but a question beat in my conscience like a distant drum. There had been more survivors. They'd been alive and waving when the search planes first spotted them. Yesterday morning it had been. If we had reached them yesterday afternoon, would they still have been alive? I thought they would have been. I thought a dozen or more men would be alive instead of just Taranov and the one other *Allende* crewman who, we learned, had been picked up by a merchant ship. And maybe a dozen more wives and who knows how many children would be saved the news that would disrupt their lives and bring them grief and loneliness. The delays probably hurt our efforts.

When my body stopped vibrating and my hearing started to return, I unstrapped and eased myself painfully out of the pilot's seat. Chris looked at me with concern. "How're you feeling, boss? Are you okay?" he asked.

I thought about it. The crews were all alive and well. We'd brought one survivor back, and that was infinitely better than none. Alexander Taranov, at least, would have a happy Christmas and see another year because we had done our job.

"I'm okay," I said.

But that ambivalence crept back into my mind, as it always does when there is loss of life. I was grateful we had gotten Taranov and Doc out of the seas. But I kept thinking of the others, and what might have happened if we had gotten there in time.

Television crews had gathered while we were over the ocean. Their lights and cameras met me when I stumbled from the helicopter. A CNN reporter asked me how I felt. I said, "We went out expecting many more survivors. We just couldn't locate any more alive." Suddenly the exhaustion and the sadness struck me all at once. "The ocean," I said. "The ocean is an immense haystack."

16

The Deep Crevasse

And slowly Arthur answered from the barge: the old order changeth, yielding place to new.

—*Alfred, Lord Tennyson*

In May 1995, in a hotel ballroom in Dallas, I rose with the two helicopter crews from the *Salvador Allende* mission to accept the American Helicopter Society's most prestigious award, the Captain William J. Kossler Award, for the year's "greatest achievement in practical application or operation of rotary wing aircraft." The search for survivors and the rescue of Alexander Taranov had set new endurance records for a helicopter rescue.

The event was dampened for the crews when Colonel Hill insisted on getting up with us to receive the award.

It was my final day in rescue.

My differences with Colonel Hill and his leadership style were past repairing. I had accepted a staff job at the New York National Guard headquarters outside of Albany, where I would be working for Jack Fenimore, my old mentor from the 106th Rescue Wing. He was a brigadier general now, and the New York National Guard's assistant adjutant general for air. By midsummer he would be the adjutant general, the top National Guard post in the state. I'd signed on as his executive support staff officer. The job would give me time to study and do research on the effects of stress on performance. In my imagination, once I had my Ph.D., I would retire and teach.

As I worked and studied, the warped sensibilities of hate continued to assert themselves. The month before the award gathering in Dallas, a homegrown terrorist named Timothy McVeigh, a Gulf War veteran, parked a rental truck packed with 4,000 pounds of diesel fuel and fertilizer outside a federal office building in Oklahoma City and walked away. The bomb exploded, killing 168 people, including 15 children at a day care center. In McVeigh's words after he was arrested, they were "collateral damage" in his war against the government for sins against his neo-Nazi ideology. In New York that fall, the blind sheik and his radical Islamic followers were tried under heavy security for plotting to blow up the United Nations Secretariat building in New York and to assassinate Egyptian and American political leaders. They were convicted, but in Los Angeles O. J. Simpson was shockingly acquitted after a 9-month trial that was a gift to tabloid headline writers everywhere.

On June 25, 1996, the truck bomb explosion at the Khobar Towers in Dhahran, Saudi Arabia, reeled my mind back to the Persian Gulf, bringing back the image of the two men I'd watched park outside the building while I sat on the balcony, oblivious to the future that, maybe on that very night, was being planned. It was the year of Whitewater and the Unabomber and the year TWA Flight 800 exploded over the Atlantic after taking off from Kennedy, sending my old squadron in a frantic search for survivors that produced only bodies and debris over a 5-mile stretch of ocean.

I was promoted to full colonel in May 1996. My dad would have been proud that his son had made it to bird colonel. Jean and I sold the Cutchogue house, from which I had been commuting weekly, and moved to the Albany area. Keith and Cavan displayed a wanderlust appropriate to their father's far-flung career. With Alexandra Bennett, Keith's future wife, they biked and camped across Scotland and Ireland. While Cavan returned to work toward a doctorate in chemistry at the University of North Carolina, and Alex to Middlebury College, where she was studying German, Keith stayed on to thatch roofs and work as a handyman. From there he went on to Taipei to teach English and study Mandarin. Later, he painted houses in San Francisco and returned to Scotland to live and study. Cavan biked across the United States, earned his doctorate, and continued studying as a postdoctoral fellow at the University of Rochester. I continued to study toward my Ph.D. in human factors and decision-making sciences, after which retirement beckoned.

But fate had other plans.

The New York Air National Guard's Stratton Air Guard Base occupies a corner of the Schenectady County Airport at Scotia, northwest of Albany. This is the home of the New York Air Guard's 109th Airlift Wing and its 139th Airlift Squadron, the only military unit in the world that flies ski-equipped transport airplanes to and from both polar icecaps.

The squadron started as a fighter unit after World War II and began cold-weather transport operations in 1975. In those days of the Cold War, radar stations in Greenland formed part of the Distant Early Warning, or DEW, line that monitored the polar skies for Soviet bombers or missiles. The 139th flew cargo and supplies to the stations from Thule Air Force Base in Greenland and became proficient at snow landings. In 1986, it added National Science Foundation sites in Greenland and the Arctic to its destinations.

Satellites killed the need for the DEW line, and the radar outposts closed in 1988. The 109th needed a new job for its flying squadron. It found it at the far end of the world, supplementing U.S. Navy cargo and transport flights to National Science Foundation research stations in Antarctica. It continued its Greenland and Arctic flights at the same time.

Antarctica is the most forbidding continent on Earth—higher, drier, colder, and windier than any other place. It is the size of the United States and Mexico combined, about 5.4 million square miles, 7 million square miles counting coastal ice. An ice sheet averaging 7,200 feet thick covers all but 2 percent of the continent. During the winter, from March through October, when temperatures at the South Pole average about 75 degrees below zero Fahrenheit, the sea at the coast freezes at the rate of 40,000 square miles a day and adds 6 million square miles to its size. Its tallest mountain is more than 3 miles high, and its lowest point 8,325 feet below sea level. It contains 90 percent of the world's ice and 70 percent of the fresh water, but gets—as snow—the equivalent of only 2 inches of rain a year. Some areas get none. The McMurdo dry valleys have had no precipitation for 2 million years. NASA tested for the Viking mission there because conditions are so similar to those on Mars. Scientists at the Soviet research station Vostock recorded a temperature of 129 degrees below zero Fahrenheit in 1983—the lowest temperature ever measured on Earth. Winds can exceed 200 miles per hour.

At the South Pole, which lies at an altitude of 9,300 feet in the middle of a high midcontinent plateau, the sun rises once a year, at about the end of September, and sets six months later. A year in Antarctica is one extended day and one extended night.

Nobody owns Antarctica. International treaties set it aside for research purposes. Nearly two hundred research projects are under way at any given time, directed by scientific teams from several nations. Many if not most of them are aimed at deciphering the effects of global climate change. The National Science Foundation oversees the U.S. research efforts. Military personnel and equipment are prohibited except to support scientific and other peaceful purposes.

Airlift at the South Pole is a huge undertaking. Getting fuel, supplies, and personnel in and out of research stations across the vast Antarctic continent is a test not only of cold-weather flying and ground operations but also of worldwide logistics that takes planes, staff, and support links on the far side of the Earth. Further complicating matters, flights must be crammed into the short austral summer, the few months between October and March when light and relatively mild temperatures make operations possible at all.

The 109th Airlift Wing saw its role grow. In the mid-1990s the navy began to transfer responsibility for Operation Deep Freeze, as the Antarctic and South Pole mission was called, to the New York Air Guard unit. By the fall of 1998, the beginning of the South Pole summer, the transition was virtually complete.

But it had not gone altogether smoothly.

That fall General Archie Berberian was the New York Air Guard's chief of staff. Prior to his 1995 appointment, he'd commanded the 109th for more than four years, and he still had strong ideas about how it should be run. He had spent much of his prior career as a staff officer at the Pentagon and headquarters of the Military Airlift Command and did not have any operational command experience before the 109th.

The ski-equipped versions of the Hercules, LC-130s, were the backbone of the 109th. He kept finding fault with his old unit and threatening to assign me to the 109th to "straighten things out." But the assignment never came.

It took an accident to end the indecision.

Osama bin Laden's name emerged as the mastermind of a worldwide terror network called al Qaeda in the wake of simultaneous bombings of the U.S. embassies in Kenya and Tanzania in August 1998. Almost two hundred people were killed and nearly five thousand wounded. Few of the dead and injured were Americans, however, and the country's attention seemed limited to the effect of the attacks on the skyrocketing stock market.

Washington that fall was fevered with talk of sex in the White House and impeachment. To his detractors, Bill Clinton symbolized 1960s permissiveness gone gray and run amok, but others just as firmly hated the methods being used to try to bring him down. Partisanship reigned in the corridors of power, while most of the country seemed to understand the president's personal shortcomings even if they didn't approve of his behavior. Good news resided in a remarkable home-run race in which Mark McGuire of the Cardinals and Sammy Sosa of the Cubs jousted to break Roger Maris's single-season mark of sixty-one. Both did, Sosa hitting sixty-six and McGuire seventy. And seventy-seven-year-old John Glenn returned to space as a crew member of the space shuttle *Discovery* more than thirty-six years after he became a hero as the first American to orbit Earth, in 1962.

At the Stratton Air Guard Base, the fall signified the opening of the Antarctic airlift season. The squadron's planes were used to support research in northern Greenland over the northern summer and with little break were shuttled back to Christchurch, New Zealand, the jumping-off point for Antarctica. From there crews flew them 2,100 sea miles over the southern reaches of the South Pacific Ocean to McMurdo Station on McMurdo Sound, the base point for National Science Foundation research on the continent. The long austral winter had just eased, and research camps that hadn't been set up, resupplied, or seen outside human beings since the previous March were again accessible.

On November 16, 1998, Lieutenant Colonel Bill Mathews, Major Karen Love, five more crew members, and four passengers climbed the steps of an LC-130 at McMurdo Station's Williams Field. One of the passengers was a polar mountain expert from New Zealand; one such expert accompanied every flight to open snow or on initial put-ins as a safety precaution. The plane also carried bags of extreme-cold-weather clothing for each person on board, a week's supply of food and water, sleeping bags, tents, shovels, and two sleds. The plane, painted light gray with red tail and wing markings, had been named for a town on New York's Mohawk River: *City of Cohoes* was painted over the crew entrance. Its call sign was *Skier 95*.

With Mathews at the controls and Love as copilot, *Skier 95* took off from the Williams skiway headed for Siple Dome, a permanent research site in remote West Antarctica near the Antarctic peninsula that reaches north toward Chile.

Skier 95 landed at Siple Dome's permanent skiway, left supplies, picked up a researcher, and charged its ATO (assisted takeoff) bottles. These were eight canisters of solid-fuel propellant, four on each side of the fuselage, that could be ignited for extra power for takeoffs in thick snow. They added the equivalent of a fifth engine for about 15 seconds.

The tasks completed, *Skier 95* took off again for the 20-minute flight to a field research site called Upstream Delta on an ice stream about 80 miles away. There the plane would off-load 12 tons of tents, fuel, and other supplies. Back at McMurdo, a team of glaciologists was waiting for the supply drop before moving to the ice stream for the summer to study its movement for evidence of global warming.

Like other remote research sites in the polar regions, Upstream Delta had no permanent skiway for landings and takeoffs. There was nothing there at all, in fact. It was just a set of coordinates in a vast expanse of glimmering white.

To land its airplanes in such open snow, the navy had developed a technique called ski dragging. The pilot would slow the LC-130 to 75 knots, drag the main skis along the snow for 30 seconds, then climb to about 1,000 feet and check out the dragged area for signs of ice crevasses under the snow. Deep fissures are normal features of the ice cap, which is always sliding slowly toward the sea, cracking as it goes. After three or four passes, if the area looked safe, the pilot would make a full-stop landing. It was a way of using a $130 million airplane as a surveying tool.

Previously the navy had done all the open snow landings. Now, in this final season of the transition from navy to Air National Guard control of Operation Deep Freeze, the guard was making the open snow landings.

Circling over Upstream Delta, Mathews identified an area that looked safe for landing. It was really hard to tell, since the snow was 8 feet deep, but the snow ridged along the crevasse lines and the low sun cast telltale shadows. The pilot did two ski drags about 200 feet apart, keeping the skis in the snow for a minute each time. For the third, he turned the controls over to Love. As she circled to approach, thin cirrus clouds moved in. The clouds dispersed the sunlight, and the shadows marking the first ski lines disappeared.

Love started the third ski drag when *Skier 95* hit fairly heavy snow and bogged down. The nose ski dropped and wouldn't lift again. Mathews decided to go ahead and off-load the cargo. He kept the engines running, which is standard in polar operations.

As the loadmasters and ground crew moved Upstream Delta's tents and fuel to pallets on the snow, Mathews and Love put on their cold-weather parkas and Gore-Tex "fat boy" pants, their muk-luks, Thermax gloves, mittens, and gauntlets, and looked around the area where they had landed. The outside temperature was about minus 30 degrees Fahrenheit. They saw that instead of being 200 feet or so from their first ski drags, they were 2,000 feet away. The idea of ski drags is to keep them close, to stay within a zone that's crevasse-free. Now they would have no choice but to ski taxi back to the area of the first drags and hope they got there.

When the research station's gear was stacked on the pallets on the snow, Mathews made a wide U-turn and taxied. The plane thumped across the dry snow on its big skis. The one at the nose was 10 feet long and the ones under the wings more than 20, and all were 5 1/2 feet wide. They were Teflon-coated to reduce drag and hinged so they could pitch up and down to follow the uneven surface. The skis on the snow sounded like the plane was moving over a washboard or one of those ridged anti-sleep strips on the highway, only slower. Suddenly the right wing dipped and hit the snow; then the plane rocked to the left and came to a halt with its left wingtip on the surface. As he cut the engines, Mathews had the odd sensation that he was moving backward.

"At first I didn't realize it at all," the Upstream Delta re-searcher who had joined the flight at Siple Dome told the *Antarctic Sun*, the National Science Foundation's polar newsletter. "It was a very slow motion. Nothing at all dramatic."

Mathews got on the radio to call for help. The mountaineer poked a long pole through the snow to locate the crevasse, then staked it out with poles tipped with black flags. It was 7 feet wide, enough to swallow anyone who broke through the overlying snow, and although she couldn't tell it at the time, 132 feet deep. The plane's left ski was lodged in the abyss. At least one engine was damaged, as well as propellers and flight surfaces.

A National Science Foundation contract pilot flying a de Havilland Twin Otter heard Mathews's Mayday calls. The dual-turboprop Otter, a small plane used to shuttle passengers and small cargo among the research sites, weighed 16,000 pounds to the LC-130's 125,000 and was less susceptible to ice crevasses. The pilot headed toward Upstream Delta.

The occupants of the stranded plane waited in their cold-weather clothing. When the Otter touched down and skied to a spot about 100 yards away, they climbed out of *Skier 95*'s escape hatch and followed a safe path away from the plane that the mountaineer had marked with poles tipped with green flags. The Otter took them out of Upstream Delta in two trips, shuttling them to Siple Dome, where they were picked up and ferried back to McMurdo.

Archie Berberian, mad as hell, sketched this out for me in a briefing in his office. The guard was just taking over Operation Deep Freeze, and already there had been a screwup. The damage to *Skier 95* would be expensive to repair, and its loss for weeks if not months would place extra demands on the remaining aircraft. The pace of polar research was increasing and the wing had planned a record-breaking 320 flights to the South Pole, where researchers lived year-round in a windowless geodesic dome. Never before had there been more than 200 flights. General Berberian didn't say it, but I knew he could hear the navy snickering.

His instinct was to blame the accident on *Skier 95*'s crew.

"What were they doing?" I asked when he had finished describing what had happened.

"They were conducting an open-snow landing, something they don't train in and have no procedures for doing," he replied with some agitation.

I asked why there were no procedures. I knew the 109th had just taken over Operation Deep Freeze, but the unit had been flying into and out of the Antarctic for 10 years, and working with the navy during the transition. And the navy had been flying cargo, fuel, and researchers into and out of the Antarctic research stations for 40 years. Somebody had procedures and training guidelines in place. It didn't make sense.

"The wing wants to develop its own procedures," he said. "But they haven't done it yet."

The 109th Air Wing had just installed a new commander. Colonel Graham Pritchard had taken over just 9 days before *Skier 95* had lodged in the crevasse. He had not, apparently, had experience in command, and it was a difficult process for him adapting to navy training and procedures.

Soon after my meeting with Berberian, General Fenimore called me to his office and announced a new appointment. He was making me vice commander of the 109th. My job was to establish crew training and operational procedures for remote-site Antarctic put-ins like the one at Upstream Delta. This was a real challenge, especially for an officer who wasn't C-130-qualified and who had never been to the Antarctic.

To prepare for my new job, I studied the Upstream Delta accident. It turned out that *Skier 95* had actually been lucky. Ground-penetrating radar had located a second crevasse, wider and longer, that *Skier 95* had been heading for when it hit the first one.

Teams of maintenance personnel, field safety experts, and military and civilian technicians took several weeks to free the plane from the crevasse and make repairs. It was a monumental effort. On January 5, 1999, Bill Mathews returned to Upstream Delta, fired up *Skier 95*'s four engines, and ski-taxied to take off. This time the LC-130 took off cleanly. Mathews flew the LC-10 the 250 miles back to McMurdo, then to Christchurch for further repairs a week later.

Meanwhile, the knives were out in Washington. When the inquiry began at guard headquarters, some Air Guard leadership targeted the crew. The senior officers wanted to blame Karen Love for missing the first ski-drag zone.

I thought the real problem was that the crews were not trained for snow landings. They had, in fact, rebuffed the operations officer, Lieutenant Colonel Verle Johnston, when he'd tried to adapt the navy's lessons.

Then I found the disconnect. Their experience was different. The pilots who were now in charge had done all their open snow landings in Greenland, where the terrain is different. Greenland's interior is like a bowl, holding the snow in and packing it. Snow depth and smoothness were problems but crevasses weren't, and a low flyover was enough to check the surface of a landing area. Antarctica was more like an upside-down ice cream cone than a bowl. The ice was always shedding toward the coasts, creeping slowly toward the sea, cracking as it went. It could crevasse anywhere.

I had no hang-ups about which snow-landing techniques were correct. My concern was the crews. It was unfair to them to schedule more than three hundred polar sorties and something like five hundred sorties overall without giving them guidelines for remote-site landings. In my experience, if the crews were out of the loop, their performance would suffer and it wouldn't be their fault. I sent our flight instructors to the navy to learn from their experience in the short term. But over time, I knew it made no sense to use a hugely expensive airplane in trial-and-error

landing surveys. Now, crews fly to remote sites in one of the Twin
Otters, mount a ground-penetrating radar detector on a sled, and
tow it behind a snowmobile to map safe research sites and landing zones.

Polar operations at Antarctica shut down in March for the long
austral winter, when the sun disappears below the horizon, not to
be seen again for six months. Temperatures plunge to 100 degrees
Fahrenheit or more below zero, and the research teams that stay
in place don't venture from their living and work quarters. The
109th's fleet of LC-130s and crews are flown home from Christchurch to be rapidly turned around, then sent to northern Greenland to support research.

This migration of crews and aircraft back north in March
1999 gave me some breathing room as I worked up training and
operational procedures.

Then, on June 16, the deepest point of the austral winter, the
National Science Foundation reached me with news that erased
the luxury of time.

17

Rescue at
the South Pole

The night is dark, and I am far from home.
—John Henry Cardinal Newman

June 16, 1999, was a beautiful day in the northeastern United States, a deliciously long day with the sun rising early and setting late. I was Dr. Fleming now, having received my Ph.D. from Walden University the month before. The summer solstice, the longest day of the year in the Northern Hemisphere, was five days away. My route to work took me down the Hoosick River Valley and across the Hudson at Stillwater, New York, near Saratoga where my father grew up and, 222 years earlier, the first incarnation of the home guard helped deal a decisive defeat to the British in the war for American independence. The valley was a soft summer green marked by a mix of forest and farm. In places you could imagine what the land had been like when it was a wilderness, before towns started up and roads threaded between them, even before the first cabins and trails.

Human affairs were the usual mix of trouble and strife, as if the human race were going all out to assert its right to chaos in the face of nature's order. In February the U.S. Senate, handed articles of impeachment by a rigidly partisan House, had acquitted President Clinton of lying and obstructing justice in his statements about his affair with White House intern Monica Lewinsky. In March, NATO began bomb and cruise missile strikes aimed at dislodging Serbs from Kosovo, where they had continued their Balkans-wide campaign of "ethnic cleansing" against non-Serbs and Muslims. The next month, two sad and isolated teenagers had turned guns on their classmates and teachers at Columbine High School in Littleton, Colorado, killing twelve students and a teacher and renewing the ongoing national debate over gun control.

Jean and I had cause for celebration in our children. Keith and Alex were engaged to be married, with the wedding set to take place early in the fall. We had seen the happiness the two of them shared when they were together and we were grateful and proud that our son had found his soulmate.

By contrast with the bright summer day through which I drove to work, the South Pole huddled in the depth of its long and volatile winter night. There were forty-one "winter-overs" at the Amundsen-Scott South Pole Station, a record since Americans established a permanent presence at the pole in 1956.

On October 31, 1956, a ski-equipped U.S. Navy twin-engine Douglas R4D—a military version of the DC-3—piloted by Lieutenant Commander Gus Shinn with a crew of six, made the first landing at the pole. Until then, it had been known as the Pole of Inaccessibility. Norway's Roald Amundsen had been the first to reach the pole, in December 1911. It took him and his party 53 days on dogsleds, and he had set up supply depots along the way earlier that year before the austral winter. British explorer Robert Scott, who was hot on Amundsen's heels, took $2^{1}/_{2}$ months, arrived in January 1912, but he and his crew died on the return trip of starvation and exposure.

Opening the pole to aircraft operations and maintenance personnel meant that construction materials, supplies, and personnel could be ferried in and out on a scheduled basis, at least during the austral summer. The 1956 landing initiated a big push to build research stations in Antarctica in advance of the so-called International Geophysical Year, an 18-month span that would mark a high point in cyclical sunspot activity. The pole station was one of six being built for year-round research, along with a logistics base at McMurdo Sound in the quadrant of Antarctica closest to New Zealand.

A construction crew of navy Seabees arrived on November 20, 1956. By March 1957 the navy had made eighty-four flights to the pole and delivered more than 700 tons of supplies, and the first phase of the first South Pole station was completed and named for Amundsen and Scott. Eighteen men stayed through the winter, beginning the continuous occupation of the pole.

In 1975, Seabees finished construction of a shiny geodesic dome over the original polar station, which was being buried in snow. The dome contained dormitory rooms, a cafeteria, a store, a library, lounges, a communications center, a computer lab, and a tiny hydroponic garden that provided a trickle of fresh vegetables. The breadth of research expanded to disciplines including upper-atmosphere physics, meteorology, earth sciences, geophysics, glaciology, biomedicine, and astrophysics, some of them housed in outbuildings.

Not all of the forty-one men and women who wintered at the Amundsen-Scott Station in the winter of 1999 were scientists. Most were support, such as construction workers who lived in a dormitory housed on stilts above the snow, and there was a doctor, maintenance and equipment specialists, and computer and communications experts. The winter-overs rarely went outside in the frigid darkness, with the mean temperature minus 76 degrees Fahrenheit, and they normally were not concerned about the weather except for scientific purposes. As far as daily living was concerned, the dome and living quarters were their entire world until the austral spring brought the outside world to the pole again at about the end of October.

* * *

But some of the people in the dome and others at the National Science Foundation headquarters in Washington had become quite concerned about the weather, as I learned when the phone rang at my desk on the morning of June 16, 1999.

Eric Chiang was on the line. Chiang was the National Science Foundation administrator who managed virtually all of the NSF's Antarctic operations. I'd never met him in person but we'd established a good working relationship by telephone. He wanted to alert me to what he called "a possible medical situation" at the South Pole station. He didn't say what it was or who it affected, only that the 109th should start planning and forming a risk analysis for a medical "airlift" if it turned out to be needed.

"What's the temperature down there right now?" I asked.

"Wait a minute," he said, and I heard him click onto a Web site. A moment later he came back on and said, "Minus 100 Fahrenheit, more or less."

Chiang knew, as I did, that jet fuel won't flow at that temperature. Even with deicing agents, it freezes to jelly. Even at McMurdo, where the winter mean was only 28 below, it was never warm enough for long enough in the winter for the fuel to flow. You couldn't spoon fuel into the tanks, and even if you could, you sure couldn't spoon it to the plane's engines when it reached the much colder pole. The cold would immobilize the plane's hydraulic systems, too. And that was just for starters among the many reasons why there were at that time no winter flights into the pole.

Nevertheless, the foundation wanted a thorough risk analysis and General Fenimore put me in charge so I called a team together. By that afternoon, a day in the seventies at the Stratton Air Guard Base, I had assembled a roomful of people whose expertise was necessary to any plan for evacuating somebody from the pole.

The possible medevac would be coordinated by Lieutenant Colonel Brian Gomula, a veteran of fourteen years of polar operations. Lieutenant Colonel Tony German, the director of aircrew standardization, knew the crews and their capabilities better than anyone. Verle Johnston was responsible for aircraft maintenance, and as a highly experienced pilot he knew what the LC-130 could do and what it couldn't. Bill Mathews, the pilot of *Skier 95*, was the safety officer and expert in risk analysis. Chief Master Sergeant Jerry Stoddard was the survival expert who put crews and maintenance personnel alike through cold-weather survival training.

As I described Eric Chiang's request, the reaction around the table surprised and shocked me. Eyes rolled in a display of skepticism. "They want to open the pole early," someone said. A chorus of voices agreed.

Many in the wing clearly feared that the NSF was pursuing a hidden agenda. They thought the foundation wanted to extend its scientific calendar and was creating a pretext to do so. The 109th was still a virgin in terms of taking full responsibility for the Antarctic airlift operations. If the NSF could persuade us to try a high-risk midwinter airlift, what would keep the foundation from wanting to do it all the time? The men around the table thought they were being asked to set a new precedent, and they didn't want to even think about it.

This mistrust of the foundation's motives was one of the prime leadership reasons for me to be sent to the 109th. "Let's not refer to it as an airlift mission," I said. "We're being asked to plan and assess a medical evacuation, not a routine airlift of cargo. It's humanitarian and it would have to be a real emergency before we'd attempt it if we could do it at all."

I felt some suspicion about me in the meeting room, too. To veteran officers of the 109th, I was a wild card as a vice commander, with completely different flying experience and a certain reputation. I felt I had to put down rumors. "I know you've heard I'm this gung-ho rescue pilot who will launch no matter what," I continued. "I'll take a risk, sure. But I'm no cowboy. I flew helicopter rescue for close to thirty years, and I'm still around to talk about it. My view of risk is that it's part of the game, but any risk has got to be acceptable."

"Headquarters will make you launch," somebody said. Aha, I thought. Not all aspects of my reputation had made their way to Scotia. I was thinking about the part that said I was independent to the point of stubbornness, another facet of my contrary Irish character.

"No. I'll never launch unless the mission is at least survivable." I knew, even if they didn't, that I'd never send crews into danger that outweighed their ability to deal with it.

The phone rang, and General Berberian was on the line. News travels fast, I thought. The general wanted to sit in via speakerphone. I keyed the machine, and we went on discussing conditions that weighed against a winter landing. There were many of them, and they were persuasive.

As we talked, the general broke in with a favorite mantra. "Let's think outside the box," he said. "Depending on your risk analysis, there's talk of an Air Force C-141 dropping medical supplies and diagnostic equipment for this sick person. But you people are airdrop-qualified. Why can't you perform an airdrop to the pole?"

"No fuel," the team said in unison. C-141 Starlifters had a longer range and could refuel in the air. They could fly to the pole and back without landing. Our LC-130s didn't have aerial refueling capability and didn't carry enough fuel to make it from New Zealand to the pole and back, and we couldn't refuel at McMurdo.

Berberian continued as if he hadn't heard. "What about this?" he said, his voice rising with enthusiasm. "We find a jump-qualified doctor and parachute him into the South Pole station." He made it sound simple.

A summer jump at the South Pole was dangerous enough. Three sky divers on a private adventure tour had died there in December 1997 when their parachutes failed to open. Parachuting anybody into the Antarctic winter was an invitation to catastrophe. The windchill charts didn't register the combination of 90-below temperatures with the 120-mile-per-hour airspeed of a jump, to say nothing of the perpetual darkness and the possibility of whiteouts that would make finding a jumper—if one did survive—a virtual impossibility.

"Sir, isn't there a doctor already there?" someone asked.

There was. She was a forty-seven-year-old divorced woman who'd seen the South Pole medical post as a way to restart her life. She shared the rough humor and camaraderie of deprivation with her fellow "Polies." When she told a patient that he drank too much and he commented on the hard truths of the South Pole, she took down the Club Med sign on her clinic door and renamed it the Hard Truth Medical Centre.

The doctor's own hard truth had started to reveal itself in March, when she'd first felt a lump in one of her breasts. Her name was Jerri Nielsen, and it would be some time before we knew that she was the possible evacuee.

Nielsen had kept quiet about the lump at first. She had a fairly good idea what it was, but she knew that the last plane had left the South Pole station for the winter. She carried on with her duties and hoped for the best. At about the beginning of June, however, she detected that the lump had gotten larger. The lymph nodes under her right arm were swollen and she was suffering from nausea and shortness of breath. Nielsen said it was hard to know whether she was "toasted"—the condition Polies call the effects of the South Pole winter, which include queasiness and hypoxia from the altitude, chronic hypothermia from the cold, and memory loss—or if the cancer had metastasized. But she was concerned enough to tell the station chief, Mike Masterman. She didn't think that anyone would come to get her. She told Masterman because she wanted to alter the work schedule to take some of the other winter-overs from their duties so she could train them in the basic medical procedures the Polies might need in case she died.

Communication with the rest of the world is intermittent at the pole. The satellites necessary for wireless e-mail communication, for example, tend to orbit along lines of latitude that go around the Earth paralleling the equator, not the lines of longitude that intersect the poles. None is dedicated to getting messages to and from the handful of people at the South Pole station. It wasn't until Nielsen got an e-mail from her parents that she learned that the National Science Foundation was going to try to get her out and in the meantime was trying to arrange an airdrop of medical supplies.

Over the next five days, we developed four rescue scenarios, which I reported to Eric Chiang at the NSF on June 21. It was the longest day of the year in the Northern Hemisphere, and the middle of the South Pole winter. Each of the scenarios carried a risk rating of extreme. None of us thought that any of them was survivable in the depth of the polar winter, and I discussed them with Chiang.

Scenario 1: Three aircraft take off from Schenectady and follow normal routing to Christchurch via Travis Air Force Base, California, Hickam Air Force Base, Hawaii, Pago Pago International, and then Christchurch. The crews who would actually fly the mission would TR (TR is militaryspeak for travel request, another way of saying the crews would fly commercial) to Christchurch. Once the crews had the proper rest, two aircraft would depart Christchurch for McMurdo. Each aircraft would have two crews on board. The first aircraft would land, refuel, and proceed to the pole. The second aircraft would land at McMurdo and enter crew rest. Once the first aircraft came back from the pole and landed at McMurdo, the two crews who were resting at McMurdo would fly the aircraft back to Christchurch. The two crews returning from the pole would fly back as passengers.

Scenario 2: Three aircraft take off from Schenectady and follow normal routing to Christchurch via Travis, Hickam, Pago Pago, and then Christchurch. The crews who would actually fly the mission would TR to Christchurch. Once the crews were rested, two crews would take off for a direct flight for the pole and back. Two other crews would remain in standby until the mission was complete.

Scenario 3: Three aircraft take off from Schenectady and fly to Punta Arenas, Chile, via Howard Air Force Base, Panama, and Santiago, Chile. Once the crews were rested, two crews would fly a mission from Punta Arenas to the pole and on to Christchurch. Two other crews would be on alert until the mission was complete.

Scenario 4: Three aircraft take off from Schenectady and fly to Punta Arenas via Howard AFB and Santiago. Once the crews were rested, two crews would fly a mission from Punta Arenas to the pole and back. Two other crews would be on alert until the mission was complete.

The extreme risk grew from several factors.

Crew rest was one problem. Long days weren't unusual for the 109th's crews on polar airlift duty, but they usually didn't go more than 16 or 18 hours without rest. Each of the four scenarios exceeded that, with crew days ranging from more than 19 to 25 1/2 hours. Crew members would have to sign a statement agreeing to waive the regulations.

Whiteout blizzard conditions were a good bet in the Antarctic winter. Even though the Antarctic is extremely dry, getting only 6 inches of snow a year on average, it never melts. Light winds stir the dry snow. Fifteen-knot winds reduce surface visibility. Winds of 25 knots or better produce whiteouts in which the surface and sky blend in an unbroken mass without shadows or contrasts, causing a total loss of depth perception. Pilots can't land in those conditions even in daylight. And at the pole, daylight was more than 3 months away, meaning a night ski landing.

A night ski landing without navigation aids or ground lighting was a maneuver reserved for extreme emergencies. Bill Mathews described it as potential suicide. The weather was impossible to predict. And once the planes were past the point of safe return, they were committed to the mission regardless of weather.

But the biggest problem was the cold. The turboprop LC-130s could use either of two types of NATO-rated fuel F-34. One froze at minus 58 degrees Celsius, the other at minus 37. The Fahrenheit equivalents were minus 72.4 and minus 34.6, respectively. Even if fuel could be pumped at McMurdo, which wasn't likely, neither type was supposed to be used at ground temperatures below minus 47 degrees Celsius, or minus 52.6 degrees Fahrenheit. The South Pole would be well below that for at least 3 more months. Oil, lubricants, and hydraulic fluid would thicken, affecting engines, flight controls, and landing gear. In the extreme cold, rubber, plastic, and fabric materials would crack, craze, or shatter under load. Adjoining metals could contract differently, again affecting flight controls.

Those were the reasons why a winter evacuation from that continent hadn't been attempted in almost 40 years. In 1961, a Soviet scientist with an ulcer was flown out of the Byrd research camp some 700 miles from the South Pole by a Navy C-130 carrying a double crew and additional emergency personnel. But it was only 6 weeks after the Antarctic sunset and in twilight, not in the blackness and cold of the dead of winter.

We continued planning, waiting for word of medical developments.

Meanwhile, on July 11, volunteers from the air force's 62nd Airlift Wing in Tacoma, Washington, flew a C-141 over the pole and dropped six parachute-rigged cases of chemotherapy drugs and diagnostic gear from 700 feet into a drop zone lighted with blazing oil drums. They threw in a case of fresh vegetables and a bundle of mail as bonuses. The temperature on the ground was 92 degrees below zero Fahrenheit, and nobody driving the snow tractors to retrieve the cases in the darkness could stay outside for more than 7 minutes at a time.

Nielsen's first step was to conduct a biopsy, drawing tissue from the lump and examining it in consultation with her personal physician in Indianapolis over satellite phone. The biopsy confirmed that she had cancer. She then began the extraordinary step of administering chemotherapy to herself in an intravenous drip with the help of fellow Polies she'd briefed on the procedure. Her hair fell out and she was nauseated, but at least it was a bloodless treatment. In 1960, a Russian doctor stricken with appendicitis during the Antarctic winter performed an appendectomy upon himself.

By now the patient's identification had leaked out along with the knowledge that she was undergoing self-administered chemotherapy. The world began to be gripped by the life-and-death drama under way at the South Pole. The next news to surface was that a dramatic evacuation from the polar deep freeze was possible. This was red meat to the media. The phones at the Stratton Air Guard base started lighting up.

As the news of Dr. Nielsen's dilemma spread and reporters started calling us about our plans, something happened that was tangential to the operation but that affected our planning and our focus on the goal of getting Dr. Nielsen out.

Suspicions deepened among some of the 109th's leadership that the National Science Foundation was using Dr. Nielsen to open the pole early. This had the effect of making an emergency sound like something routine. It meant that if Dr. Nielsen's condition deteriorated and turned into an actual emergency, the approvals to move crews and equipment to bring her out would be harder to obtain. This troubled me. Somewhere up the line, somebody was going to take issue with the foundation's medical analysis based on a built-in prejudice. I'd been in the business of saving lives my whole career and I'd rarely let bureaucratic judgments interfere. I didn't want it to happen now.

More than that, I had some experience with cancer in my sister Lynne's long illness and with my dad's illness. I knew its ravages, and I identified from afar with Jerri Nielsen. Our progress was being impeded and I was feeling very frustrated.

Fortunately for everyone concerned, Dr. Nielsen stabilized under the effects of chemotherapy. The regular NSF updates reported that her condition was unchanged. Berberian told me that there would likely be no medevac at all. Still, we continued planning. I wanted to know the absolute lowest temperature at which we could safely operate. I knew we couldn't eliminate all risk—that would be impossible—but I wanted to know where the thermometer would have to be to give us a fighting chance.

Meanwhile, the NSF airlift and logistics experts looked for ways to heat the frozen fuel supply at McMurdo. None of them was good enough. They couldn't liquefy the fuel enough to pump more than 50 gallons a minute. An LC-130 with its engines running—and they'd have to be kept running—burned more or less the same amount.

The answer kept coming back the same. Minus 50 degrees Celsius, or minus 58 degrees Fahrenheit, was the cutoff. There was no way we could refuel until the mercury rose above that point. We and Dr. Nielsen were prisoners of the calendar.

This was frustrating to me, but I could only imagine how Dr. Nielsen felt as she marked her days and tested the continued success of her treatments. Time in the confinement of the polar station must have moved excruciatingly slowly. Despite the chemotherapy's effects, however, she was able to continue working. And the camaraderie of life under the dome asserted itself in a party in which she was presented with a variety of hand-knit caps, including one with ears, to hide her baldness.

On September 23, the sun would barely break the horizon at the South Pole for the first time in six months, beginning the dawn of its long summer day. This would remove one major safety problem that stood in the way of an evacuation—the absence of a visible natural horizon that could cause a fatal landing error.

Now the NSF and its contractors would begin gearing up for a new research season. Weather support would return, air traffic control navigational aids would be set up and put into operation, and support personnel would begin their annual migration to McMurdo, on the edge of the Antarctic continent. The stirrings of a new research season mitigated many of our medevac concerns. But it was still too cold—minus 65 degrees Fahrenheit. We needed 7 more degrees of warmth.

At the pole, unbeknownst to us, Dr. Jerri Nielsen was running out of time. Her response to the initial regimen of chemotherapy had changed after four or five rounds. The lump had grown larger. Switching to another drug, which she took both intravenously and orally, had arrested the cancer but made her so sick she could barely stand. She started coughing and developing back pain. Once, trying to cook, she fell into the stove and burned herself. She believed her kidneys were beginning to malfunction. Worst of all, the veins into which she was taking the chemotherapy were starting to collapse.

The day before the twenty-third, Eric Chiang called with the dire news: Dr. Nielsen needed to be out by October 15 to start a new and aggressive treatment regimen.

I received the news from Chiang with a mixture of emotions. I felt the anticipation that always comes with the run-up to an intricate and hazardous operation. We had done a good job of planning and knew the essential variables. But I couldn't let the anticipation and the wish to get it done overwhelm the first and paramount concern: to do it right and safely.

October brings the year's worst weather to McMurdo Station. As temperatures are slowly warming, a semipermanent low-pressure system 16,000 feet over the Ross Sea hurls climatic thunderbolts at the continent. It's the same thing the Aleutian and Icelandic lows do to North America and Europe, respectively. It's impossible to know what to expect.

We went into final preparations. Scenario 1, the first choice all else being equal, was our guidepost. We planned to launch from Scotia with two LC-130s on October 6. A third was already standing by in Christchurch.

The crew who would fly the final leg to pick up Dr. Nielsen had been chosen. Major George McAllister, known as Robby to his friends, was the pilot, and Major David Koltermann the co-pilot. McAllister was the unit's chief of standardization, a job that routinely goes to the best and most experienced pilot. Koltermann also had a long history of polar flights and ice landings, but he had an extra incentive for volunteering for the mission. Koltermann's mother had had cancer; he wanted to do whatever he could to help someone else who was battling the disease—whether it was a friend or stranger didn't matter. Lieutenant Colonel Bryan Fennessy would navigate. Chief Master Sergeant Michael Christiano was the flight engineer.

Tony German, who would serve as the field mission commander, left for Christchurch with a sheaf of commercial airline tickets in his pocket. He would stand by until conditions allowed operations from McMurdo. Two planes would depart Christchurch for McMurdo on October 12. The next day one of them would fly to the South Pole. If all went well, Dr. Nielsen would be back in the United States and undergoing treatment by the October 15 deadline.

Everything depended on the temperature and the weather. At least that's what I thought until a series of side issues started popping up with a regularity that would have been comical if they had not threatened our ability to get the mission off on time.

On October 1, I ran through the ORM—operational risk management—checklist and concluded that the operation fell in the high to moderate risk category. I had sent the same assessment to the National Science Foundation. However, another of our officers, who had not been involved in any of the planning, ran the same checklist and came up with an "extreme risk" rating. He sent flags up everywhere.

This concerned me, but I thought I was right.

Then Sergeant Paul Terpening, a life support equipment expert, briefed me on a new regulation that came out of nowhere to catch me by surprise. It required parachutes, ML-4s (seat packs with individual life rafts and some survival gear), survival vests, and other items on all LC-130 flights. The regulation went into effect October 1. We had ordered the equipment, but we didn't have it yet, and everybody was surprised.

The LC-130s had flown safely for years without all this. I told the sergeant to get the regulation waived.

The 109th's commander provided the next last-minute glitch. Graham Pritchard announced that he would replace one of the pilots and fly the LC-130 that picked up Dr. Nielsen from the pole. When McAllister and the rest of the designated crew threatened a mutiny, Pritchard graciously relented, though he said he would still join the mission as an observer.

On October 4, two days before we had to launch, I called mission coordinator Brian Gomula to ask if we were ready.

"The crews and aircraft are all ready," he said. "But we've got no authorization to do the mission yet." He said we needed a tasking message from Colonel Rich Saburro in Christchurch, the theater commander of Operation Deep Freeze, and aerovac approval from the regular air force at Yokota, Japan.

There it was again, the differentiation that from the beginning I feared would threaten our ability to get the mission off the ground. "But it's an emergency medevac," I said. "Why aren't we dealing with the Rescue Coordination Center and Air Rescue?"

The air force's Rescue Coordination Center at Langley Air Force Base in Virginia coordinated the kind of "hot pursuit" rescues I was most familiar with, where approvals often came after the mission was launched. Waiting for a slow-moving bureaucracy to approve a mission that had been planned for months and was ready to go had me tapping my feet in frustration.

Brian gave me the answer I expected. "Everyone I have talked to is treating it like an airlift mission, not a medevac," he said.

The next day, with the clock ticking down to launch time, Brian called again. "Colonel Flemmmming," he said, drawing my name out as he did when there was something wrong, "we still have a problem. We don't have any air force authorization yet. We can't launch without a mission number."

The aide keeping track said, "We have a mission number from the National Guard Bureau, but we still need a tasking and mission number from the air force. I've not seen any yet."

Except for Colonel Hill and *Salvador Allende*, I'd always found that if you launched, the paperwork would follow. "Well, Bri," I said, "we will launch tomorrow because there's an emergency at the South Pole. We told the NSF we would, and Dr. Nielsen needs us. Is Tony German in Christchurch yet?"

"Yes."

"Good. Crews and aircraft set?"

"All set. Except for no authorization from air force in Yokota, the plan is working."

"Good; we're going to launch."

It felt good to say that. The decision was clear in my mind, and to set the wheels in motion was what needed to happen. It was no time to be timid, and waiting would do nobody any good. It was always a relief to move forward.

I arrived at the base on October 6 at four-thirty in the morning. Television news trucks were parked outside the gate. Sleepy-looking crews were dragging cables and aiming microwave transmitters in preparation for their coverage of the mission launch. They would be covering the departure of the backup crews, but the LC-130s would look good taking off.

When I arrived at Operations, the crews who would fly the two planes to Christchurch were making their final preparations. The pilots were rechecking the weather and clearances for the first day's flight to California. The navigators were calculating times and distances. Loadmasters had secured baggage and equipment in the two aircraft, and the flight engineers had finished their systems checks.

There was a vague feeling of disappointment in the air. The crew members moved and talked with none of the excitement or anticipation that usually precedes a rescue. These men and women knew they were the backup crews. McAllister and his team, along with Wing Commander Pritchard, were on the first leg of their journey to New Zealand aboard a commercial flight. The crews they left behind knew they were required for the mission, but they felt like second-stringers.

I knew that the men and women preparing to leave Scotia were important pieces of the rescue—they just didn't believe it yet. I gathered them for a predeparture pep talk.

"You are departing on a very long mission," I said. "You may not be flying to the pole, but you're still participating in the rescue. McAllister and his crew are only flying the last 480 miles of the mission. You men and women are flying the first 16,000. Without your aircraft at the bottom of the world, there will be no rescue.

"So when you take off remember that it is not so that the rescue can begin several days from now. When you take off the rescue will have begun. It begins with you. It starts right now."

Later that morning, I watched the two LC-130s lumber down the runway bound for the far ends of the Earth and felt both relief and satisfaction. The planning and the games were over. Somebody, somewhere, was still worrying about approval, but I knew the mission wasn't coming back.

The call from Albany came right on cue, at three o'clock that afternoon. A distraught colonel at New York Air Guard headquarters informed me that I did not yet have approval for the operation. I said I was aware of that. "It's an emergency, after all," I told him for probably the tenth time.

The colonel fired off a memo to General Fenimore. He showed it to me later, and I had to laugh. The subject line on the memo read, "Early Opening of the South Pole Station." Confusion between routine airlift and an emergency ran right into the launch time.

*   *   *

Day by day, the media attention grew. *Today* called on the second day and in turn *Good Morning, America*, the BBC, CNN, MSNBC, National Public Radio, and a host of other outlets. Mine was one of several talking heads they wanted. An admiral in Washington saw me on *Today* and called to chew me out for launching ahead of time.

Four days of relentless flying took the crews to Christchurch. The Hercules isn't that fast to begin with and the weight and fairings of the skis on the LC-130s reduced their cruising speed by a good 10 knots. From Christchurch, two of the planes launched to McMurdo the first time the weather gave an opportunity. Then the final game of weather tag began.

While the aircrews rested in McMurdo and waited for the temperature to climb, maintenance crews had to keep the aircraft ready. There were no warm hangars in which to store the planes or for them to work in. They worked day and night in temperatures of about 60 degrees below zero Fahrenheit, with 20- and 25-mile-per-hour winds.

On October 12, a violent storm hit McMurdo with winds of more than 40 knots and blowing snow that buried the skiway. On October 13 and 14 the temperature rose to minus 55 degrees Fahrenheit, but no amount of watching and hoping moved it any higher.

Meanwhile, at the pole, Nielsen was aware of the risks that were involved in her evacuation. She had pressed her doctor, Dr. Kathy Miller at Indiana University, with whom she had been communicating primarily by e-mail, to tell her if she was dying. If so, Nielsen had agreed with her family to call the mission off to avoid placing the crew in danger. "I didn't want to risk people's lives," she said. "The pole had become my home and I wanted to stay there if it meant putting other people's lives in danger."

Miller and Nielsen's colleagues at the pole convinced her not to take that course. And when it became clear that a rescue effort was going to be launched, Nielsen changed her mind. "I turned around," she said. "I got really excited. I thought that I might live, and that this rescue might really happen."

In preparation, the polar crew deployed snow tractors to clear the winter's accumulation of blown snow from the skiway.

I was ready to let McAllister take off when the temperature rose to minus 52 degrees Fahrenheit. Suitable conditions at McMurdo, at sea level, didn't mean suitable conditions at the pole, but he could circle the pole to wait for the right conditions if he had to. But Rich Saburro, the theater commander, wanted it to be minus 50 before the plane left McMurdo. We jousted back and forth by phone and e-mail. Finally I said, "Look, we're not airlifting toothpaste and gum. This is a humanitarian mission, no matter what the approval says. There's some risk to this, but there's some risk in life."

It was minus 53 by one gauge and minus 52 by another before noon on October 15 when McAllister led his crew through the crew entrance of an LC-130 with the name *City of Christchurch, NZ* painted above the door. Its call sign was *Skier 96*.

McAllister powered the LC-130's four turboprops and steered it down the Williams Field skiway, headed for the pole. They reached the pole after a 3-hour flight but couldn't land. The mountaintop on the bottom of the Earth was laced by ground blizzards that forced *Skier 96* back to McMurdo.

Blizzards of blowing ground snow and whiteout conditions occurred again, on the sixteenth. But the temperature was right or close to right at 53 below and after consulting with me Tony German told McAllister to try again. *Skier 96* took off at 10:26 A.M. McMurdo time.

At the pole, the temperature was closer to minus 60, but McAllister and his crew decided to attempt a landing. As he dropped toward the surface, a windstorm blew snow, blotting out the horizon. It was too late to do anything but try to land.

Skier 96 descended surrounded by white. Fennessy called out speed and altitude. McAllister later said he felt like he was flying inside a Ping-Pong ball. He figured the risk at eight or nine on a scale of ten. There was a shadow that looked like the horizon, but he wasn't really sure he'd hit the skiway until the altitude gauge hit zero and he felt the skis on the snow. He threw the props into reverse.

The Polies at the research station knew that the plane had left McMurdo. They had put on their extreme cold weather gear, left the dome, and gone outside to the flight deck when the wind came up and the sun and everything else disappeared. They heard the plane's engines overhead but no one thought that it would land. They stayed out only because they knew they had but a few minutes to get Nielsen aboard the plane if by some miracle it did land. Joel Michalski, a station scientist who composed a weekly e-mail and Web report, wrote, "We were shocked when without warning we heard the distinct sound of props in reverse, a roar much louder than the blowing wind. Immediately, everyone realized the plane had landed. We started cheering, clapping, and throwing our hands in the air."

The LC-130's landing lights appeared; then the plane emerged from the whiteout and stopped a hundred yards from the entrance to the dome. McAllister looked out from the plane and saw the Polies in their bright red weather suits jumping up and down.

The research station crew hurried to get Dr. Nielsen and her luggage aboard as McAllister kept testing the hydraulics and the flaps. Two loadmasters off-loaded mail, fresh food, and vegetables. In her 30 pounds of thermal clothing, the doctor was too stiff and weak to climb aboard by herself. The station's heavy-equipment mechanic, mohawk-sporting "Big John" Penney, lifted her and literally threw her into the plane, where she sprawled on her hands and knees. Two other members of the station crew also joined the flight, and the station's new doctor left the plane to begin life in the dome.

The LC-130's doors closed and McAllister revved the engines to taxi for takeoff. The plane didn't move. The pilot had a sinking moment. The friction of landing had melted the ice enough to weld the skis to the surface. McAllister retracted them, pulling them straight up to break the grip of the ice, leaving the wheels on the ice before dropping the skis back down. *Skier 96* was free.

Twenty-two minutes after landing, the LC-130 was once again on the skiway taxiing for takeoff. McCallister fired the ATO boosters. On the ground, Michalski and the other Polies saw "the plane shooting skyward, leaving a trail of aggressive fire and smoke."

The flight nurse, Major Kim Terpening, had volunteered for the mission because she had lost a son to cancer when he was six. His death had been a part of everything she'd done since then. She, like the rest of the crew, was curious about Jerri Nielsen, the woman they'd come all this way and risked their lives for. She thought at first that the doctor had boarded the plane with surprising vigor for a cancer patient. Then the doctor took off her insulated cap and revealed the ravages of chemotherapy.

Terpening, Chief Master Sergeant Michael Casatelli, the chief of the 109th's clinic, and Master Sergeant Kelly McDowell had strapped Nielsen into an inward-facing jump seat for the dangerous takeoff. She tried to look out the window but couldn't. "I wanted so much to see the South Pole one last time," she said.

Casatelli found Nielsen warm and talkative. "She was bubbly," he said. "She was so happy to be on the plane." In the first minutes of the flight after the LC-130 had reached altitude, Nielsen entertained a stream of visitors. The pilots came back from the cockpit to meet her. Someone gave her a gift package from McMurdo Station—more hand-knit caps.

And then she said, "I just got very tired, and they let down one of those beds from the side of the plane and they made up the bed and I went to sleep."

When *Skier 96* took off from the pole, it was early afternoon on Friday at McMurdo, which shares a time zone with New Zealand. In Scotia, New York, the calendar had not yet flipped. It was still the day before. I got periodic updates from the chief of staff, Bob McInerney, and I'd walk from my office in the headquarters building across the parking lot to operations, where I'd relay them to the planning team. The tension rose throughout the day. By early evening, the atmosphere was stifling.

At about seven-thirty, McInerney tapped on my office door and leaned inside. He was beaming. "They got her," he said. "They took off and they're headed back to McMurdo."

Relief combined with a sense of exultation. It felt wonderful. The wait was finally over. For just a second I was overwhelmed at what we'd done; the plans and the women and men and machines combined in an incredibly complicated effort that was the equivalent of combat, all for the incredibly simple task of taking one person from harm's way. Full of joy, I sprinted across the parking lot to spread the news.

Gomula, Mathews, Johnston, and the rest were scattered around making work, with their minds 10,000 miles away. They looked up when I ran in. "They got her," I said, repeating McInerney's words.

"*Yes!*" The room full of exhausted men erupted. They pumped their fists, high-fived, and cheered at the signal that they'd crossed the finish line of a long race. I heard a collective sigh of escaping tension. It drowned out all the suspicions, all the planning problems, all the frustrations of waiting for the weather, all the piggybacking on the mission by people who wanted its glory to shine on them and their careers, all the sound bites and television lights.

It drowned out everything and left shining the beautiful fact at the heart of the matter. The Air Guard had done the job its people had signed up for. A person who seriously needed our help had gotten it.

The rest was anticlimactic. *Skier 96* touched down at McMurdo a few hours later. Terpening and Casatelli transferred Nielsen to a waiting Air Force C-141 from the 62nd Airlift Wing and stayed with her on the flight to Christchurch. The slower LC 130s headed back to Christchurch, too, and McAllister and his flight crew slept during the 8-hour flight.

At Christchurch, the National Science Foundation handed Nielsen over to her two brothers, who shielded her from the media as they transferred her to the international hub at Auckland and then home, where she retreated from the public eye. She issued a statement a day or two later through the NSF, thanking the 109th for its role in returning her to family and friends and treatment for breast cancer, which she said had been confirmed.

The flight in and out was 9 days earlier than any previous flight to the South Pole. Did 9 days buy a life? Maybe. Dr. Nielsen underwent a mastectomy and wrote a best-selling book, *Ice Bound*, chronicling her ordeal. She continued to travel to the far ends of the Earth, she lectured in the wake of her experience, and when she was interviewed in 2003 for the preparation of this book, she remained cancer-free.

Back in Antarctica, the Air Guard continued moving its equipment into place. Soon the regular work of the austral summer was in full swing—the wealth of essential research that was helping to paint a picture of our planet and its health as it hurtles through the years. Before the season ended, the 109th's LC-130s had made more than five hundred trips to research sites at the South Pole and all over the continent. None of them fell into ice crevasses.

I was grateful for *Skier 95*'s mishap. I might not have gone to the 109th without it. Jerri Nielsen's medevac essentially ended my career in rescue and I rejoiced for myself as well as for her when she lifted off from the South Pole.

I retired from the Air Guard a few months later. It's hard to launch a mission you can't fly, hard to order troops into battle when you can't lead the charge. It would have been harder to go out pushing papers in a headquarters staff job.

I am very grateful to have been given the chance to direct the Nielsen mission. It allowed me to do what I always loved the best in my career—taking the pieces and shuffling and reshuffling them as weather and people and machines brought new realities to bear. I loved it because what you came out with at the end of all the shuffling was the precious jewel of life.

Epilogue

After Jerri Nielsen, I was thrust into the helicopter world again, proving, I suppose, that as much as things change, they often recycle back to the beginning. The occasion was another reminder of the risks of helicopter flight and of the game of chance that rescue crews play daily with their lives.

On November 23, 1999, barely a month after Dr. Nielsen was medevaced from the South Pole, an Army National Guard unit based in Ronkonkoma, Long Island, suffered a fatal helicopter crash. A pilot, copilot, and two crew chiefs had gone up in a UH-1, one of the Bell helicopters known as Hueys, to get in some training time on instrument approaches. The weather was dicey. It wasn't violent, but the South Shore of Long Island had been socked in with fog for three days. The fog lifted slightly, and because they wanted to log training time, the crew went up. They flew approaches at East Hampton and at Westhampton when the fog rolled in again.

With the fog, the Huey crew's options disappeared. The Huey didn't have the instrument array of one of the Air Guard's MH-60s and the pilots didn't have the actual instrument experience to deal with the conditions. And the Huey didn't carry an awful lot of fuel. There wasn't enough left to fly inland out of the fog. The pilot headed to the unit's home base at Islip–MacArthur Airport, hoping for the best.

It didn't happen. The Huey crashed, killing the pilot and one of the crew chiefs. The copilot and the other crew chief were miraculously thrown from the helicopter when it hit the ground. Otherwise they, too, would have been crushed in the remains of the Huey. General Fenimore assigned me to investigate the accident.

By November 25, I was at the Suffolk County coroner's office and morgue, being briefed on the horrendous causes of death. Later, in the residual gray fog, I walked along the path of mangled metal, flight equipment, and the crew's effects strewn on the edge of the airport. The Huey had hit the ground at cruise airspeed in an extreme nosedive that generated sixty times the force of gravity. The aircraft furrowed the ground for 80 feet, rose into the air again, and then crashed some 130 feet farther.

As I surveyed the wreckage, I thought how many years I had battled weather and conditions like the ones that led to the Huey's crash. I was sad for the crew members who died and for their families. The sacrifices they made were way too common. At the same time, I felt overwhelmingly fortunate still to be alive after too many helicopter flights to count.

What stood out to me was the disconnect between the physical reality that the Huey crew faced and the administrative reality that made them fly. The physical reality was persistent fog over several days, an aircraft without the instruments to deal with it, a crew that wasn't experienced in those actual conditions, and a fuel capacity that wouldn't let them fly to safety. The administrative reality was the perceived need to complete a training cycle.

The wrong choice between those realities left two men dead and a multimillion-dollar helicopter a twisted pile of scrap metal.

Reality must take precedence over public relations or administration, for nature cannot be fooled. That, in effect, is what physicist Richard Feynman said after he concluded his report to Congress concerning the 1986 *Challenger* disaster. He meant that physical realities of a space shuttle flight are absolute. In *Challenger*'s case it was the cold morning and the cold-stiffened O-ring that let exhaust flames leak to the hydrogen in the external fuel tank, causing the explosion. The administrative reality that day—

man's rule versus nature's—was that a live television appearance had been planned between President Reagan and the crew of *Challenger*. The pressure to make the appearance coincide with the State of the Union address trumped engineers' warnings that it was too cold to launch the space shuttle.

I listened to recordings of the radio transmissions between the Huey and the Islip tower. The transmissions from the helicopter became increasingly stressed as the crew tried one approach after another without ever finding the break in the fog they hoped for. The source of the stress was all too common. Administrative demands had run up against physical reality, and once again, nature was going to have her way.

This is what I talk about in the courses I now teach in leadership studies at Empire State College in Saratoga Springs. Good leaders don't confuse man's rules with nature's. They know that the two things are of a different order. Knowing when one applies and takes precedence over the other—and not being afraid to say so—may not always be the smoothest course. But it allows the men and women under you, for whose lives you may be responsible, to focus on the hard realities, and it may keep them alive.

I retired shortly after that investigation. As I look back, the career I backed into turned out to be as satisfying and fulfilling as any I have ever been able to imagine.

I get Christmas cards each year from Alexander Taranov. He sends me pictures of his children. I appreciate them more because my boys are men now, one with children of his own, and I know how much it's meant to me to be there through all the stages of their lives. I followed Jerri Nielsen's story through her wonderful book, and I rejoice in her health and the career she's found in the wake of the South Pole rescue.

My life is calmer than it was. Besides my teaching, when I'm not too busy writing I provide expert testimony in cases involving aircraft crashes and human performance under extreme stress.

That reminds me of all the years spent flying. And other reminders sometimes hit me in the face, such as on the day of the September 11 attacks on the World Trade Center and the Pentagon when the evil designs of worldwide terrorism thrust themselves into the nation's consciousness in a horrifying and unprecedented way and I returned, in my mind, to the Khobar Towers.

But they are reminders from afar.

Jean and I live on a hillside near Cambridge, New York. It's near Saratoga and the border with Vermont and we look out on the Green Mountains. I still run and lift weights, but we get the greatest pleasure from being with our family and hiking together in the mountains. The mountains are somehow less threatening now. Keith and his family and Cavan, who's still single, come to see us, and for a time the quiet of the house is joyously broken with voices that are both familiar and young and relatively new. We hear questions about the life we've lived. I love the curiosity of children. We hear the bark and patter of new dogs exploring places that are new to them. I don't want to go back to the cockpit.

As a rescue helicopter pilot and as a commander, I joined with copilots, flight engineers, pararescuemen, and untold numbers of supporting players—tanker pilots and their crews, maintenance and ground crews, air controllers, weather forecasters, fuel haulers, radio operators, and more—to save hundreds of people from floods, mudslides, avalanches, typhoons, hurricanes, and other storms, disasters at sea, and all manner of other catastrophes.

I never met most of them. I never got to follow their careers. But the exchange was always the same whether the survivor was a person who later became noted, a Korean peasant, a military pilot or sailor, a merchant mariner, a fisherman or fisherwoman, or a soldier in the Philippine Constabulary.

In every case, I always thought that rescue was a place where humanity met humanity, halfway between need and the ability to meet it. I wouldn't have wanted to do anything else.

Glossary

airspeed: The speed of the aircraft relative to the air through which it is flying. The speed the aircraft is making through the air. This is often different from ground speed.

altitude: The height of the aircraft.

attitude: The position of an aircraft in relation to the horizon.

autorotation: Helicopter flight with no engine power driving the rotor systems, where the rotors are kept turning at a sufficient rpm by pilot control inputs and the wind approaching from below the rotor system.

blade: Rotorblade.

ceiling: The height above Earth's surface of the lowest significant (hides more than approximately half the sky) layer of clouds.

checkride: A flight evaluation given by a designated flight examiner to a crew member to ensure that they maintain the safe performance standards set for all maneuvers and missions.

clock positions: A sighting, such as a survivor, outside the aircraft is always described using clock positions, with the nose of the aircraft being twelve o'clock. Then, visualizing the clock face, three o'clock is directly out the right side of the aircraft, six o'clock is straight behind the aircraft, and nine o'clock is directly out the left side of the aircraft.

collective: Control stick located to the left of the pilot. Movement of the collective upward increases power; movement down lowers power.

coriolis illusion: Condition when the head is abruptly moved from one plane to another while the body (aircraft) is in rotation. This causes the illusion of spinning when no spinning motion actually exists.

cyclic control: Control stick located between the legs of the pilot. Its purpose is to control the horizontal motion of the helicopter in a desired direction. Moving the cyclic forward makes the helicopter fly forward; moving it back makes the helicopter fly backward, and so forth.

deadman's curve: Chart that depicts the combination of altitude and airspeed from which structural damage will occur in the event of power loss.

detent: A position on the engine speed selector where the engines are at ground idle, and while inflight the engines are no longer driving (turning) the rotors.

ditching: Emergency landing in the sea or other large body of water.

downwash: Airflow deflected downward by the turning of a rotor, caused when lift is created.

drogue: A heavy reception coupling at the end of the air refueling hose normally extending from the HC-130 aircraft.

flameout: Refers to the condition where the engine stops running, often due to fuel problems.

flapping: The motion of the blade upward and downward. In certain low-rpm and high-energy maneuvers, the downward flapping blades may strike the aircraft.

flight engineer: Aircrew member responsible for the aircraft preflight, systems management, flight monitoring, performance computations, hoist operations, and various other duties as required.

flight examiner: A person qualified to give others evaluations or check-rides as well as instruction; the highest qualification of any crew position.

force protection: As used here, the responsibility of a commander to take all necessary actions to protect his unit from attack.

forest penetrator: The rescue device attached to the end of the hoist cable that contains three seats and three straps. The survivors (if ambulatory) are strapped on and straddle the penetrator to be hoisted up into the helicopter. It is named forest penetrator because it was designed to be able to penetrate through thick trees to reach a survivor. With a flotation collar, it is also used for water rescues.

formation: Two or more aircraft flying in close proximity and treated as one aircraft for coordination and control. The primary purposes for formation flight are mutual support and increased lift capability.

formation lead: Flight leader responsible for the safe and successful conduct of the mission, and for all aircraft and crew members in the formation.

ground speed: True airspeed corrected for wind, the speed the aircraft is making across the ground. This is often different from the airspeed displayed on the airspeed indicator.

hooch: Slang referring to a living quarters.

horizontal reference: Aircraft attitude.

hovering: Remaining stationary in the air.

knot: Unit of speed equal to one nautical mile (6,000 feet) per hour, or equivalent to 1.15 statue miles per hour.

lift: The force that supports the aircraft in the air caused by the dynamic action and reaction of the wing and the air mass.

mission commander: The person who is required to control actions taken during contingencies or other operations.

night vision goggles (NVGs): Night vision devices based on the principle of light amplification.

night water hoist: A night overwater hoist rescue involving hovering over a moving sea while trying to position the helicopter over a moving survivor. It is considered the most high-risk maneuver, and in the past, only select crews were qualified.

off-line: Refers to a condition where the engines are no longer driving the gearboxes and rotors but have not flamed out.

pararescue jumper, or PJ: Elite rescue crew member of the air force, Air Force Reserves, and Air National Guard. Pararescue jumpers are highly trained in all rescue techniques, as well as being survival and emergency medical experts.

radar vector: A heading issued to an aircraft to provide navigational guidance or aircraft avoidance.

rotor: A system of rotating wings which provides the source of lift, propulsion, and control in helicopters.

rotor hub: The rotor driving and supporting structure, to which rotor-blades are attached. It includes the control linkage.

rpm: Revolutions per minute.

SAR: Search and rescue.

SAR (Inland Region): Inland area in which the USAF Air Rescue Service exercises the coordination and control function.

SAR (Maritime Region): The area, normally over the seas, in which the U.S. Coast Guard exercises the coordination and control function.

spatial disorientation: Term that refers to the condition in which the pilot confuses illusion with reality.

tail rotor: On some rotary wing aircraft, a rotor located on the tail to provide antitorque. The antitorque compensates for the torque generated by the main rotor; without the tail rotor, control of the aircraft would be lost.

thrust: The rotor force perpendicular to the plane of the rotor disk.

vertical reference: Aircraft altitude.

vertigo: Condition of dizziness or spinning experienced as a result of some physiological abnormality.

vortex ring state (settling with power): The airflow condition that may occur in a moderate to high vertical descent when the rate of descent overtakes the rate that the rotor can accelerate air downward and produce positive lift. Can result in high rates of descent and, if left uncorrected, loss of control.

yaw: Movement about the vertical axis of the aircraft. This movement is similar to that of a weather vane.

Index

Printed in the USA
CPSIA information can be obtained
at www.ICGtesting.com
JSHW011540051223
53300JS00009B/209

9 781684 425846